TEACHING WHAT WE DO

ESSAYS BY AMHERST COLLEGE FACULTY

Teaching
What We Do

■

ESSAYS BY

AMHERST COLLEGE FACULTY

Amherst College Press   Amherst, Massachusetts
1991

CONTENTS

FOREWORD

IN WORLD WAR II, seamen of the Royal Navy used a brisk, deck-swabbing chant as they worked, beginning

> Yehudi Menuhin
> Knows what he's doin' . . .

—heavy emphasis on the penultimate syllable in both lines. This is a satisfying chant in every way, reflecting credit both on the violinist and on the sailors who invoked his name. At first glance, it is a humorous nod to the world of the arts from the working man. But looked at more closely it reveals, perhaps, an assumption that their two worlds are one: a nod of recognition from one professional to another.

As far as the world at large and the world of higher education are concerned, it might not be safe to assume that any such recognition of solidarity is in place today. Hence, we hope, the usefulness of this volume; as teachers and scholars, we want to spell out what we are doing. Those who are interested in our work can then make their own judgment on its worth—whether they want to come and share in it, or they want their children exposed to it, or they wish to continue supporting it.

Perhaps a few words first about our perceptions of the particular climate in which this book appears.

It is not an easy time to be an academic in the Arts and Sciences, and the point is confirmed by the growing reluctance of college graduates to become one. According to figures reported by William G. Bowen and Julie Ann Sosa, in many fields American colleges and universities are within a few years of having less than one candidate for each position (0.71 of a candidate in the humanities and social sciences by 1997, to be precise, and 0.83 for all disciplines).*

There are many reasons for this decline: the difficulty of finding academic appointments in the seventies inclined many to look elsewhere, and the inclination has probably been cemented by the lengthening of the time required for the Ph.D. degree. By the year 1987, the median time spent to earn a doctorate (from the award of the B.A.) was 9.5 years for all disciplines, 12 years for the humanities. Another factor is economic: one hears complaint in some quarters that professors are overpaid, but there is no doubt that the academic profession has lost ground financially against the other professions over the last twenty years (Bowen and Sosa confirm this, too). If you take the case of Amherst, it was only in 1989 that the faculty finally made good the losses of the seventies, and in real terms regained the value that its salaries had in 1967. There cannot be many professions for which that is true. These two factors alone explain a lot: the longest training for the smallest salary is not a winning formula for attracting the strongest talent into the field.

But there are other, more disquieting reasons for the hard times of academe, and they have to do with diminished regard in the eyes of our countrymen. There is strong ambivalence towards higher education. Our schools are still eagerly sought for the accreditation they provide at the end of a degree; but for the education they offer in the course of it, there is strong suspicion, perhaps even disdain. There have always been hostile skirmishers along these lines in America, but they have recently become more concertedly regimented.

Critics of the academy attack on two fronts—against failure of mind, and against failure of will. The first criticism amounts to the charge that the American intellectual community has lost its way. Increasing specialization (the argument goes), burrowing ever deeper into narrower seams within a discipline, has robbed members of a faculty of any sense of connection with a common enterprise, or with each other; they could not now define educational priorities, let alone an overarching educational philosophy, if you asked them. The situation is compounded by a wash of vague, trendy, liberal permissiveness, encour-

---

* See their book, *Prospects for Faculty in the Arts and Sciences: A Study of Factors Affecting Demand and Supply,* Princeton University Press, 1989.

aging a million doctrines to flourish unjudged, with no real structure or priority at all.

The second criticism falls more heavily on professorial delinquency—especially in the matter of teaching. In this view, it is not so much a question of faculty not knowing what they ought to do as of their unwillingness to do it. At home and abroad, the argument goes, research is everything, and teaching can be left safely to graduate students; otherwise it interferes with airline schedules. The bargaining position of star professors in the great research universities has developed to the point that they rarely have to teach at all—a large irony: the more you are thought to have something to say, the less you may be obliged to impart it to the students who have paid to hear it.

I have written about some of these criticisms elsewhere and do not intend to engage them directly now. Every major college and university puts in the front of its catalog or admissions material the claim that the institution is dedicated to excellence in teaching and research. It is clear that imbalances, excesses and delinquencies occur, and it is in the public interest that we attend to them. But there are still institutions where the balance is maintained, where both sides of the commitment are honored. Amherst is one. It seems worthwhile at this juncture to explore the tensions in a professor's life, when the balance is in place—when he or she takes the teaching obligation seriously, even passionately, and tries at the same time to remain at, or close to, the front of a discipline by active research. Are the tensions creative, or do they enforce a kind of schizophrenia, two sides of the brain, each resenting time spent on the other? What is the focus of your research, what are you driving at? Can students help you with it, or does it have to be watered down to bring it within their reach? What can you bring from your research into the classroom in terms of content or methodology and emphasis? And what are you looking for from your teaching—apart from light relief or blue books to correct?

Those are some of the questions the authors of these essays address from their own perspectives, throwing an individual accent sometimes on one side of the balance or the other. All of them speak articulately for themselves and are worth listening to carefully, as one would in their classes. But first, it is worth setting them more generously in the context of the life they lead.

People who become academics do not usually do so primarily because they are attracted to the life-style, although it often seems compellingly attractive to outsiders—especially "the leisure of the theory class," in Riesman's phrase. But there is more hazard, pressure and adventure in this supposedly sedentary profession than is evident from the outside. The pressure arises exactly from the challenge that drew young scholars to the field in the first place—the chance to "think new" about a body of material that had already engaged them with its importance and interest, and on which they had already shown their talent. The pressure, then, is mostly psychological, and in a sense self-willed. Most academics have been told at least from their undergraduate years that they are bright. They often become the favorite sons and daughters of the departments in which they major, and are recruited into the field as "having something to offer." The thought that they will break new ground in their further studies is an enormous stimulus; but it is also an obligation, which the institutions they enter, from their graduate departments onward, will endorse and insist on. "What original contribution does this dissertation make to the field?" is often an early question at a doctoral defense, and it is a question that every reviewer of everything they write thereafter will raise as well. Passing these various hurdles, including the large one of tenure, they are launched on a career that must be fueled and constantly refueled by private obsession. Academics are seen as expert in a chosen area and are still expected to devote much of their time and energy pushing against the limits of what they have learned so far. One needs to have some imagination for the kind of interior strain that expectation induces: it is not easy to keep thinking new, all the time, for a lifetime. Several older professors have confided to me that a hard moment came in their career when they had to accept the fact that they could not deliver what they set themselves to do, and that sometimes indeed their own field had moved ahead of them faster than their capacity to keep up with it, let alone make gains within it. In G.H. Hardy's fine *A Mathematician's Apology,* this note of regret is explicit—he apologizes for having to write about mathematics, now that he can no longer *do* mathematics.

But why does an undergraduate institution insist on this research aspect of a professor's work, especially if it is attended by all that strain and disappointment? Why not just let them teach undistracted by other claims? There are, in fact, many colleges that offer fine instruction and attend closely to their students, without imposing the requirement of research on their instructors.

The college which does impose in this way has a different view in sight. It does not ask for research as a kind of public relations gimmick, because that is the way you get your institution known (although I believe some research universities come dangerously close to espousing this view). It asks its faculty to commit themselves to research because it wants them to instill the attitude of "thinking new" and probing the conventions of a discipline in the students they teach. The ideal is this: you look for the most gifted faculty and put them together with the brightest students you can find; if you find the right ones, both groups will be attracted to each other. Once together, the independent mastery of the professor challenges the students to reimagine what they have learned so far—to handle evidence more dexterously, to make inferences more strongly, to form hypotheses more boldly and test them more ingeniously and rigorously, to see associations and connections more insightfully—until they are capable of forming judgments that are fully their own. One wants all the powers of mind and spirit and sense to be awakened to new alertness and rise to new confidence, because that is the only way we realize all the possibilities within us. It is unlikely that more than a few students in a generation will aspire to follow their teachers into the academic world, but that was never the point. The point is to instill in them strong habits of mind and spirit, so that for the rest of their lives they will think and feel and judge for themselves. That is good for them and good for any society they live in.

These encounters are also good for the faculty who teach. There is a large psychological, as well as principled, error in an institution or a policy that uncouples research from teaching. Certainly, undergraduates cannot be given all the findings of anyone's research; in several fields, the technical sophistication of the work puts research out of reach to all but fellow specialists. Research can be a solitary matter and will often lead down blind alleys to an impasse. But imparting what one knows often fuels creativity towards new knowledge. Publication also plays this beneficial role; but there is perhaps a special incentive for yourself as a professor to confront the mild curiosity of the good-natured young in the classroom, and see it rise, in the face of your own interests and insistences, first to eagerness and then to the sort of passion you remember, and hope to sustain, in yourself.

We hope by this sample of essays to give a sense of what faculty do in their classrooms, what they do on their own in research, and what kind of relationship between the two they fashion in their lives. The contributors wish to thank Richard Todd and Douglas C. Wilson for their interest and professional editorial assistance, Suzanne Auerbach for design and production of this volume, and Nicholas Evans of the Amherst Board of Trustees for funding the project.

Peter R. Pouncey

President and Professor of Classics
Amherst College
April, 1991

ENGLISH AND THE PROMISE OF HAPPINESS

Benjamin DeMott
Professor of English, Emeritus

> ... *the process of reading is not a half-sleep, but, in highest sense, an exercise, a gymnast's struggle.* ... *The reader is to do something for himself, must be on the alert, must himself or herself construct indeed the poem, argument, history, metaphysical essay—the text furnishing the hints, the clue, the start or framework. Not the book needs so much to be the complete thing, but the reader of the book does.*

> —Walt Whitman

> *We animate what we see, we see only what we animate.*

> —Ralph Waldo Emerson

I

I WAS ABOUT TO SAY that patience is all, but this would be disingenuous. You also need—for English as I conceive it—a sense of what's meant to happen in a good class and a rudimentary grasp of how to make it happen. In a good class the efforts of student and teacher bring an imagined human innerness alive. Animation takes. A ghost walks. The collaborators enjoy a stretch of intelligently active, sympathetic engagement with a fictive being—and with each other.

If this sounds rather like meditation or incantation, no problem: meditation is involved. After many years of teaching I still intrude clumsily on classroom silences, muttering students' names, framing half-audible queries, creating a mildly twitchy atmosphere that's inimical to the basic undertaking. I blame this bad habit of mine on others: those who down the years have persuaded students young and old to mistrust any version of school other than teacher talks/students listen. The muttering and hovering are intended to reassure the class that the teacher understands his obligations and will begin piping up shortly. . . .

But I also interrupt because aware that in the basic classroom work meditation and articulation are interdependent. Most people don't know what they feel, hence feel nothing, said D. H. Lawrence, reflecting on the link between emotion and knowledge, feelings and names for feelings. In the silence student and teacher are engaged in imaginatively constructing and drawing near; the bridging tools and materials are words (gestures and movements as well); once the foundation is in—meaning, once the labor of construction is launched—talk is indispensable.

Talking publicizes and to an extent routinizes an otherwise more or less exotic activity: searching one's own intimate experience and private knowledge to comprehend the intimate experience of others. By naming and "discussing" the condition of feeling they're attempting to summon, by talking their way into treating the labor of imaginative penetration as run-of-the-mill, people moderate inhibition and adjust more comfortably to their obligations as animators. One, small, self-protectively objectifying chirp—we're perverse creatures, after all—enables us to shed embarrassment and live with a feeling from which ordinarily we'd retreat.

THE LAMB

Little Lamb, who made thee?
Dost thou know who made thee?
Gave thee life, & bid thee feed
By the stream & o'er the mead;
Gave thee clothing of delight,

Softest clothing, wooly, bright;
Gave thee such a tender voice,
Making all the vales rejoice?
Little Lamb, who made thee?
Dost thou know who made thee?

Little Lamb, I'll tell thee,
Little Lamb, I'll tell thee:
He is called by thy name,
For He calls himself a Lamb.
He is meek, & he is mild;
He became a little child.
I a child, & thou a lamb,
We are called by his name.
Little Lamb, God bless thee!
Little Lamb, God bless thee!

Little Lamb, Little Lamb . . . On opening day students who are asked to step inside this moment of speech and call up the attendant feelings are likely to resist. Their recently attained adult selves wince at babytalk. Their will to be left alone, notetaking, is offended by my intrusiveness. *Why is this man, this teacher, in my face? What's the point of regressing to infancy in front of buddies? Shouldn't he be embarrassed for himself?*

Sensible questions. Yet as long as the student's adult self persists in holding center stage, frozen in "proper" impersonality, this lyric moment will remain elusive. Childlike being needs to be recovered—a small person given to miming teachers (laying on condescension and mnemonic aids, that is) when dealing with dolls, pets, or other adored dependents. Only if the child-teacher comes alive can the animator participate in the movement—the childlike deliciously impulsive movement from preceptorship to tenderness. Only if we take the lamb-creature into our arms, as the speaker does, through tone, can we touch the unembarrassed, unprotected, loving quickness of response that is called innocence.

The function of conversation—searching for terms, pretending to exactitude, criticizing and celebrating each other's offerings—is to re-situate a deeply private enterprise on a public stage. Talking reassures the hardnosed self, prevents it from shaking off the possibility of feeling that "The

Lamb"—like many another lyric poem—exists to create. Gradually an understanding takes hold: this odd activity is *social,* people stay at it, they actually ante up as though unashamed. Words, grown-up joke words, allow the feeling to be evoked without infantilizing effect. Distance is at once kept and closed. With the aid of *cuddle,* for instance—as in: "It's a nice cuddly feeling"—I draw closer to what I imagine to be the appropriate response, awakening a soft pretty defenselessness that cries out to be touched, hugged, pressed close, kissed. And I also smile knowingly at myself. Teasing the fear of innocence, I bring innocence alive, thus letting myself in the back door of the penetralium.

A minute or two have passed, not more. Relief from pressure is near. Relief in this class tends to take the form of approved Western Civ chatabout—remarks on the relationship between the imagination of innocence, the rejection of worldliness, and the Christian and Blakeian visions. Accredited Education. But the real work, obviously, is that which has previously been done, ideally without fuss. For a moment or two the classroom explores a possibility of feeling, living back briefly into the courage of tenderness and the certitudes of innocence.

As the example may suggest, one pleasure of the classroom work is that of bringing your own variousness into play, exploring your range, discovering your delicacy. My own pay, not measurable, is hearing a student say —this has happened—that "I never really knew what lyric poetry was *for.*" Always the important classroom goal is that of increasing imaginative mobility, learning to accommodate and comprehend feelings and conditions of being that can, within seconds, touch extremes. Or, putting the same point differently, learning to read Shakespeare.

Lighter-than-air spirit-stuff is what one is on the balcony in *Romeo and Juliet,* bringing the lovers to life—longing to fly from self, aspiring to utter vulnerability (Romeo: "I would I were thy bird"). But from moment to moment come inklings of the entailments of devotion—imminent seriousness, a strong new rooted sense of personal worth. Completing the lovers means more than soaring—means taking on solemn, sacramental substance, as in Romeo's priest-like blessing:

Sleep dwell upon thine eyes, peace in thy breast.

On occasion the teacher lobbies shamelessly for imaginative mobility as a "value," proposing it as the ground of moral or even spiritual advance. The New Testament story of Mary and Martha (as told by the wonderfully vivid author of the gospel according to Luke) strongly supports this position:

> Now as they went on their way, he entered a village; and a woman named Martha received him into her house. And she had a sister called Mary, who sat at the Lord's feet and listened to his teaching. But Martha was distracted with much serving; and she went to him and said, "Lord, do you not care that my sister has left me to serve alone? Tell her then to help me." But the Lord answered her, "Martha, Martha, you are anxious and troubled about many things; one thing is needful. Mary has chosen the good portion, which shall not be taken away from her."

How much we discern in Martha's mind and nature that's known to be good! The proudly dutiful sense of responsibility, realism that refuses to be seduced by lah-dee-dah calls to Higher Things, stern awareness that somebody has to cart the garbage. Martha is pure *im*mobility, the genuine article, and the human richness of Jesus of Nazareth is hard to miss in those opening words: "Martha, Martha—" Frustration, patience in impatience, fondness, pity, understanding . . .

But not warm approval. Properly judged, pure immobility, the genuine article, is no good, and learning how to move oneself imaginatively—at this stage what else can Mary have learned?—is lifegiving.

There's no need, though, to build the case for our kind of classroom work on lofty ground; in a world of negotiating positions and bargaining chips the secular uses of the skills of close imagining are patent.

II

AS FOR METHODS: they are simplicity itself. The armory boasts a few, conversation-generating questions, and little else. —What's going on here? What do you make of so and so? What's happening to this person? What happened a moment ago? Does the person understand what just occurred? Does the person understand her feelings here and now? Why? Why not? Is the person about to commit some action? How will the person explain this moment of feeling and action in the future?

Good sense avoids questions that lead toward judgmental conclusions, because they tend to distance situations and feelings. *Is she insensitive?*

Poor question. The minute I say, "She's insensitive," I cut the flow of feeling that I have to depend upon to carry my imaginings beyond perfunctory, letter-of-reference cliché.

Good sense also preoccupies itself with change. What change do you imagine to be occurring here and why? What were the earlier attitudes and feelings? Can you invent the "causes" of change? Do you say that the person knows that a change is occurring? What would it feel like to undergo such a change?

Certain changes, to be sure, don't abide questions—indeed, they mock questions as piddling and smallminded. *Now,* says Shakespeare's Cleopatra, *now from head to foot/ I am marble-constant.* And a moment later:

> Give me my robe, put on my crown, I have
> Immortal longings in me.

Without an imagination of transcendence we're helpless here. But it's important to realize that, even in these circumstances, the effort to penetrate may not be pointless; in English as in life it's by arriving at our borders that we discover ourselves. Unanswerable or not the key questions must be pressed. They are (to repeat): What is this person *to herself?* What would it be like to be this person, occupying this moment in time?

III

THIS MOMENT IN TIME. The initial working assumption, namely that moments of feeling are timeless and need not be set in relation to author or to age, is of course indefensible. Just now I spoke of the glimpse of the rich humanity of Jesus of Nazareth offered in the exclamation "Martha, Martha." But that humanity is inseparable from cultural tradition—from the art, music, worship, prayer, and commentary of two millennia that have fashioned Western imaginings of a Savior. We see and animate through this tradition. Space has to be made, therefore, in the classroom, for confrontations with the fallacy of timelessness. The reader and imaginer must know themselves—as well as the poem or story—in their genetic contexts.

And they must know better than to consent to the segregation of "appearance" from "reality." We deal ceaselessly and inevitably with shadows, images, projections, versions, since this is the "human condition" (obtaining even in Chapel 31, our classroom). Some versions of St. Augustine, for instance, obsess themselves with his role in the history of sexual repression; they speak of "morbid eccentricities" and of the man's regrettable influence on a thousand years of reflection concerning "original sin." This style of history—history à la village atheism—competes with pious history; professional historians scorn both styles, preferring to quarrel with each other. And where exactly are we, young Emersonians and Whitmanians?

Well, we're at a distance, certainly, from epistemological puzzles and methodological fretting. Our labors are practical rather than abstract; we keep remembering (in obedience to Whitman) that we're exercising, developing ourselves, engaging in a gymnast's struggle—not settling questions.

When reading Augustine's *Confessions,* we practice the struggle against received truths of our own "liberation"—finding the heroic in ancient battles against indulgence and desire. No way to do this without attempting to enter time. Might the Augustinian battle in its own day have been enlivening and exhilarating—the opposite of what's now read as morbid? Is it mindless to think of history as a series of awakenings in which people brainier than their grandfathers best superstition? These are not our questions, although we hover on their outskirts. We are "merely" animating, grappling with the remote:

"I tore my hair and hammered my forehead with my fists; I locked my fingers and hugged my knees; and I did all this because I made an act of will to do it . . . Yet I did not do that one thing which I should have been far, far better pleased to do than all the rest. . . ."

"In my heart I kept saying 'Let it be now, let it be now!' "

"I was held back by mere trifles, the most paltry inanities, all my old attachments. They plucked at my garment of flesh and whispered, 'Are you going to dismiss us? From this moment we shall never be with you again, for ever and ever. From this moment you will never again be allowed to do this thing or that, for evermore.' What was it, my God, that they meant when they whispered 'this or that'?"

And then finally:
"I was asking myself these questions, weeping all the while with the most bitter sorrow in my heart, when all at once I heard the sing-song

voice of a child in a nearby house. Whether it was the voice of a boy or a girl I cannot say, but again and again it repeated the refrain 'Take it and read, take it and read.' . . . In silence I read the first passage on which my eyes fell: *Not in revelling and drunkenness, not in lust and wantonness, not in quarrels and rivalries. Rather, arm yourselves with the Lord Jesus Christ; spend no more thought on nature and nature's appetites.* I had no wish to read more and no need to do so . . . It was as though the light of confidence flooded into my heart and all the darkness of doubt was dispelled."

To seek to draw near to Augustine in these passages, imagining the intensities of torment and release, isn't to "do" history in any conventional sense. It is, however, to practice the invention of time, deploying intelligence and passion at the task of creating a non-contemporary self. In our class such practice is frequent, and I believe it may moderate illusions of mastery arising from lectures on "historical backgrounds."

IV

THE CLASSROOM I'VE BEEN SPEAKING OF came into being as the result of decisions about what English is not that were influenced by reading and teaching, as well as by lucky friendships with a few genius-teachers—people who generously passed along what they knew. (I am thinking particularly of Mina Shaughnessy, James Britton, and Barbara Hardy.) Among the pertinent negatives are these:

English is not centrally about the difference between good books and bad. It is not centrally about poetics, metrics, mysteries of versification, or the study of balance and antithesis in the Ciceronian sentence. It is not centrally about philosophical systems as these can be deduced from abstracts of selected great works. Still more negatives: the English classroom is not primarily the place where students learn of the majesty of Shakespeare and alas for Beaumont and Fletcher. It is not primarily the place where students learn to talk about the structure of a poem or about the logic of the octave and sestet, or about the relation between the narrator and author and speaker and mock-speaker and reader and mock-reader of the poem. It is not primarily the place where students learn to mind their proper manners at the spelling table or to expand their vocabulary or to write Correct like nice folks. It is not a finishing school, not a laugh riot with an entertainer at the front of the room, not an archaeological site, not (once *our* theory has been straightforwardly outlined) a museum of theories.

It is the place—there are few others in most colleges and universities —wherein the chief matters of concern are particulars of humanness: individual human feeling, human response and human time, as these can be animated with the help of writing (at many literary levels) by people living and dead, and as they can be invented and discovered by student writers seeking through words to name and compose and grasp their own experience. English in sum is about my imagined distinctness and the imagined distinctness of other human beings. Its function, like that of some books termed great, is to provide an arena in which separate persons, single egos, can strive at once to encounter the world through art, to decide what if anything they uniquely are, and what some brothers and sisters uniquely are. The instruments employed are the imagination, the intellect, and texts or events that rouse the former to life. And—once more—the goal is not to know dates and authors and how to spell *recommend;* it is to expand the areas of the human world—areas that would not exist but for art—with which creatures of our kind can feel solidarity and coextensiveness.

V

NOT EXCLUDING COEXTENSIVENESS WITH GREATNESS. Lines need to be kept clear, naturally; catching an intuition about the insides of genius doesn't make the intuiter a genius. The pursuit of felt intimacy with greatness often has as its result the clarification of limits: better understanding of what separates immortals from ourselves.

But the pursuit can also define potentialities of one's own nature not perceived hitherto. The capacity for intensity, for one thing—the force of feeling already spoken of in connection with Augustine. Or the capacity for self-transcending fury. (The close imaginer of Marx the ironist finds out about self-transcending fury when evoking, as a reader of *Capital,* Marx's attitude toward panegyrists of nineteenth century "progress" in regulating child labor.)

What's quite often discovered is that a great man's or great woman's gift for infinitely complicated response—the ability, say, to be moved, equally and at the same time, by scorn, pity and hopeless love—isn't finally beyond us. When reading Freud on "what the common man understands by his religion," for instance, we ascend a summit of humane magistrality; the journey demands shedding both conventional tolerance and conventional reproach. ("The whole thing is so patently infantile, so foreign to reality, that to anyone with a friendly attitude to humanity it is painful to think that the great majority of mortals will never be able to rise above this view of life. It is still more humiliating to discover how large a number of people living today, who cannot but see that this religion is not tenable, nevertheless try to defend it piece by piece in a series of pitiful rearguard actions.") Or again: the reader of George Eliot's *Middlemarch* must rise to a level of supreme alertness to the interacting forces (class, history, personal convictions, "character") that constitute us—the alertness modeled in nearly every sentence of that book.

Close imagining of gifts on this order can stimulate decent, proportioned ambition in those of us with no prayer of ascent to comparable achievement. The English classroom exists partly to facilitate that imagining.

VI

A YOUNG WOMAN IS EXPLAINING a moment in the opening scene of *Lear* in class, telling us what's going on within Cordelia as the King her father bears down on her. —*Now, our joy,/Although our least and last . . . What can you say to draw/A third more opulent than your sisters? Speak.* She, Cordelia, says the student, is in rebellion, yes, but that's not *her* idea of herself. She won't flatter her father—but think how much harder on him she could be than she's being. Actually she's not saying one half of what she could. Not telling him what everybody can see, that he's vain and fatuous . . . Oh she's rebelling but she has herself under wraps as she's speaking. She's pressing *down*. In spite of everything—being stony and brusque—she knows she's being good. She feels *forbearing*.

A sound of assent comes into the stillness.

When class is going well, this is what an auditor hears. First the teacher reads aloud—a poem, or a bit of a scene in a play, story or novel, or a patch of Marx or Freud or whoever. Next there's the predictable pause over one or another line: *Good lord,/ You have begot me, bred me, loved me.* Comes then the usual question (What do you make of, etc.?), a silence, a hand or two, and some talk. People listen to each other, add, contend, qualify; on occasion a consensus is reached; at moments as many as a half-dozen minds work collaboratively, installing themselves within remote emotions, tightrope-walking through inner space that's nerved or jokey or fiery or frigid as readers create and cross it.

Needless to say, the proceedings are not to everyone's taste; if it's early in term individual students bring up their misgivings, politely, after class. Is this it? This is the *course*? They're in dead earnest and deserve respect. (Fortunately, because we're in Five College valley, I can inquire about special interests—the Jacobean stage? the editing process? history of Shakespeare studies?—and offer a suggestion about other courses at other places nearby that will meet the need.) I attempt to explain that, after many years of teaching, this is where I have "come out," and that I'm aware that other teachers come out elsewhere. Implicit is that as teachers grow older, they—like others—find changing their ways difficult. Especially difficult if, at various times in their past, they have tried to think the issues through with what ranks, for them, as the utmost seriousness.

In my office, after a class that has gone well, I reflect on the substance. I jot a word or two in the crowded margins of *Lear* (I,i): "C.-forbearing," with the young woman's initials—and look out the window at the Octagon and down the hill. I try to examine the word *forbearing*, setting it on edge like a rare gold coin on my mental palm. I realize not simply that this is a good student who will have more and more to give but that it will be better not to think of "teaching her." The point is to stay with her, being equal to what comes. I realize also that I am trembling. It's because this is English as I conceive English that my student was free to think her thought, to work up its implications, to be unhurriedly serious about serious things in the company of attentive others. The purpose of the retrospective pleasure and self-congratulation that I describe is to bring myself gently down—to restore my calm. What just happened in my classroom—Cordelia walking among us—was to me intensely exciting. Not even the lad who asked the question up at the desk afterward (This is the *course*?) took the edge off it. We were together, nearly all of us. The student who gave us Cordelia spoke to us and for us. A murmur of approval—comprehension—went across the rows. There was more than one sound of assent: I decide that I'm certain of this. We shared a life-quickening experience of art and response-to-art. To this day such moments seem to me beyond price or valuing; they are the promise of happiness fulfilled.

THE DRAGON

George Greenstein
Professor of Astronomy

THE STORY IS TOLD that as he lay upon his deathbed Goethe called out for more light. The shutters were flung wide. Blessed sunlight dispelled the sickroom's shadows.

Fear of the dark is so widespread I imagine it is biologically ingrained. City dwellers that we are, with light available at the touch of a switch, we tend to forget its power. From time to time, however, to reestablish contact with what I suppose to be a more primitive element in my nature, I intentionally put myself into a situation guaranteed to call it forth.

A small forest threaded with a network of trails abuts the playing fields of Amherst College. One of my favorite walks home from work takes me through it. The forest is a tiny patch of civilized wilderness: I share the trails with jogging undergraduates. Not long ago, however, I walked home after sunset without a flashlight.

The night was dark and moonless. Neither a jogger nor a streetlight in sight. Pale starlight filtered down through the arching branches. Barely sensed, the path wound into the gloom. I felt my way. I had walked that route for years, knew every turn of the trail. I could have negotiated it happily blindfolded. But I was not blindfolded, and I was not happy. My skin crawled. I kept resisting an urge to look behind me.

A sudden sound off to one side. I halted. Something gigantic, vague and indistinct loomed beside the trail. Was it moving? Try as I might, foolish as I knew it to be, I could not resist the thought: *there may be dragons here*.

BLESSED SUNLIGHT DISPELS the gloom of night. It floods the inner portions of the solar system. But it does not penetrate everywhere. Most of the universe is dark—darker than my forest. Planets situated farther from the Sun than we are receive less light than we do. High noon on Mars, whose orbit lies just beyond that of the Earth, is still relatively bright; but on Jupiter it is dimmer, and in the distant reaches of the solar system—out by Pluto, say—stars can be seen in broad daylight. Day out there is oppressively dark.

Furthermore, in relative terms even Pluto sits positively huddled beside its lightbulb. Out beyond the orbit of this, the most distant planet, stretch the dark immensities of interstellar space. A hypothetical interstellar traveler would voyage a long way before encountering the next source of light —the next star. He would, in fact, spend a far greater proportion of his voyage in darkness than in light. In relative terms, the volume of space brightly illuminated by stars constitutes a mere 0.000000001 of a percent of the total volume of our Galaxy. Put it another way: for every place that is brilliantly illuminated, there are one hundred billion places which are not.

Farther out, in the gulfs of intergalactic space, the darkness grows deeper. Astronomical photographs give the impression that the universe is peppered throughout with the brightly glowing pinwheels of galaxies. The impression is false: those photographs are time exposures. Actually, an astronaut magically transported into intergalactic space would be capable of seeing only the few closest galaxies, and these merely as faintly glowing patches. And the light they cast is so faint that he would be unable to see his hand held before his face. His body would be invisible to him. The astronomical universe is a universe of stygian darkness.

You could hide a lot of dragons out there.

BEYOND THE VICINITY of the Sun, the only things that immediately leap to our attention are those that emit light and other forms of radiation such as radio waves: stars, galaxies, and so forth. Things which do not generate their own emissions, on the other hand, are by their nature invisible. Such things might lie all about us and nevertheless have escaped detection.

But there are more ways than one to find a dragon. If the forest is dark, you can always listen for the gigantic murmur of its breath. In the astronomical context, it is gravitation that enables us to detect the invisible. Newton taught that matter exerts a gravitational tug—all matter, whether it be the tree in the forest that I see or the thing beside it that I do not see; a brightly shining star or some astronomical object, darkly hidden, of which I am entirely unaware. The more matter one is talking of, the stronger its tug: while the method is not much help in finding relatively small Earth-bound things, it is eminently suited to the searching out of gigantic astronomical objects.

It might be wise, then, to take a gravitational census of the cosmos. What one searches for is an excess attraction, a tug of gravity over and above that which can be accounted for by all the known objects in the cosmos—by all those planets, stars and galaxies that more traditional observations reveal.

How to measure the force of gravity? The simple act of hitting a golf ball provides a clue. The ball travels some distance down the course before falling to the ground. It falls because the Earth attracts it; and had the Earth's force of attraction been stronger, the ball would have travelled a shorter distance before landing. The moral is that the path a flying body takes can tell us the gravitational force acting upon that body.

And in the astronomical realm everything is flying, is orbiting. So to find unseen things, one studies the orbits of seen things, such as stars and galaxies. Anomalies in these orbits reveal the presence of unsuspected matter in the universe.

When one studies the orbits of nearby stars, there turns out to be a good deal of unseen matter in our vicinity—an astonishing quantity, in fact. Accompanying all the normal matter that we see in our corner of the Milky Way Galaxy, there is a fully equal quantity of matter that we cannot see. It is like inviting twenty couples to a party and discovering that another twenty, quite invisible, have accompanied them into the room. Nor is this all. If one surveys the orbits of stars over larger distance scales, one can probe for the presence of unseen matter, not just in our immediate vicinity, but in the Galaxy as a whole. Here there turns out to be fully ten times more invisible than visible stuff: for every ton of matter that we can observe in our Galaxy, ten more tons float unseen. When we survey the orbits of galaxies about each other, the situation grows even more unsettling: for every ton of visible matter, several hundred tons lurk unseen. And finally, the so-called "inflationary" theory of the universe as a whole implies that it contains a thousand times more invisible than visible matter.

The gravitational census, which began as an innocuous research project, has led to ominous results. We astronomers normally rely on telescopes in our study of the universe, and the picture they give us is already rich and complex enough. But the gravitational census has revealed that by using telescopes we have missed the whole point. All those planets, all those moons, asteroids and comets, the stars and galaxies and quasars and interstellar clouds—all these add up to no more than a fraction of a percent of the real content of the universe.

It is like walking through an old, familiar forest and unexpectedly coming upon a dragon. More than that: it is like discovering that the forest one thought one knew so well amounts to no more than scruff on the nape of the neck of a dragon.

But what is it? What is the dragon?

THE FIRST COURSE I EVER TAUGHT at Amherst, which was the first course I ever taught anywhere, was a doozer. I had prepared for it six ways from Sunday—astronomical slide sets one day, film clips the next, and in-depth reporting of the latest astronomical news on the third. I lectured enthusiastically; chalk dust flew. As for the students, they leaned back in their chairs and promptly fell asleep.

My mistake, I eventually realized, was in thinking that my task was to keep them engaged. I was trying to entertain them. Nothing is wrong with entertainment, but it's not education. The students' response to my first efforts had been what we all do before the TV set—they became passive. But as my teaching style has evolved over the years, one guiding principle above all others has emerged: keep students active. They have to *do* science, not just hear about it.

In this regard, the presentation of a mystery such as that of the unseen matter in the cosmos is a marvelous instructional technique. Students find it hard to keep themselves from proposing solutions. Some of my best classroom experiences come when my students find themselves gripped suddenly by the lure of a delicious enigma. Once this has been achieved, the function of the instructor is no longer to "effectively communicate the material." It is no longer to "maintain the students' interest." It is to control a stampede.

The urge to solve problems appears to be innate, and, in my experience, common to us all. There are those who speak in reverential tones of the nobility of science, of the selfless dedication of the scientist. The profession is sometimes held up as a shining example to a world steeped in venality and sin. But I would disagree with this view. So far as I am concerned, there is nothing noble about science at all. Scientists, in truth, are merely behaving according to their innermost natures.

In claiming that the urge to solve mysteries is common, I am far from saying that every student is really a closet scientist at heart. I am rejecting the notion that people are of two sorts: normal humans on the one hand, and on the other those who by some strange quirk are "interested in science." I am claiming that there is nothing remotely unusual about the impulse which motivates the scientist—and that this is what makes education possible.

"It is not at all true that the scientist goes after truth," Sören Kierkegaard once commented. "It goes after him."

TO DO SCIENCE, to solve the mysteries of astronomy, one must use mathematics. Mathematics is the key to understanding in science. The calculations performed need not be complex. But the insights that are reached in the course must emerge from doing the calculations, not *ex cathedra* from the lips of the instructor. In the present instance, note that the problem of unseen matter in the cosmos would never have arisen had quantitative measurements not been made. A detailed mathematical analysis of the orbits of stars and galaxies is essential to the discovery of the excess gravitational attraction. A more intuitive approach, on the other hand, would have gotten us nowhere; after all, the astronomical universe seen through a telescope *looks* perfectly innocuous.

In my view, the sole distinction to be made between advanced courses and those specifically aimed at non-scientists is in the level, but not the amount, of mathematics to be used. Even courses for non-scientists must employ mathematical reasoning, and regularly at that. A student whose curiosity has been piqued by an unsolved problem is helpless to solve that problem unless provided with the tools needed to do so. It is worth pointing out in this regard that even those who claim to be mathematical ignoramuses in fact have quite a respectable array of techniques and instruments at their disposal. Anyone who has attempted to multiply two numbers expressed in Roman numerals, or has glanced at the pages upon pages of laborious calculations performed by Kepler without the aid of a ten-dollar pocket calculator, will understand what I mean.

BACK TO THE GRAVITATIONAL CENSUS. It has revealed the presence of immense quantities of unseen matter in the universe. But what is this matter?

The difficulty is that the gravitational census, which alerted us to the existence of the unseen matter, tells us nothing about it. This is because the force exerted by an object is utterly independent of that object's nature. A ten-ton truck exerts the same (microscopic) gravitational attraction as a ten-ton heap of hay, a comet the same as an asteroid of equal mass. All that counts is quantity of matter; everything else is irrelevant.

So we will never learn much about the nature of the unseen stuff from a study of its gravitational properties. We know that it is present and that it emits neither light nor any other form of energy, and we know a little about its distribution in space. It is termed dark matter, which gives it at least a name. Beyond this, we are on our own.

The only thing for it is to propose a few possibilities and see what becomes of them. Begin at the beginning. I spoke metaphorically when I termed the dark matter a dragon; but suppose I had inadvertently stumbled upon the correct answer? Could the dark matter be a lot of dragons flying about the cosmos?

—But that's nonsense! you expostulate.

—Prove it, I respond.

—The dragon is a mythical beast! No one has ever found one! you persist.

—Not until now, say I (noticing all those exclamation marks—always a sure sign that, while you may be sure of what you say, you are finding it difficult to say just *why* you are sure).

—All right then, you say (calming down). If this insane suggestion is to be taken seriously, we must allow these extraterrestrial beings to obey the laws of biology. One of those laws is that animals must breathe. But space is a vacuum. Ergo, nothing can live in outer space.

—Fish don't breathe, I respond.

—No, but they take in water through their gills. There's no water in space either.

—But why do we breathe? Why do fish take in water? Could it be that whatever we obtain in these ways might be obtained by a space-dwelling organism in some other way?

Suddenly the conversation has taken an unexpected turn. If conducting a class, I would leave things as they stand, with the charge to research the above questions in time for the next session. For now, I change the subject and point out that all living beings require energy, and that the ultimate source of this energy must be at a higher temperature than their own (this can be demonstrated using the laws of thermodynamics: depending on the class level, I would or would not give the proof). It is sunlight that provides the energy in the case of life on Earth, captured by plants through the mechanism of photosynthesis. Animals, in turn, get their energy by eating the plants. Similarly, my hypothetical dragons would have to get energy from starlight. What does this imply?

—It implies that they would cluster around stars.

—And do they?

—Well, they don't cluster around *our* star. There are no dragons flying about through our solar system. If there were, we'd see them.

—Not necessarily. Dragons might be bigger than we are, but they are tiny by astronomical standards. If our solar system were filled with them, would our telescopes be powerful enough to discern them?

Here is an opportunity for a calculation. The answer turns out to be Yes. This presents a severe problem for the dragon hypothesis. And now a second problem emerges from the discussion. The gravitational census revealed more and more dark matter as the cosmos was probed over larger and larger scales of distance. The stuff acts as if it is avoiding our neigh-

borhood and preferring intergalactic space. But that is just the opposite
of the distribution expected of living beings, which would need to cluster
about stars.

Death of the dragon hypothesis. More hypotheses: could the universe
be littered throughout with stones, pebbles? Or how about ultra-dim
stars, so faint as to have escaped detection? A tenuous, all-pervasive intergalactic gas? Ever more sophisticated arguments are brought to bear.

THAT IS AN EXAMPLE of the sort of interchange I might attempt to
conduct during a class meeting. I have not always taught that way. Until
recently my teaching style was the straight lecture. This is the preferred
method of instruction in the sciences, in which such an enormous body
of information must be conveyed.

But a curious paradox stands at the heart of the problem of education
in the sciences. The student must learn all the multitudinous facts and
techniques of the field; but science develops so rapidly that, by the time
that student has finished graduate education and embarked upon original
research, the facts will have changed. Especially will they have changed
by, say, the midpoint of his or her career. (I am astounded when I open
the textbooks from which I learned the trade, so obsolete have they become.) How to prepare to enter a field that transforms itself so rapidly?
How to bend the bow, so as to launch an arrow into ecstatic, productive
flight for a lifetime?

I would say it's impossible. It's impossible because that's the wrong
metaphor. A better metaphor would be that of preparing a person to
undertake a voyage—a voyage lasting a lifetime; a voyage to unknown
lands, in circumstances that cannot possibly be predicted. Instruction in
the mathematical techniques, instruction in the facts: these are means to
an end. The end, the most important task facing the teacher, is to em-
power the student, to provide him or her with the means for solving *any*
problem that comes along.

And the way to learn how to solve any problem is to get practice
solving problems on your own. You don't learn how to play the violin by
reading books about it—you learn by picking up the instrument, gritting
your teeth, and producing those (initially) horrible sounds.

I want to emphasize the role of conversation in the process of research.

The popular image of the scientist as an isolated individual, lonely and aloof in the laboratory, is mistaken. Science is a community, and the business of that community is argument. The arguments take place over lunch and in the hallways, by long-distance telephone and at scientific meetings, and especially in the pages of the professional journals. Ideas are proposed and criticized, revised and criticized anew. Out of this perpetual interchange, the truth is hammered out.

The classroom equivalent of this interchange is the seminar. It is, of course, a method with many perils. Discussions are time-consuming; and because there is a great amount of material that must be covered, panic inexorably rises within the instructor as the end of the semester draws near. As for the students, they are often impatient with such dialogue. They want to push through what often appears to be little more than wrangling, and get down to results. But the method has so many virtues that I find myself using it more and more.

I DON'T WANT TO GIVE the wrong impression. Most astronomy classes are not *salons* at which tantalizing mysteries are debated in dazzling conversation. I want in this essay to analyze how a scientist worries away at a problem, and what attitudes and skills must be communicated to the student who wishes to take part in the process. But there's more than this to be done: most class time is taken up with instruction in technique, and with the complex array of facts these techniques have revealed. If truth be told, a lot of drudgery is involved.

In many ways the experience of being a student is difficult and fundamentally unsatisfying. My guess is that this is particularly so in the sciences. Students often feel that science is sterile and uncreative, and that people who enjoy giving free rein to their creativity ought to enter another field. To an extent these students are laboring under a misconception: the creation of a piece of music, say, requires fully as much rigorous discipline as any scientific endeavor. Nevertheless there is an element of truth in the attitude. In the sciences there is indeed such a thing as the right answer to a question, and the student who does not get that answer has simply Not Done It Right. A sterile perfection will get you a perfectly good "A": it will get you a perfectly good lifetime career.

The best scientists, of course, are immensely creative. They have highly refined faculties of intuition and taste. One often hears about how important such matters are to the practice of science. It's all perfectly true—but only at the cutting edge of research. The student of astronomy, on the other hand, is by and large denied the opportunity to exercise these talents.

Even now I recall the bitter sense of inferiority, of uselessness, that oppressed me when I was an undergraduate. I felt there was nothing I could say to my teachers that they did not already know. I felt that I had not the slightest possibility of producing an original thought. My only role was that of the learner.

I was right, and the same is true of students today. The problem, of course, lies not with them but with the nature of the field they have elected to study. The student who cannot possibly suggest something new to me about electromagnetism is perfectly capable of achieving insights in a philosophy course that would send the instructor into hours of cogitation. It is one of the worst things about the life of the science student. Nor do I know of any cure. It is a situation the student is simply forced to live with.

I KNOW A MAN who has spent most of the last two decades in the study of pulsars. He is perhaps the most brilliant, inventive and prolific of all the workers in that field. Indeed, he is so inventive that he keeps changing his mind about them. Not one of his theories has survived more than a few years before he—*he*—has demolished it.

Has he been erratic and inconsistent? Has he spent his career hopping foolishly from one chimera to the next? I would argue that he has steadfastly held true to a single course. As best he could, he has worked out his ideas concerning the nature of pulsars—and then has evaluated those ideas, found areas that required modification or extension, and gone on to explore his new theories. If his progress has seemed erratic, so too does the progress of anyone exploring an unknown land.

To solve a mystery such as that of the dark matter, it is not enough to be creative. It is not enough to think of a new and ingenious explanation. The important thing is to evaluate the evidence for and against that explanation. This incessant testing of hypotheses is the hallmark of science.

In this regard, nothing is more beneficial for students than the chasing down of wrong ideas. I regularly devote a certain amount of class time to the analysis of a notion that I know will turn out to be false. (It's not cheating, because the notion was presented not as the truth, but as provisional.) The sequence of events is instructive. There will be an initial commitment to the notion, but then a recognition that it fails in some essential respect. There follows an attempt to save it by modifying it in various ways, and finally a decision—arrived at only with reluctance—that the truth lies elsewhere.

Students will not long remember the facts they have been taught in class. I certainly have only the haziest of memories of my undergraduate education. What they will remember is the habit of probing for inconsistencies. For the one enshrined virtue of scholarship is skepticism. You must doubt everything.

There is nowadays a program of research projects designed to undermine our most cherished advances. Enormous sums are spent on experiments probing for weaknesses in the theories, for instance, of Einstein. And although Einstein is held by scientists in a regard that borders on religious adoration, there is nothing heretical about these efforts. On the contrary, they are a tribute to his greatness.

IF EVERYTHING IS SUBJECT to doubt, let us not be diffident: let us doubt the very *existence* of dark matter in the universe. Could it be there is actually no mystery to be solved? Could it be there are flaws in the analysis that led us to the enigma in the first place?

Here's a possible flaw: perhaps there is something wrong with our ideas about gravity. The gravitational census of the cosmos employed the full mathematical theory of gravitation, and if that theory happens to be false, conclusions derived from it will be false. But what is the evidence for the correctness of that theory?

Part of the evidence involves laboratory experiments. Masses have been placed near each other and the force between them measured. The results are in accord with theoretical prediction. But is this sufficient? A skeptic would point out that the theory has been confirmed only under certain limited circumstances: with masses of a few pounds or so, over distances of a few feet or so. Couldn't gravity behave differently when the objects attracting each other are the size of planets, and the attractions operate over distances of hundreds of millions of miles?

Probe further. Tests have been carried out within the solar system. The orbits of planets have been tracked and the results compared with theory. Here, too, the theory is confirmed—but here, too, only with certain masses and over certain distances. So the list of tests grows longer. Orbits of stars about each other are analyzed, orbits of galaxies. In every instance, the theory is confirmed.

—But hold on, the skeptic interjects. You're going too fast. Just *how* do you track the orbits of the planets?

—The most accurate means we possess is radar, I reply.

—Then maybe your ideas about radar are where the error lies. How does radar work?

—We send off a signal, it hits the planet and bounces back, and we detect the returning echo. What we measure is the time delay between sending off the signal and receiving the echo. That tells us how far away the planet is: the more delayed the echo, the more distant the planet.

—Hmm . . . you are assuming that you know how fast the radar signal travels?

—Oh, but we do know. Radar travels at the speed of light.

—Prove it.

Panic rises within me. The velocity of radar signals has been measured in the laboratory, and found to be that of light. But over distances of hundreds of millions of miles? Why could not the signals "grow tired" in traversing such inconceivable gulfs? I'll have to think this one over for a moment. But before I get my thoughts in order, the skeptic continues:

—And tell me something about this tracking of the orbits of stars about each other. How do you do that?

—Oh, that's easy. We just look at them through telescopes.

—So you're using light. How do you know it travels in straight lines from the stars to the telescope?

In fact there are good arguments that radar travels at the speed of light, and that light travels in straight lines. But these arguments themselves depend on other assertions, which in turn depend on others, and so forth. At what point do we stop and declare our theory of gravitation absolutely and finally correct? At no point. A scientific theory is an enormous scaffold of interconnected assertions—and each one of them is subject to some degree of doubt.

This is not to say, however, that we are entirely ignorant. For the assertions making up the scaffold interrelate with each other closely. They confirm one another in complex ways. The scaffold as a whole possesses a remarkable inner consistency: it is stronger than any of its parts. My belief is that there are no major holes in our understanding of gravitation, and that we are indeed faced with a mystery concerning dark matter in the universe. But there is a certain degree of uncertainty attached to that belief.

I WANT TO EMPHASIZE THE ambiguous nature of our position with regard to the dark matter. The hypothesis that it consists of dragons can be rejected unambiguously. But things do not usually turn out so cleanly. Most of the other suggestions cannot be rejected at all, and are left as viable—and mutually contradictory—hypotheses. Yet other suggestions run into partial objections, and are left in an unclear state.

To the working scientist it's a familiar situation. In the long run the practice of science brings certainty, but the researcher at its cutting edge lives in a world of perpetual ambiguity. So will our students when they graduate and move on to their professional careers, whether these careers turn out to be in science or elsewhere.

But I do not often teach ambiguity in my courses. There simply is not enough time. There are too many techniques to be taught, and too many facts revealed by these techniques. Under the press of necessity, mostly what I teach is certainty.

For this reason I value the Introduction to Liberal Studies courses I have taught. These seminar courses, required of every freshman and intended to explore the deepest questions of liberal thought, are an opportunity to try out nonstandard forms of instruction. My most recent experience of this sort has been in a course dealing with the extinction of the dinosaurs. The central fact here is that we do not understand what killed them off. Rather, we have a wide variety of hypotheses—again, all mutually contradictory—together with evidence that is fragmentary and incomplete. So the point of the course is not to learn the truth. The point is to give the students practice in dealing with ambiguity.

But no one likes ambiguity. It is painful, and the urge is universal to resolve it. I have encountered two common ways of trying to do so. Some people prefer retreating into a comfortable sense of certainty, and will adopt the very first suggestion that comes along and cling to it. At the other end of the spectrum are those who retreat into an equally comfortable sense of universal skepticism. "After all," these people say, "when you get right down to it, we don't know anything for sure."

The problem is that both the claim to certainty and the claim of total ignorance are spurious. The first suggestion that comes along is likely to be false. No matter how seductive it may appear, the most rigorous evaluation is required before we should accept it. On the other hand, it is equally the case that we are not totally ignorant. There are plenty of things we know for sure, and even though they do not provide the answers we are looking for, we should not abandon them. A healthy balance between these poles is the goal of the Mass Extinctions course. I would like to work more of this into my other teaching.

A REMARKABLE INSIGHT into the nature of the dark matter comes from an apparently unrelated consideration: the abundances of the chemical elements in the cosmos.

According to the big bang theory of the origin of the universe, the cosmos began composed of the lightest of all elements, hydrogen. But, shortly after the big bang, nuclear fusion reactions took place which transmuted some of this hydrogen into heavier elements of the periodic table. One can calculate mathematically just how many of them were formed. This calculation turns out to depend on the amount of dark matter in the universe. If a moderate quantity is present, the calculations agree perfectly with the presently observed abundances of the elements. If, on the other hand, the universe contains as much dark matter as the gravitational census implies, the predicted abundances come out wildly wrong.

It is difficult to be sure how seriously these calculations should be taken. To comprehend the outcome of processes taking place during the first few minutes of the history of the cosmos requires a gigantic extrapolation of our ideas into unknown territory. Nevertheless, most workers in the field are inclined to take the calculations very seriously. What should we make of the dilemma they pose?

Their implication is that what we have been calling dark "matter" must not be matter at all, in the normal sense of the word. All of the previous discussion has turned out to be irrelevant: it cannot be dragons, and it cannot be planets or ultra-dim stars or any of the other possibilities. All these objects are made of *stuff*—and the dark matter cannot be stuff at all.

Rather, it can consist only of material lying at the very frontiers of modern research. Neutrinos are one possibility. They are known to flood the cosmos in great numbers. Neutrinos were originally thought to be utterly without mass, but a recent experiment has raised the possibility that they might possess mass after all. The experiment has been disputed; as of this writing, the evidence is unclear. A second possibility is the notion of immense numbers of black holes filling space. Meanwhile, not to be left waiting on the sidelines, the elementary-particle physicists push for their latest inventions: particles with dream-like, romantic names such as photino, axion, or the yet more mysterious cosmic strings.

The mystery of dark matter in the universe is one of the central conundrums intriguing astrophysicists today. It is customary to say that we have not the slightest idea what the stuff could be. That's not quite true. We have lots of slightest ideas—far too many, in fact. What we do not have is a persuasive idea, one that sweeps aside all the others. And most important of all, we do not have enough evidence.

"GO EENA KUMBLA":
CARIBBEAN WAYS OF SEEING AND KNOWING

Rhonda Cobham
Assistant Professor of Black Studies and English

"So how do *you* like teaching at Amherst?"

AFTER NEARLY FOUR YEARS, the inflected question still comes, reminding me that for many of the inhabitants of my college community, I remain an exotic outsider. How to explain that I've lived in Amherst for almost as long as I've lived anywhere else since leaving Trinidad at eighteen, and that I've lived and worked since that age almost exclusively in academic communities of three thousand students or less? From that perspective, Amherst seems a lot like everything else in the rag bag of assorted colleges and cities—Port of Spain, Kingston, St. Andrews, London, Brighton, Bayreuth—that I refer to in certain contexts as "home."

My education in Trinidad at an elite girls' school modelled on the British public school system prepared me for export to Europe and America as surely as cocoa and sugar cane exist to make Cadbury's chocolate. Many well-known West Indian intellectuals have written at length about the odd social ruptures created by this educational process: C.L.R. James in *Beyond a Boundary,* George Lamming in *In the Castle of My Skin,* the historian and politician Eric Williams in his autobiography *Inward Hunger,* and Derek Walcott in his long poem *Another Life.* The narrator in V.S. Naipaul's novel *The Mimic Men* explains the process in this way:

> It was difficult at that school and with those boys. We had converted our island into one big secret. Anything that touched on everyday life excited laughter when it was mentioned in a classroom: the name of a shop, the name of a street, the name of street-corner foods. The laughter denied our knowledge of these things to which after the hours of school we were to return. We denied the landscape and the people we could see out of open doors and windows, we who took apples to the teacher and wrote essays about visits to temperate farms. Whether we dissected a hibiscus flower or recited the names of Isabellan birds, school remained a private hemisphere.

Almost any West Indian professional living outside of the region can tell a version of this story. It's one of the ironies of our colonial legacy that islands so small continue to lavish so large a portion of their scarce resources on the education of a group of people who can best use their skills by distancing themselves from their home communities for most of their lives.

From the perspective of ten years teaching in the Caribbean, Europe and America, however, my schizoid colonial education seems different only in degree from the discontinuities that mark the intersection of private and public worlds in the lives of most of my students. Like them, I've often found it difficult to relate the experience of the classroom to the reality of my life. That gulf forced me to invent ways to keep learning about other people's worlds while teaching myself retrospectively about my own society. For most of my students, however, this process of retrospective integration remains a problem. Their lives seem, if anything, more complex than mine. Yet, growing up in the age of the sound bite, in a world that reduces politics to a face-off between the good cowboys and the bad Injuns, they seem to find it difficult to escape the illusion that they live (or should live) in a coherent moral universe. I watch them sort their teachers into feminists, "old fogies," late sixties' radicals and postmodern theorists, and wonder if they ever think about the ways in which such categories overlap or even create each other.

For me growing up, the categories rarely seemed so clearly defined. I was in high school in 1968, and watched as my teachers and peers swung through impossible about-turns around issues of race and class before I was even sure what those terms meant for me. And people didn't always belong to one side or the other. The headmistress who introduced me to Jane Austen was also the first person I met who had lived and worked in Africa. I was fascinated by both of the worlds to which she gave me access. The professor who read Anglo-Saxon sagas with me at the University of the West Indies was involved in research on African-derived oral traditions, and there was no clear divide between the pleasure I got out of those wonderful alliterative mouthfuls in *The Seafarer* and the excitement of discovering a Caribbean oral tradition.

Later, the most conservative of political agendas enabled some of my most radical learning experiences. As a graduate student at the University of St. Andrews in Scotland, I was encouraged to work on Caribbean Literature because an eccentric Scottish professor (who thought typewriters were the work of the devil) was convinced that nothing worth reading had been written in Britain since Shakespeare. In Germany I developed an expertise in gender issues in African literature because the German government, having missed out on the colonial era, decided to invest heavily in research on Africa at a time when, from the perspective of recent motherhood, I was anxious to explore my feminism. I moved to America in search of a job in the mid-1980s when Imperial America, like Matthew Arnold's British Empire a century before, was trying to master the complexities of the states and societies it dominated. Within the academy this agenda created a demand for people who could teach the kinds of things I knew about race, gender and non-Western cultures.

The doors that allowed me to make these connections were opened by chance. They could just as easily have been traps for another person, or insurmountable barriers for me at another time or place. But the intellectual developments they made possible have shaped my approaches to knowledge. Although I now describe myself as a teacher of African and Caribbean literatures and feminist theory, I find myself in the classroom and through my research in an ongoing conversation with all the texts and places that have been a part of my education. This dialogic process forces me constantly to re-situate my understanding of the subjects I teach in response to the shifting, often contradictory modes of apprehending experience that characterize the many different societies and intellectual traditions with which I have come into contact.

Some of my most formative learning experiences have been those which for whatever reason forced me to distance the familiar. Paradoxically, I acquired this perspective in part in response to the contradictions of a colonial education that constantly challenged me to make familiar what was foreign. As an English major at the University of the West Indies, when I learnt about the world of seventeenth-century England that produced Milton, I took it for granted that if I studied hard enough I could incorporate his cultural experience into my own, in the way that my Chinese Jamaican professor obviously had done. It was only when I attempted the same process in my graduate work at the University of St. Andrews on the Victorian poet and essayist Matthew Arnold that I realised that such cultural divides could not always be crossed without consequences. Sometimes my teachers and fellow students in Scotland found it difficult to accept my desire as an outsider to participate on an equal footing in what they thought of as their intellectual world. It was easier for them to place me in the category of Samuel Johnson's dancing dog than to question the assumption that there had to be a "natural" link between their participation in Western culture and the biological accident of their being "white" and/or "male." What would they have made of Jean Rhys, I wonder, a white West Indian author whose immersion in Caribbean culture—a culture within which she was ostracized as a "white cockroach"—made it difficult for her to identify with the ways of perceiving reality she encountered in Western Europe? Rhys's heroine in *Voyage in the Dark,* who shares her creator's "white" racial and "black" cultural background, tries to describe this perceptual difficulty:

> England, rosy pink in the geography book map, but on the page opposite the words are closely crowded, heavy looking. Exports, coal, iron, wool. Then Imports and Character of Inhabitants. Names, Essex, Chelmsford on the Chelmer. The Yorkshire and Lincolnshire wolds. Wolds? Does that mean hills? How high? Half the height of ours, or not even that? Cool green leaves in the short cool summer. Summer. There are fields of corn like sugar cane fields but gold color and not so tall. After summer the trees are bare, then winter and snow. White feathers falling? Torn pieces of paper falling?

More frequently, however, my British colleagues took my enthusiasm for their literature as evidence that their culture had a "universal" appeal: that any outsider would recognize it as inherently superior, offering sweetness and light in quantities not approached in "provincial" non-European cultures. As Matthew Arnold puts it in his essay on "The Literary Influence of Academies":

> To get rid of provinciality is a certain stage of culture; a stage the positive result of which we must not make too much importance, but which is, nevertheless, indispensable, for it brings us on to the platform where alone the best and highest intellectual work can be said fairly to begin. . . . The less a literature has felt the influence of a supposed centre of correct information, correct judgement, correct taste, the more we shall find in it this note of provinciality.

When he penned these lines in the late nineteenth century, Arnold considered British culture philistine in its intellectual taste and barbarian in its pursuit of physical pleasure. In this passage he is actually upbraiding his fellow Englishmen for their provinciality in comparison to the French and Germans. But by the time I was reading Arnold's words a century later, it was not only my British peers who assumed that British culture was beyond provinciality. Looking back, I think that I, too, may have taken this position for granted. At any rate there was certainly a connection between my easy participation in Western intellectual discourse and the ambivalence with which I alternately embraced or effaced my personal connection to Caribbean culture. The Jamaican-born poet Claude McKay confesses to a similar ambivalence in an autobiographical essay collected in *My Green Hills of Jamaica,* when he recounts how his British mentor Walter Jekyll encouraged him to abandon the writing of cramped, imitative romantic verse in favor of poetry in Jamaican Creole. McKay enjoyed the freedom of this new genre, and he won public acclaim for elevating the local language to the status of Art; but, he remembers, "I used to think I would show them something. Some day I would write poetry in straight English and amaze and confound them."

In the end, it was the endearing, albeit misplaced, chauvinism of my eccentric Scottish professor that forced me to reconstitute my Caribbean heritage as a valued object of intellectual scrutiny. He had never forgiven the English for continuing to produce writers after Shakespeare and, to spite them, he encouraged me to abandon Arnold and the Victorians for the study of Caribbean literature. Fortunately for him, he retired before I had finished my thesis; and since he had never encountered the work of any West Indian writers, he was spared the pain of discovering that their literary mentors were the Victorians and Romantics and (horror of horrors) the English novelists of the eighteenth and nineteenth centuries. Perhaps it was homesickness that made me follow his advice, but in elevating Caribbean writing to the same status that I had previously reserved for English literature and culture, I made myself work at mastering its nuances and complexities from an academic perspective. Reading my way through West Indian novels, newspapers and colonial documents in the British Library, I began to understand who I was, why I liked the things I did, why I did not know which part of Africa my ancestors came from, and why that wonderfully balanced Arnoldian prose had made so much sense to me in the first place. For the first time, I was able to link those parts of myself that were about academia and literature to going to church with my mother and being excited and terrified by Carnival, and going to music lessons on Thursdays and the beach on Saturdays and "going-away-to-England-to-study" and sitting up all night with my cousins and sisters talking about "Life."

One of the immediate results of this process was that it demystified my attachment to British literature. Now, when I read Matthew Arnold, I could see that he was struggling to articulate a new way of thinking about spirituality in an age of doubt and change similar in many respects to the age in which I lived. But I was also painfully aware of his blindness and partiality about the subjectivity of others—Orientals, the Irish, the masses —whom he relegated to the status of non-persons in order to buttress his own uncertain sense of self. The double vision my new understanding made possible did not destroy my appreciation of English Literature. In fact it heightened my responses to some of these writers. My discovery that they, too, were capable of self-indulgence and partiality made their achievement seem less perfect, more tangible, more humanly compelling. I never could bring myself to enjoy Tennyson again, but it was possible to read a whole new layer of acknowledged and unacknowledged blindnesses in the closing lines of Arnold's poem "Dover Beach."

> Ah, love let us be true
> To one another! for the world, which seems
> To lie before us like a land of dreams,
> So various, so beautiful, so new,
> Hath really neither joy, nor love, nor light,

Nor certitude, nor peace nor help for pain;
And we are here as on a darkling plain
Swept with confused alarms of struggle and flight,
Where ignorant armies clash by night.

My new sense of cultural empowerment brought a world of aesthetic possibilities within my grasp and I seized it with both hands. I had done enough work in linguistics as an undergraduate to teach myself the basics of Creole linguistics. It was pure delight to rediscover and name the patterns of my own Creole speech and to recognize the ways in which these patterns had been codified in the work of West Indian writers. I like to think that this discovery of a way to name linguistic patterns and to manipulate their contrapuntal interaction with the rhythms of Standard English is what gives this early sonnet by Derek Walcott for me—in spite of the tragi-comic sordidness of the scene it describes—its freshness and panache:

Poopa, da was a fête! I mean it had
Free rum free whisky and some fellars beating
Pan from one of them band in Trinidad
And everywhere you turn was people eating
And drinking and don't name me but I think
They catch his wife with two tests up the beach
While he drunk quoting Shelley with "Each
Generation has its angst, but we has none"
And wouldn't let a comma in edgewise.
(Black writer chap, one of them Oxbridge guys.)
And it was round this part once that the heart
Of a young child was torn from it alive
By two practitioners of native art,
But that was long before this jump and jive.

Can you hear the syncopated rhythms of Caribbean speech when you read this sonnet, I wonder, answering like a tenor solo on a steelband pan the steady five-beat, walking meter of an invisible metronome? And do the multiple ironies of that final quatrain make sense? ("Get it, Mummy, get it?" My delight reminds me of my six-year-old daughter as she demands that I share her mastery of the latest "why-did-the-chicken-cross-the-road" joke.) I know both of those rhythms, and the beach; I recognize those "native practitioners," and the music they were playing at the fête; and the school that test (fellow) must have attended if he was misquoting Shelley—and the Shelley! All of it is mine. "Adam's task, of giving things their names," Walcott calls it in *Another Life,* stealing the quotation from another West Indian writer who probably picked it up somewhere along the line during his own colonial education. But that very eclecticism and sense of inhabiting a world not yet named are the qualities that create my special bond with the writers and intellectuals of the Caribbean.

In the classroom, my students are occasionally overwhelmed by this passionate private relationship I seem to share with the texts I teach. "We'll never get it the way you do," is a common complaint. I try to explain that growing up in a culture doesn't necessarily entitle anyone to "get it." There was a time when I did not "get" Walcott or Naipaul, and another time, when reading Chaucer was pure delight because I felt I "got it" without having to think of why each word meant what it did. Part of the excitement of teaching Caribbean literature has become the challenge of making students see their unreflective participation in any cultural milieu as a short cut. Their struggle with the eclecticism of Caribbean writing may encourage them to think about the imaginative literature of their own worlds as alien texts with which they too can become passionately involved through careful reading and thought.

To that sense of linguistic delight and cultural empowerment, my time in Britain added an understanding of Marxist theories about culture. In fact, it wasn't really quite Britain, but the Barbadian novelist George Lamming, who befriended me in London and introduced me to the work of writers like Gramsci, Eagleton and Raymond Williams. Through the prism of class, these writers challenged me to acknowledge that, along with the Anglophilia that had been imposed on me as part of the colonial legacy, my cultural alienation was the product of a deliberate strategy of the "brown" West Indian middle class to which I belonged. I knew from my own upbringing how resolutely this class had fought to separate itself from its origins in the Caribbean peasantry. There was no love lost within it for those who were black and poor. Though we resented our colonial situation, we knew how to gain status and privilege by aligning ourselves with the external sources of power which still controlled the labor and resources of the former slave population.

My reading of Marxist cultural theories brought into focus another layer of intellectual issues that constitute an ongoing preoccupation in my work. From the perspective of large segments of the population in my society, I am one of the "oppressors." Where does my privilege end and my oppression begin? And how is it possible to represent in language the experience of occupying simultaneously the position of victimizer and victimized? I've encountered a parallel uncertainty in the responses to exclusion and inclusion of students who consider themselves social or racial outsiders at institutions like Amherst College. Not to be accepted in an environment like this may be painful, but how much more terrifying is the guilt of knowing that one in fact fits in better here than back home! One of the ways in which I address this ambivalence in the classroom is by examining the uneasy alliance between protest and patronage embedded in such relationships as that between the Jamaican Claude McKay and his English mentor, Walter Jekyll. Is a writer who speaks out about injustices in his society compromised by the fact that his patrons are representatives of the institutions he assails? What kinds of strains and ruptures does this create in the texts produced? And can these strains be transformed or deflected into new ways of manipulating language or structuring narrative?

The writers George Lamming and Wilson Harris offer different responses to these questions in their work. In Lamming's novels the archetypal relationship between colonizer and colonized which he reads into Shakespeare's *The Tempest* provides an allegory of the Caribbean condition. Unlike Fanon and Manoni, who, from different perspectives, identify Prospero with the colonizer and Caliban with the colonized, Lamming dramatizes the ways in which each of his characters simultaneously occupies the roles of Prospero/Caliban/Miranda—even Ariel, depending on which of their relationships we privilege at any given moment in the text. So, for example, in the novel *Water With Berries* the Old Dowager, who provides a home in Britain for the stranded Caribbean artist Teeton, is united with him through their different relationships of subjugation to an absent "Prospero" figure; but, at later junctures in the text, each plays Prospero to the other's Caliban. Structurally this tension enacts itself as a rupture in another of Lamming's novels, *Season of Adventure,* which is set in the Caribbean. Having traced the rise of the fictional lower-class character Powell from the position of victim to that of tyrant, Lamming abruptly enters his novel in what seems to be his "own" voice to comment:

Until the age of ten Powell and I had lived together, equal in the affection of two mothers. Powell had made my dreams; and I had lived his passions. Identical in years, and stage by stage, Powell and I were taught in the same primary school.

And then the division came. I got a public scholarship which started my migration into another world, a world whose roots were the same but whose style of living was entirely different from what my childhood knew. It had earned me a privilege which now shut Powell and the whole *tonelle* out of my future. I had lived as near to Powell as my skin to the hand it darkens. And yet! . . . Instinctively I attached myself to that new privilege; and in spite of all my effort, I am not free of its embrace even to this day.

I believe deep in my bones that the mad impulse which drove Powell to his criminal defeat was largely my doing. I will not have this explained away by talk about environment; nor can I allow my own moral infirmity to be transferred to a foreign conscience, labelled imperialist. I shall go beyond my grave in the knowledge that I am responsible to my brother.

Powell still resides somewhere in my heart, with a dubious love, some strange nameless shadow of regret; and yet with the deepest, deepest nostalgia. For I have never felt myself to be an honest part of anything since the world of his childhood deserted me.

Lamming's abrupt first-person intervention has worried many of his critics. His refusal to distance himself from the social malaise he describes unsettles the relationship between reader, author and story; between "fiction" and "real life." The effect of this strategy on the narrative is to collapse the certainties of its plot inward in ways that threaten to leave the reader without a guide through the spiritual morass he invokes.

Lamming urges vigilance, but often communicates despair. For the Guyanese writer Wilson Harris, by contrast, the dissolution of the boundaries between victim and victor in the Caribbean context makes possible an apocalyptic vision in which all fossilized hierarchies are collapsed, and man is faced with the terror and promise of re-imagining community. In his essays on *Tradition, the Writer and Society,* Harris asserts that "man will never pass beyond pre-historic conditions until all his gods have failed, and their failure, which puts him on the rack, opens up the necessity for self-knowledge." He is insistent in his rejection of the way in which the traditional form of the novel seeks to establish a narrative time and space that creates the illusion that real life can be reduced to a fixed, linear progression. For him, this "novel of consolidation" offers its characters a spurious freedom of choice within the parameters of "an accepted plane of society [which] we are persuaded has an inevitable existence." Instead, Harris argues for the novel of fulfillment. He takes the figure of the individual slave, separated from any communal identity by the depersonalization of his enslavement and the linguistic barriers between himself and other slaves, as the starting point for a new sense of subjectivity based on the search for an inward dialogue and space—a new vision of consciousness:

> This vision of consciousness is the peculiar reality of language because the concept of language is one which continuously transforms inner and outer formal categories of experience, earlier and representative modes of speech itself, the still life resident in painting and sculpture as such, even music which one ceases to "hear"—the peculiar reality of language provides a medium to *see* in consciousness the "free" motion and to *hear* with consciousness the "silent" flood of sound by a continuous inward revisionary and momentous logic of potent explosive images invoked in the mind. Such a capacity for language is a real and necessary one in a world where the inarticulate person is continuously frozen or legislated for in mass and a genuine experience of his distress, the instinct of distress, sinks into a void.

Harris's fiction enacts this process of revisualizing, or re-articulating, experience from within. In novels about explorers, painters, land surveyors and East Indian peasants, set in every imaginable past or present metropolitan and Caribbean location, he takes his readers past their fear of a life in which no meanings are prescribed, on to a more difficult, constantly elusive moment of potential renewal somewhere on the frontier between nihilism and hope. Because Harris challenges them to resist the conventional surface meaning that narrative structures impose on experience, many students find his work bewildering and disorienting. Indeed, few critics can describe its effect without slipping into Harris's idiosyncratic, often abstruse, language. Harris's method, however, helps me as a teacher to encourage students to appropriate language as a personal resource, and to use it to imagine a space beyond the predictable polarities of what Harris has called "victim/victor stasis" from which to assess their worlds.

The six years in Germany that followed my time as a graduate student in Britain were also the years in which I "discovered" Africa, as a physical space and as an intellectual concern. There were wonderful ironies and an unexpected pleasure in this juxtaposition. From a New World island perspective, Europe and Africa presented startling similarities. There was a sense of geographical vastness for me in both continents which was exacerbated by the complex ways in which their inhabitants negotiated between multiple languages and cultures. Both places also offered a new understanding of ethnicity. To say that one was Prussian or Igbo carried with it quite different implications than to say one was Jamaican as opposed to Trinidadian or that one's grandfather had come from Asia or Africa. Here place was important, even when place, as with Prussia, or Biafra, no longer existed. The kinship ties that this Old World sense of place embodied went back for centuries in the oral histories of both continents. In Germany and Nigeria I encountered individuals whose families had been displaced by war. Twenty, fifty, one hundred years after the moment of dislocation, the status of outsider remained a powerful marker, surviving in the meaning of a surname, the location of a dwelling, or as casual epithet in daily conversation.

There seemed also to be literary consequences for these broadly generalized areas of intersection. In the classic New World narrative, the accident of exile is read as a necessary precondition for the discovery of self. By contrast, in Chinua Achebe's *Things Fall Apart* or Gunter Grass's *Tin Drum,* the displacement of exile becomes a metaphor for psychic disintegration. From this perspective, Harris's visionary embrace of chaos seemed profoundly American: closer to the magical realism of Latin America or the wilderness tradition of the U.S.A. than to the Old World myths from which much of his imagery was borrowed. Until this time I had seen few connections between my Caribbean world and the American continent, but now I began to feel that my own identity had been shaped by forces substantively different from the European and African heritages that were the source of so much celebration and agony in Caribbean literature. In my research I encountered surprising affinities between African women writers and some nineteenth-century European feminists, especially in the way that both groups maintained a vested interest in the establishment, or used their power within traditionally defined spheres to re-negotiate the delicate balance between reform and the *status quo.* In spite of overt racial continuities and the shared experience of colonialism, the links seemed more tenuous than I had envisioned between this African writing and the iconoclasm and innovation of Caribbean and African American women writers.

But there was another side to my encounter with these worlds—worlds which seemed, on the surface at least, to be so much more unified through their histories and cultures than the islands I had left. On both continents, there was a sense in which I embarked on an archaeological foray into my own forgotten history. In Germany I re-encountered the songs of my childhood. It was disconcerting to discover that "Fox you must bring back my goose" was really "Fuchs, Du hast mein Gans gestohlen," and that the song had as much to do with the Bavarian village where I was living as it did with my memories of music period in a stuffy room through whose windows I could see lizards and hummingbirds. Other kinds of connections and relationships were preserved in the name of a museum benefactor which until then I had known only as the name of a powerful firm back home in whose dusty corridors no paintings hung. In West Africa, as well, I found myself placing the shards of my fractured Caribbean experience alongside the seemingly intact vessels of the African reality. Slowly I was able to bring into focus patterns, continuities and meanings that I found I had been acting upon without ever knowing why.

The phenomenon had its pragmatic and mystical sides. Many Caribbean Creole words that I used in specific contexts back home turned out to have their linguistic counterparts in specific West African languages. Their meanings were roughly the same but the African etymologies and associations added new dimensions. I shared *Jane and Louisa will Soon Come Home,* the novel by Erna Brodber from which the title of this essay comes, with a Nigerian friend. One of the central metaphors in this work is the Kumbla, a code word that Anansi, the spider man in Caribbean folk tales, uses to protect his only son, Tucumba, from being eaten by the King of the Sea. Every time Anansi says, "yu face fava—Go eena Kumbla!" (you are despicable, go hide yourself from me!) the king thinks that Anansi is cursing one of his children before handing him over. In fact, Anansi uses these words as a code to tell Tucumba that he should slip away and change his disguise. In the end the king is convinced that Anansi has willingly given up all but one of his sons, and he allows Anansi to take the "last" son back with him to earth.

The term Kumbla, "this round, seamless calabash that protects you without caring," is an Afro-Caribbean syncretism of Brodber's invention. It serves as a metaphor for the often disfiguring devices that New World blacks have used over generations to protect their children and ensure the survival of the race. The name Anansi has well-documented West African origins. Indeed it is the African cultural survival most often invoked when Caribbean people talk about their connection to Africa. But Tucumba? Until then I had registered only that it was the name always given to Anansi's son: maybe an invented one, like Kumbla, maybe a generic one, like Kofi or Kwesi, which are *Akan* day names, the equivalents of Smith and Jones. But my Nigerian friend told me that in Yoruba the name Tucumba means "the one born away from home," a common name now in Nigeria for children who were born while their affluent parents were resident abroad. Within the Caribbean context, however, this must have been the generic name for the child born into slavery: the one, unlike Anansi, without direct access to African culture, who had to be given new forms of protection to survive the Middle Passage. It was uncanny to discover that we had passed on these stories about our survival without knowing that we had named ourselves as survivors in the process.

Faces, body language, ways of cooking, private rituals, political process. In spite of the foreign, even exotic feel of West Africa, there were these recurring moments of recognition. One of the most dramatic was enacted back in West Germany when a Nigerian friend and a Trinidadian colleague (the same professor who had taught me Anglo-Saxon and introduced me to Caribbean oral traditions when I was an undergraduate) met at my house to puzzle out the meanings of some religious chants my former teacher had collected in Trinidad. She knew they were in Yoruba, but in spite of her own linguistic skills and a year's work with translators at the University of Ife in Nigeria, she had been unable to formulate English meanings for the esoteric, elliptical chants which she could by now sing with precision. My Nigerian friend was an artist and *olùfọkànsìn*, a devotee of Yoruba traditional religion. When my colleague began to sing the chants he literally freaked out. He explained that the words she was singing were connected with secret devotional cults to which only a select group of Yoruba people could dare claim access. To hear them in Germany, sung by a West Indian woman who had picked them up from an aged derelict in Trinidad, must have been like overhearing one's secret Masonic codes being used in a conversation between two Chinese-speaking travellers on the Orient Express in the middle of Turkey—or, worse yet, like discovering that a confidential departmental review is being used as a writing sample in the freshman English course! Listening to the excitement and unease with which my friends approached their discovery, I began to grasp how close I was as a West Indian to the experience of slavery and to the historical reality of Africa.

My encounters with Europe and Africa brought me back to the work of poets like Derek Walcott and Edward Kamau Brathwaite. In an early poem called "A Far Cry from Africa" Walcott had asked rhetorically:

> I who am poisoned with the blood of both
> Where shall I turn, divided to the vein?
> I who have cursed
> The drunken officer of British rule, how choose
> Between this Africa and the English tongue I love?
> Betray them both, or give back what they give?

In later work he went on to claim his right to use English as a West Indian language, deliberately highlighting the linguistic tensions and overlaps between his Afro-Caribbean and European heritages. Brathwaite's work had described another trajectory. He had spent several years teaching in Ghana, after studying at Cambridge University and going through a process of distancing from British culture not unlike my own. The experience had created a longing for cultural certainties. The Africa of his imagination became a desperate necessity; a place where spiritual wholeness might be attained. Once in Africa, however, he had to come to terms with unexpected gulfs between his Caribbean cultural experience and the African reality. At the same time, he recognized, as I had, those vestiges of Africa in the Caribbean that stood spontaneously revealed in a gesture or familiar word.

Brathwaite is an historian by training, so he was able to complete that process of archaeological re-entry where I had merely stood at the threshold. In his poetry, he battles with the need to demystify his romantic expectations of Africa, while creating powerful new myths of African continuity through the language and history he incorporates into his New World Trilogy *The Arrivants*. His poems are spectacular oral performances that make use of the sounds of trains, elephants, jazz horns and sonorous African words. But some of my favorite lines come from a poem in *The Arrivants* called, simply, "South," written in Ghana at a time of nostalgia for those fragmented, incomplete islands which, in spite of amnesia and inconsequence, we still call "home." On the surface the poem is about the stream of history that connects the islander to the African continent. But if we read the urchins and thatched houses of the final stanza quoted as being on the New World rather than the African shore of the Atlantic Ocean, we can sense the undercurrents of emotion that reverse the flow and incorporate the continent into the islands:

> We who are born of the ocean can never seek solace
> in rivers: their flowing runs on like our longing,
> reproves us our lack of endeavour and purpose,
> proves that our striving will founder on that.
> We resent them this wisdom, this freedom: passing us
> toiling, waiting and watching their cunning declension down
> to the sea.
>
> But today I would join you, travelling river,
> borne down the years of your patientest flowing,
> past pains that would wreck us, sorrows arrest us
> hatred that washes us up on the flats;
> and moving on through the plains that receive us
> processioned in tumult, come to the sea.
>
> Bright waves splash up from the rocks to refresh us,
> blue sea-shells sift in their wake
> and *there* is the thatch of the fishermen's houses, the path
> made of pebbles, and look!
> small urchins combing the beaches
> look up from their traps to salute us:
> they remember us just as we left them.

My experiences in Africa and Europe have made me much more cautious about the ways in which I assume connections or oppositions between cultures and texts. Nowhere was this clearer than in my work on feminist theory which formed the other part of my research project in Germany. The idea of an essential feminist experience, defined by the universality of patriarchal oppression, was a particularly seductive one at this time, as I was struggling with the confusion and disorientation of new motherhood, and all the economic, physical and psychological limitations it can entail. There was something to be said for a world view that made sense of the way in which, literally overnight, I ceased to be someone who read books and engaged in intellectual debates and was relegated to the ghetto of faculty wives on the fringes of academia, talking about nappy rash, grocery lists and vacuum cleaners. What did it mean that I had never actually registered the existence of this group before I was pushed into it? Or that I felt somehow that talking with these women about our lives was inherently inferior to gossiping with the men about the academy?

Theorists like Helene Cixous provided me with frameworks for talking about the psychological process by which such values are assigned and internalized. It was a simple step to integrate these frameworks into my readings of fiction by African writers. Granted, the ways in which gender difference was constructed varied across cultures, but an underlying pattern of privileging the masculine seemed difficult to ignore. The cross-cultural ways of thinking about gender that have become the hallmark of our courses in Women's and Gender Studies at Amherst became salient for me during this period of my life. As women at an institution whose public identity has long been incontrovertibly "masculine," many coeds in my classes have also been happy to seize on such theories. And yet at times I have found these ideas somehow reductive. I felt my students also recognized the problem when, in a course on "Feminist Theory and African Literature," we discussed how Cixous at one point assumes a parallel between the experience of oppression of European women under patriarchy and the experience of Africans under apartheid. My readings of the works of Lamming and Harris had made it impossible for me to overlook the ways in which thinking about oppression through the construction of binary oppositions reproduced the very relationships it sought to assail. Clearly, there was a way in which it was possible to read apartheid as the ultimate form of patriarchal oppression, but did that make the comparison true: that blacks and women experienced the same forms of oppression; or, even, that black and white women shared an agenda? What seemed even more invidious was the way in which constructing an identity through the category of victim could produce a subjectivity which understood itself as being somehow beyond participation in the socio-symbolic contract. What was the nature of the sisterhood that Cixous claimed with black women in South Africa if it subsumed white women's involvement in racism into the narrative of a shared oppression under patriarchy?

Within the feminist debate, Cixous's position has not gone unchallenged. "[When] feminist currents [refuse] homologation to any role of identification with existing power no matter what the power may be," writes Julia Kristeva, another feminist theorist, "[a] female society is constituted as a sort of alter ego of the official society, in which all real or fantasized possibilities of *jouissance* take refuge." Because Kristeva shares with Cixous an understanding of human experience predicated on neo-Freudian interpretations of reality, her critique of the kind of models presented by theorists like Cixous seems to me to lead her back to certain "masculine" modes of thinking about the origins of desire and language. But, as the American theorist Donna Haraway points out in her "Manifesto for Cyborgs," "the political struggle is to see from both perspectives at once, because each reveals both dominations and possibilities unimaginable from the other vantage point."

Novels like the South African Bessie Head's *A Question of Power* seem to take up this challenge in infinitely more creative ways than many of the feminist theorists I read and teach. Head's harrowing recreation of the process of psychic disintegration and recovery of Elizabeth, a "colored" exile from "white" South Africa in "black" Botswana, calls into question racial and sexual hierarchies in ways that make it impossible to reduce one category to the other or to ascribe to women or blacks a claim to what Harraway calls "an original language before violation." In courses on "Black Women Writers" I try to map the recurrence of such textual strategies in order to reveal connections between African and New World Black women writers that often remain elusive when we see these writers as unified only by some essential racial or gender identity. Head's narrative experiments are repeated and elaborated in the work of the African American writers Toni Morrison and Toni Cade Bambara, as well as in the Kumblas of Erna Brodber's vision. But there are also unexpected continuities between her work and that of the German writer Christa Wolf and the New Zealanders Janet Frame and Keri Hulme, as well as a few of the familiar established names within the canon of male Caribbean writers. What binds these writers together is not merely their involuntary participation in mutually exclusive categories of oppression, but their ability to imagine worlds which hold such contradictions in creative tension, and to resist the need to locate meaning in static, self-replicating modules.

I came to Amherst College in the mid-1980s to find that America had rediscovered Europe in the guise of "Theory." There were uncomfortable parallels between my earlier Anglophilia and the way in which many American critics and students appropriated and mystified as absolute truth selected utterances in a provisional and contested philosophical debate taking place in another place and time. I was bemused by the passion with which my brightest students seemed to devour the most abstruse and convoluted academic arguments about the nature of desire or subjectivity without evincing the slightest excitement about the literary texts around which their gurus pontificated. Names like Derrida, Foucault, De Man and Bakhtin were solemnly recited like a litany of magical formulae that promised access to a secret shrine.

I had encountered the ideas connected with some of these names in Europe, but this had happened casually, in the context of wider academic debates or even at the level of anecdote. Codified and reified within American intellectual discourse these names and theories became another set of vaguely "familiar" objects that had to be distanced and mastered. Once again, the experience challenged me to systematize my understanding of a body of knowledge that I previously had taken for granted. Though I still wince when one of my senior thesis advisees invokes the name of a particular theorist with all the assurance of being among the elect that I associate with the fundamentalist preachers of my childhood, my teaching has profited from the uses students have been able to make of new theoretical ideas in my courses.

Many of the theories currently in vogue in the American academy are attempts to grapple with the same problems of identity and subjectivity that I encountered in the works of Caribbean and African writers. They challenge us to ask whose truth is being constructed in any given narrative, and encourage us to think about models for speaking of these issues that escape or undermine static or linear notions of reality. My readings of Caribbean authors gave me a language for thinking and writing about these issues for myself. Theorists like Mikhail Bakhtin, who creates a dynamic model for representing the way that words produce and react to potential meanings, or Gyatry Spivak, who attempts to integrate the language of deconstruction into worlds beyond the margins of Western discourse, have provided me with words and images for communicating my insights about the nature of language and aesthetic pleasure within the post-colonial experience to a whole new constituency of potential readers.

American students who come from the mainstream of their society are seldom given the opportunity to see themselves and their cultural assumptions from outside of that mainstream. The result is a kind of paranoia, which interprets every attempt to question or relativize their privilege as an act of aggression. Whatever their background, American students are rarely allowed to claim aspects of each other's traditions out of curiosity or affection. The result is a tendency to limit the range of their intellectual interests to those preordained by existing categories. Black students are expected to eschew all that is not "black enough." WASPs are expected to apologize for an enthusiasm for Black literature or culture or, worse yet, to claim an interest only out of a need to assuage racial guilt. Perhaps most seriously, for American students who come from dissenting and/or oppressed traditions in relation to the mainstream, the encounter with their own traditions remains mediated by desperation: the need to hold on to something that is theirs in the face of imminent dispossession; the longing for an uncomplicated sense of cultural wholeness instead of that two-ness or liminality about which Du Bois has written so eloquently in *The Souls of Black Folk*. The truth is that the world is no longer big enough to accommodate mutually exclusive realities. It has always been too small to contain the violence inherent in utopian visions of a life without contradiction. I think that students stand to gain from my attempts to institutionalize some of the accidents that have characterized my education. The process may help them find ways of claiming the paradox at the heart of their cultural heritage without rationalizing its partialness or erasing other worlds; to fashion from such necessary, albeit painful, Kumblas the tools both of self-knowledge and of mastery.

CROSSING BOUNDARIES:
TEACHING LAW IN THE LIBERAL ARTS

Austin Sarat
Professor of Jurisprudence and Political Science

CONSIDER THE SAGA OF MRS. PALSGRAF and her children innocently waiting on a railway platform for a train that would take them on a day trip to Rockaway Beach only to have their lives turned upside down when a man running to catch an already moving train tried to jump aboard. A conductor reached for the man and pulled him forward while a railroad employee on the platform, in some desperate contortion, pushed him from behind. While the unidentified man was saved by these acts, a package he was carrying dislodged and dropped from his grasp. The package contained fireworks which, unfortunately for Mrs. Palsgraf, exploded on contact with the rails. The explosion, in the rather bland words of Judge Benjamin Cardozo, "threw down some scales at the other end of the platform, many feet away. The scales struck . . . [Mrs. Palsgraf], causing injuries. . . ." Subsequently, Mrs. Palsgraf sued the Long Island Railroad, claiming that the acts of the railroad's employees were negligent and that the railroad was responsible for her injuries. Cardozo and the Court of Appeals of New York ruled otherwise, and denied compensation to Mrs. Palsgraf.

As a law teacher outside a law school, I am grateful for such stranger-than-fiction cases that regularly bring me and my students face-to-face with philosophical puzzles, linguistic morasses and soap-opera-like melodramas which only the most ingenious, or deeply perplexed, minds could invent. As a law teacher outside a law school, I try to help students avoid the transfixing, paralyzing search for legal right answers in such cases and, instead, to engage with the human lives, as well as the intellectual challenges, hidden beneath the arcane jargon and authoritative style of judicial opinions and law's other artifacts. Poor Mrs. Palsgraf! Like many of the names without faces, the persons whose identities become fixed and flattened by their inscription in such cases, her fate is forever tied up with some of the most vexing ideas and complex prose ever generated in a legal decision. The initial challenge of teaching about Mrs. Palsgraf and *Palsgraf v. Long Island Railroad,* the case that bears her name, is to take on such ideas—ideas about foreseeability, harm and causation—and explain the alchemy through which they are put together to define duties that the law says we owe to one another as persons. There is, of course, also the thrill of engaging the intellectual prowess and legendary reputations of judges like Cardozo.

To do this means getting students, in this age of hyperlexis, the litigation explosion and the insurance crisis, to think about Mrs. Palsgraf as something other than an unscrupulous, if unfortunate, victim of circumstance reaching for the brass ring from the opulent railroad. Try as I might to overcome, or get my students to suspend at least momentarily, this hard-nosed, unsympathetic reaction to poor Mrs. Palsgraf, the almost uniform "life-is-tough" reaction turns out to be less easily dislodged than the package of fireworks whose exploding contents occasioned this classic of legal education. My efforts to describe Mrs. Palsgraf in sympathetic terms evokes the gentle skepticism of those who might already see me as too liberal, too soft-headed, or just not wise enough in either the ways of the world or the ways of the law.

This skepticism came alive not long ago when one student approached me, after what I thought was both a particularly illuminating rendition of the philosophical complexities of *Palsgraf* and a particularly heart-rendering description of Mrs. Palsgraf. His agitated appearance should have told me that something was not sitting right with him, but I was still off guard when he explained, in that peculiarly Amherst-like combination of politeness and dogmatic insistence, that he thought my rendition of the law of

Palsgraf was probably wrong, and that I should not be so sympathetic to "money-grubbing people like Palsgraf." In response I provided some further explanation of the circumstances of the case and logic of the decision, but he remained unconvinced. As he began to move away, he looked back over his shoulder, as if to shield himself, and told me that he was going to call his father to check out my interpretation. Falling into the trap, I asked whether his father was a lawyer. "He's a *law* teacher," he said in a tone that said, as between me and his father, his father was the real law teacher. "He teaches at a law school."

As a law teacher in a liberal arts college I sometimes feel, perhaps never more so than in the presence of the skepticism of the law school teacher's child, a little out of place. Law teachers, after all, really do seem to belong in law schools. At least since the beginning of the twentieth century, the authority to pronounce about things legal has been lodged with the organized profession and with the appointed guardians of its wisdom, law professors. And if there is any doubt about this official placement of authority, one needs only to look at the treatment of law professors in contemporary culture. Not only do they make higher salaries than liberal arts professors do, but late-breaking developments in the Supreme Court almost inevitably lead the media to the law-book-lined office of a law professor for instant commentary rather than to one of us in a liberal arts college. Moreover, when a crisis or scandal sweeps the legal profession, law professors are called upon to say the ritual incantations and staff the committees that propose needed reforms. For law teachers in liberal arts colleges the law school thus looms as a symbol of privilege and as the reputed repository of all legal learning. There is, of course, some compensation for this life outside the law school—at least in those popular culture portrayals where the law professor turns out to be Kingsfield, crusty master of the arcane detail of legal doctrine, while the college professor instead is Indiana Jones, venturesome hero defying professional norms by being out of place, on the wrong side of a boundary.

The possibility of a professional life spent on the wrong side of a boundary was introduced to me, unfortunately without the Indiana Jones twist, during my days as a graduate student in political science when I decided to concentrate on what was then rather gingerly called public law. While there were, at that time, esoteric debates about whether the law we studied was in any meaningful sense more public than the law that was left to others, conversation generally focused on the larger question of whether the study of law, public or private, really belonged in political science at all—or whether it should be left to law professors. There was, to be sure, a tradition of great teaching and scholarship about law done by persons with my disciplinary pedigree (Edwin Corwin, Karl Loewenstein, Earl Latham); but that in itself did not still the feeling that teaching about law really did not belong there—that my teachers were not the *real* law teachers, and that if I succeeded in this field, at best, like them, I would always be facing the skeptical questions of students as well as my own self doubt.

I wanted then as now to cross the boundary separating law from the liberal arts and to do so not by respectfully avoiding someone else's territory but by claiming that territory as my own. Law teaching outside law school could be worth doing only if one were not cowed by the very claims that made law schools so powerful. To do it right required resisting the allure of the law school model, but also mustering the hubris to think beyond my own disciplinary training, to cross disciplinary boundaries and to find, or invent, a new space for law.

It was in this preoccupation with being on the right side of the divide between law schools and the liberal arts that I found my initial energy. I believed then, as I believe now, that the abandonment of law teaching to law professors would be a great mistake, that law had to be saved from its profession and its professionalization. I believed then, as I believe even more strongly now, that there is an important difference between teaching law to students so that they can use it as a tool in their professional lives, and teaching undergraduates about law as a social institution and about what happens when law is learned the way lawyers learn it.

I saw my teaching as, among other things, a resistance to the professionalization of legal learning and its almost exclusive location in law schools. For me this meant keeping one eye on those guilded (and gilded) ghettoes as well as attending far too many conferences where I was the only non-law professor. It meant keeping up with the law reviews and frequently conversing with former students as they endured their own professional training in law.

Thus, when I decided to go to law school several years ago, it seemed almost inevitable, like the working out of a fate sealed when my own teachers spent so much time trying to prove the legitimacy of their own scholarship and teaching. Such mid-career moves now seem common, or at least not surprising. Mine, however, was not a mid-career move: it was more like a three-year voyeurism, an ethnography of the tribe that has occupied such a large space in my thinking about what I do. I went with no aspiration to practice law; I went to learn lawyer's law, to cross the boundary and experience professional education for myself. Nevertheless, I worried at least a bit that I would never return. Facing such concerns, I pretended that I was a spy gone undercover in search of trade secrets or insider information, and that this would make it possible for me to understand more fully the terrain that should not be ceded to law professors. And, if nothing else, a law degree might make my commentary on the Supreme Court, and other great matters of law, more credible to my students and more attractive to CNN.

There is, of course, much to say about such an experience, much to report from the field. But what is most pertinent here is the confirmation I found. What I saw confirmed my sense of the danger of allowing law schools and law professors to exercise a monopoly on legal education. Recently my colleague Hadley Arkes recounted a story that illustrates, in vivid detail, that danger.

Hadley tells of watching the Public Broadcasting System's ten-part series on *Ethics in America,* in which panels of journalists, government officials, lawyers and other professionals went through a series of moral issues framed as hypothetical dilemmas by a series of Socratic moderators. He describes, in detail, one particular dilemma as well as the response of a well-known lawyer:

> . . . in a case of murder . . . the killer claims that he killed reluctantly; he seeks counsel, and every lawyer extends, to this client, the protection and shield of his confidence. As (the moderator) kept turning new corners, with new, disturbing facts, the lawyers on the panel preserved their willingness to shelter their client and hold back information from the authorities. Particularly adamant here was Mr. James Neal from Tennessee. . . . The killer finally reveals to Mr. Neal that he was responsible for yet another inadvertent killing; that another man had been convicted for his crime; and that the man who was wrongfully convicted was about to be executed. With the unpeeling of these facts, one could sense the mood altering in the room. Still, even in the face of these reports, Mr. Neal held his ground; he would not yield up information, even to save the life of an innocent man; . . . his reflex was to hide behind the "Code of Professional Responsibility." He reminded his

auditors that his reactions were all quite consistent with the Code. . . .
Would he really let an innocent man be executed? "Absolutely . . . people die every day. It may sound harsh, but we have values to serve."

Retelling this story is not meant to suggest that every lawyer would respond like Mr. Neal (indeed there is some doubt about the strength or
accuracy of his interpretation of the Code of Professional Responsibility),
or that his response is in any sense the product of deficiencies in his legal
education. It is rather to suggest that Mr. Neal's response exemplifies what
it means to "think like a lawyer," and it shows the way law is most often
taught in law school and the way lawyers learn the conventions of their
profession.

Law schools generally try hard to undo the naive, innocent impulses of
their entering students—in particular their impulse to think about law in
moral or political terms. Much of the effort of law professors is devoted
to differentiating law from moral reasoning or political argument, to fo-
cusing the mind of the would-be lawyer on the content of the positive
law, and to teaching the skills of manipulating, distinguishing, and evad-
ing rules. While this is, even in law schools, contested terrain, and while
many influential legal philosophers continue to press the case for connecting law to moral argument, the goal of professional education is to sever
the connection between the question of what is good or right and what
the law permits or prohibits.

Mr. Neal's way of thinking is the antithesis of the humane judgment
and political engagement that teaching law in the liberal arts should seek
to cultivate. Law teaching in this setting works to reveal the very connection of the legal with the ethical and the political which law schools try to
mystify and undo. Crossing the boundary from professional school to the
liberal arts thus frees the teacher of law from preoccupation with techniques for manipulating rules. It provides an arena in which the complex,
contingent and varied ways in which law expresses, and/or represses,
moral judgment and political position, can be brought to the center of
concern.

In doing this, students are asked to think about how their concerns for
justice and visions of the good polity can be translated from abstract
commitments into a community's taken-for-granted, governing rules.
They are asked to keep normative concerns perpetually at the front of their
thinking, and to ground them in practical efforts to create communities
where persons with different moral and political visions can live together.

They are invited, if you will, into the mess of moral and political life and reminded that the just community, if it is ever to earn such a name, cannot be constructed by those with an unquestioning reverence for laws or, for that matter, any other set of rules, roles and conventions.

There is no certainty, of course, that such teaching sticks, or even that teaching law is a particularly good way to cultivate these concerns. Indeed, from my experience teaching *Palsgraf,* sometimes I have my doubts. Moreover, I know that many of my best students will choose to make their careers in law, and that some, all too eagerly, may end up speaking Mr. Neal's lines. As a result, I occasionally imagine that it would be better for everybody if students got their professional education in law first and then came to Amherst. In that way, teaching law outside the professional school would be a chance to engage in a little counter-socialization, to carry on a guerrilla war against the effort that law schools make to turn otherwise sensitive, decent human beings into lawyers like Mr. Neal, persons who cling so tenaciously to rule and convention that they can countenance the sacrifice of innocent life.

Yet the story of law teaching inside and outside law schools is not quite as simple as the us/them narrative I have thus far presented. Law schools have lived, almost since their inception, in an ambivalent relation to the organized profession and to the universities where they are housed. That ambivalence concerns the central question of how much of law teaching could, or should, be other than an entry way into the world of legal practice; it also concerns what legal practice requires in the way of training and preparation. This is not to say that law teachers never take on law in a broader, more intellectually capacious way. Many do. It is only to say that there is a certain limiting of vision and cramping of style that comes with the territory marked out by the professional school.

The law teacher in the liberal arts college escapes such constraints only to face a different set of challenges, in particular the challenge of pre-professionalism, of students who are already primed and eager to think like lawyers or who believe that the path to the Supreme Court begins right here at Amherst. Some of these students come to my classes with the view that law is to be found in some encyclopedic compilation which, if only I would produce it, would provide security, certainty, and a refuge from the confusions they find in their other classes. One sees at a very early stage, then, the will to have law simply be a matter of rules and to turn rule-following into a way of living and the anchor of social life.

Other students, not altogether different in temperament, come to my classes with the belief that learning law is easy. For them every legal question is merely a more formal version of common-sense moral judgment. Such students generally bring with them an unarticulated sense of the nature of law's boundaries. For them the question of boundaries is, of course, not yet a question of professional identity or career; it is, instead, a question of the way moral and political judgments inform and shape legal ones, and of the permeability or resistance of law to their own sense of right and wrong. For these students the idea that law should be connected to morals and politics is both obvious and welcome. They are, however, quite perplexed when they are introduced to the messiness of moral judgment and political argument, and to the complex ways in which law resists as well as incorporates such judgments and arguments.

For these students and others, teaching law involves an effort to make the familiar and the seemingly easy strange and uncomfortable. One begins where they feel comfortable and makes their thinking about law more complex by making the subject of law more difficult. Thus I place the nature of law's boundaries at the center of my teaching concerns and, in so doing, begin by puzzling out law's ambivalent and shifting, though undeniable, relation to morality and politics.

Law's boundaries are sometimes imagined to be almost completely permeable to moral concerns. Law, at least the law of democratic societies, is thought by some to reflect judgments shared by political majorities: to be, if you will, an apt reflection of democratic preferences. For others, law is more than the reflection of such fleeting preferences. It is, when properly understood, the embodiment of fundamental and enduring ethical commitments and moral judgments. While these views differ in identifying the source of law, they share an understanding of law as open and responsive to outside forces.

Paralleling these understandings is a somewhat different view, a belief that law respects, or should respect, the claims of individual conscience, and that it should permit, if not encourage, individuals to escape its constraints when rules conflict with conscience. One hears the voice of Antigone opposing Creon's will in the name of family, honor and fidelity to the gods' laws; one hears Thoreau's insistence that the only life worth living is a life in which conscience is valued and followed, in which man is "thought-free, fancy-free, imagination-free," and in which the "only obligation which I have a right to assume is to do at any time what I think is right." Law's boundaries, then, should be open.

For the teacher of law these are difficult matters. One tries to show how law both mirrors and helps to constitute our political preferences and our moral understandings. One tries to illuminate the ways law is both resistant and permissive in dealing with the claims of conscience. It is, in fact, this capacity of law to be many things at once that needs to be communicated, in order to counter the view that law is the final terrain of stability and certainty and the last bastion for those seeking externally imposed answers.

This requires looking at law close-up; it requires literary readings of legal texts. Here another disciplinary boundary is crossed as students are invited to become familiar with the judicial opinion as both rhetorical performance and interpretable artifact. Students are invited to inquire about the language of law as well as the way law constructs and understands the world beyond its boundaries.

Among the cases that I teach is *Yania v. Bigan*. While *Yania*, unlike *Palsgraf*, is neither a classic of legal education nor the written product of famous judges, it provides a fine illustration of the rhetorical ingenuity of law. It seems that Yania and Bigan were both engaged in strip-mining coal. As part of that business, large cuts or trenches were created to expose deposits of coal beneath the earth's surface. The trenches filled with water which had to be pumped out regularly. One day Yania visited Bigan at his strip-mining site to discuss what the Supreme Court of Pennsylvania calls a "business matter." While he was there, Bigan asked him to help start a pump in one of the trenches. After some dispute, and apparently without explanation, Yania jumped from the bank of the trench into the water, falling approximately eighteen feet and drowning.

In the ensuing suit, Yania's widow sought damages for the wrongful death of her husband and claimed that

> The death by drowning of . . . [Yania] was caused entirely by the acts of [Bigan] . . . in urging, enticing, taunting and inveigling [Yania] to jump into the water. . . . After [Yania] was in the water, a highly dangerous position, having been induced and inveigled therein by [Bigan], [Bigan] failed and neglected to take reasonable steps and action to protect or assist [Yania] or extricate [Yania] from the dangerous position in which [Bigan] had placed him.

The court, invoking the judicial equivalent of the maxim that "sticks and stones can break my bones but names can never hurt me," quickly discounted the first part of the claim by suggesting that Yania was an adult "in full possession of all his mental faculties": taunting and enticement could not in themselves constitute "actionable negligence" even where they result in demonstrable harm.

The court found the second part, concerning the failure to rescue, only somewhat more troublesome. It continued to insist that Yania had "voluntarily placed himself in the way of danger . . . [and thus] the result of his ignorance, or of his mistake, must rest with himself. . . ." The court went on, however, to draw a sharp distinction between what it saw as Bigan's limited legal obligations and his more extensive moral duties. It concluded that, while Bigan had no legal duty in the absence of a recognized legal responsibility, he did have a moral "obligation or duty to go to [Yania's] rescue." Like James Neal's insistence that his obligation as a lawyer was defined solely by the rules, and Cardozo's opinion denying compensation to the injured Mrs. Palsgraf, the court insulated Bigan from any legal duty by linking the scope of that duty to his lack of legal responsibility for placing Yania in the position of peril from which he claimed a right to be rescued.

Confronted with *Yania,* students almost instantaneously choose up sides on the question of whether there should or should not be such a solid boundary between law and morals. Some insist that the court got it right—that Bigan might be condemned for his moral obtuseness but not punished for a harm which he did not bring about. Others believe that Bigan should be subject to a legal punishment for his unforgivable indifference. Instinctively, students want to say what the rule should be; they want to argue it out on grounds of morality, the place of law in society, or the requirements of fairness. It is this desire that becomes the stuff of legal education in professional schools, where it is first highlighted and then challenged in the hope of domesticating it.

But there is another issue often ignored in such discussions, and in the law school approach—an issue which suggests, in a direct way, the vexing quality of law's inescapable relationship to morality. This issue surfaces in the *Yania* court's own rhetorical strategy. It is that court, after all, which discusses the nature of Bigan's moral duty. The court does so even though its jurisdiction does not extend to the realm of ethics, and even though the discussion is irrelevant to its own understanding of the correct legal disposition of the case. By asserting its right to make such a moral judgment, the court blurs the boundary which it seems to want to create. It thus brings morality into the law even as it tries to assert its irrelevance. The allegedly clear boundary between law and morals becomes less clear when one sees, in this case, that the realm of ethics is placed first outside the law, as a separate sphere of obligation, and then inside the law making a claim that the court, I think erroneously, works to resist.

One might, of course, find that in *Yania* the court simply said too much, that it suffered from its own excesses, and that a more prudent and careful opinion could have avoided this blurring of boundaries. Perhaps. But there is more here than one court's lack of artfulness. The blurring of boundaries between the legal and the ethical is not an isolated and idio-syncratic phenomenon, a problem limited to the Supreme Court of Pennsylvania. It is a historically specific but nonetheless important aspect of the life of law itself.

Demonstrating the relationship of moral concerns and legal judgments, and the blurring of boundaries that arises in the very attempt to separate the two, does not of course explain the "proper" resolution of any particular case. Yet it does expand the agenda beyond lawyer-like searches for relevant precedents and existing rules of law. It opens the way to explore connections between the law's principles and broader conceptions of the good. In so doing, it brings together the study of law's rhetoric and performance with enduring questions of political and moral philosophy. It gives law teachers and undergraduate students of law the space to explore those issues, and it opens up for them the question of why law has insisted for so long on its distinctiveness, and on the irrelevance of such questions. We take as our subject, then, law's own response to morality even as we try to illuminate the way the two express themselves in each other's domain.

Beyond this, the kind of close reading necessary to understand such interactions means that teaching about law inevitably raises questions about language, about the power of words to bind legal decision-makers. This attention to language is brought forth by judges themselves, in their denial that they need to make moral judgments, and in their insistence that judicial decisions are "compelled" by law itself. Judges to this day regularly deny the role of human agency, namely their own, in speaking the law. They act as if they have attained Thayer's version of a lawyer's paradise "where all words have a fixed, precisely ascertained meaning; where men may express their purposes, not only with accuracy but with fullness; and where, if the writer has been careful, a lawyer, having a document referred to him, may sit in his chair, inspect the text, and answer all questions without raising his eyes."

Such judges would keep our eyes fixed on the edifice of law itself, like Dorothy in the *Wizard of Oz* just before the revelation of the little man behind the smoke-blowing, noise-making, awe-inspiring visage of Oz. In so doing they command another crossing of disciplinary boundaries, this time to investigate the meaning and power of language in law; for, as Peter Pouncey recently put it, "the very formalization of language in legal procedures removes it from the regular give and take of daily discourse, renders it arcane, and gives it a kind of institutional force; the language of the law moves beyond verbal communication, and becomes a kind of enactment, like the recitation of a spell."

So I am driven as a teacher of law to confront the vast mysteries of language itself, to engage again with a discipline far removed from my training as I ask students to consider the play and plasticity of law's own language. This is difficult for students who want to believe in the determinate meanings of words and the power of language to fix and transmit those meanings across history and cultures. The rich engagement with the twists and turns of language, and with the almost infinite possibilities of shaping new meanings out of the arrangement of particular words, which may be cultivated in literary studies, is all too quickly abandoned when students confront the hard face of the law. Like Kafka's man from the country, they are transfixed, frozen and held before law by its "possibility and impossibility, its readability and unreadability, its necessity and its prohibition."

Here students need to be prodded and inveigled to reawaken their literary imagination. Here, paradoxically, teaching law in the liberal arts most resembles the job of the teacher of lawyers who imparts the following two messages to his students: first, when the law seems, on its face, to be on your side, insist that there is, and can be, one and only one meaning; second, when that language stands in your way, make it dance and insist that literal meaning has no place in this or any other universe.

Occasionally, but all too rarely, judges themselves make visible the plasticity of legal language and, in so doing, provide an antidote to the spell that law casts on young minds. Occasionally they explore and explain the dangers of Thayer's fantasy as they reason their way through particular cases. Thus the California Supreme Court forcefully turned its back on such a fantasy when, in a recent case arising from an alleged breach of contract, it argued that contractual obligations flow only from the intentions of the contracting parties rather than from the words of the contract. The court went on to explain that it is not feasible to determine intention from words alone by saying that "If words had absolute and constant referents, it might be possible to discover contractual intentions in the words themselves. . . . Words, however, do not have absolute and constant referents. . . . Judicial belief in the possibility of perfect . . . expression . . . is a remnant of a primitive faith in the inherent potency and inherent meaning of words."

Judges sometimes openly display their own manipulation of legal language. For instance, Judge Jerome Frank, in a contract case involving the so-called parol evidence rule, said, "Candor compels the admission that, were we enthusiastic devotees of that rule, we might so construe the record as to bring this case within the rule's scope." For the law teacher these are precious moments. When the indeterminacy of legal language is thus exposed, students confront law as something more than a system of rules. They see it as a system of human choices and moral or political judgments shaped, constrained by, and constructed out of social institutions and practices.

In precipitating such a confrontation, law teachers profit from the Tocquevilleian idea that legal learning is as indispensable to the cultivation of democratic citizens as it is to the practicing lawyer. While the legal learning that Tocqueville had in mind bears little resemblance to the kind of learning available to students in liberal arts colleges, a partial solution to the perplexing question of how to cross the boundary separating law schools from the liberal arts is suggested by Tocqueville's discussion of the kind of learning once associated with serving on a jury. Indeed it was on my first reading of his description of the jury "as a gratuitous public school" that I could imagine what law teaching in a liberal arts college might really be about.

Tocqueville wrote about the jury and jury service to defend another boundary crossing, this time a crossing represented by the entrance of amateurs, of citizens temporarily extricated from their daily pursuits and preoccupations, into the domain of law itself. The jury, Tocqueville wrote, cannot

> fail to exercise a powerful influence upon the national character. . . . The jury . . . serves to communicate the spirit of the judges to the minds

of all citizens; and this spirit, with the habits which attend it, is the soundest preparation for free institutions. It imbues all classes with a respect for the thing judged, and with the notion of right. . . . It teaches men to practice equity; every man learns to judge his neighbor as he would himself be judged. . . . The jury teaches every man not to recoil before the responsibility of his own actions. . . . It invests each citizen with a kind of magistracy; it makes them all feel the duties which they are bound to discharge toward society, and the part they take in its government. By obliging men to turn their attention to other affairs than their own, it rubs off that private selfishness which is the rust of society.

As I understand Tocqueville, he believed that what the citizen learns from his contact with the law is the discipline of judgment rather than a body of rules or doctrines. It is, after all, the "spirit" of the judges that is communicated, that spirit which understands the need to empathize with the person judged even as one accepts the responsibility of imposing judgment. The discipline of judgment requires making particular decisions by applying abstract ideas of right conduct to concrete human experiences with all of their ambiguities. Teaching law then involves teaching practical judgment, teaching the discipline of making judgments that count in the world. These can result in the confiscation of property, the loss of liberty and, all too often, the sacrifice of life. Encountering law's rigors and consequences focuses the mind as no mere philosophical exercise could do.

Tocqueville's musings about the jury and his hope that it would serve as a school "to form the judgment and increase the natural intelligence of the people" set a large agenda for the imagination of any teacher, young or old; but for me they were the key I had been looking for, a powerful statement of what it might mean to teach law outside a professional school. Nevertheless, Tocqueville's reflections do not sit well with me in all their particulars and nuances. They are a little too patrician, a little too respectful of the judges and a little too suspicious of the intelligence of the citizens. Tocqueville was too comfortable in his assumption that citizens had something to learn rather than something to teach, too concentrated on the problems of those who must decide the fate of others and, alas, too removed from the experience of those being judged, those whose fate is being decided, who will feel the pain inflicted after law's judgments are made. Crossing the boundary from law school to liberal arts is not rightly done unless and until that pain is made clear, made part of teaching law, in a way that might never happen where training lawyers is the main order of business.

Yet oddly enough it is a voice from within a professional school that spoke most eloquently about the need to acknowledge this pain in our understanding of law. As Robert Cover, a professor of law at Yale, put it, the work of law always "takes place in a field of pain and death." This stunning phrase is not merely rhetorical. Cover himself recognized that law's relationship to pain and death is deeply perplexing. Law deals in pain and death as a "counterpunch" to the pain and death that is done outside law. And law seems to dispense pain and deal in death with great reluctance and considerable scrupulousness, imposing on itself elaborate procedures and providing various safeguards and protections for its potential victims.

Because Cover's reminder has had a powerful effect in shaping my scholarship and teaching, I would explicate it in some detail. His essay, "Violence and the Word," calls for an expansion of the concerns of the legal academic, a shift in understanding, a movement away from the familiar (though by no means easy) parsing of judicial opinions toward an understanding and articulation of law from the perspective of its acts, not just its words. Cover tried to think about the doing of law as more than a problem for judges and jurors. He asked how law is given meaning by the convict sent off to await execution, by the welfare mother told that she no longer qualifies for state assistance, by people like Mrs. Palsgraf, or by the homeless man who is branded as a loiterer and told to move on. As Cover put it, the acts of judges and jurors

> signal and occasion the imposition of violence upon others. A judge articulates her understanding of a text, and as a result, somebody loses his freedom, his property, his children, even his life. Interpretations in law also constitute justifications for violence which has already occurred or which is about the occur. When interpreters finish their work they frequently leave behind victims whose lives have been torn apart by these organized, social practices of violence.[1]

---

[1] Extracts from Cover's essay, "Violence and the Word," are reprinted by permission of The Yale Law Journal Company and Fred B. Rothman & Company from *The Yale Law Journal*, Vol. *95*, pp. *1601–1629*.

Cover warned that "neither legal interpretation nor the violence it occasions can be properly understood apart from one another." On the other side of the boundary separating what I teach from the education of lawyers, too little attention is paid to the violence that accompanies the interpretive act. This is not to say that at Amherst it is easy to focus attention on that violence and the pain it produces: here, after all, one typically confronts students who identify themselves more easily with law's interpreters than with those who are on the receiving end of law's violence.

But that is more than a local difficulty. It is, I think, nearly impossible, here or anywhere, to convey the pain that law routinely imposes because —as Elaine Scarry reminds us—

> for the person in pain, so incontestably and unnegotiably present is it that "having pain" may come to be thought of as the most vibrant example of what it is to "have certainty," while for the other person it is so elusive that hearing about pain may exist as the primary model of what it is "to have doubt." Thus pain comes unshareably into our midst as at once that which cannot be denied and that which cannot be con- firmed. Whatever pain achieves, it achieves in part through its unshare- ability, and it ensures this unshareability in part through its resistance to language. . . .

Despite this difficulty, one can describe the nature of law's enterprise. Here the philosopher's effort to connect law with morals and politics, and the linguist's concern to explore the interpretive conventions as well as the plasticity of legal language, give way to an interest in the social organiza- tion of violence and law's role in it.

Law's role in the social organization of violence begins with its own effort to substitute an organized, orderly, perhaps domesticated violence for the violence imagined to exist outside the law. One of the most im- portant tasks of my teaching is to explore with students the way law constantly makes and remakes our imaginings of violence on the other side of law's boundary and keeps those images before our eyes. In making and remaking those images, law authorizes its own use of force and its own imposition of pain as gentler, or at least more rational, and thus preferable.

Here the story of a Hobbesian state of nature is explored not as an accurate recounting of a particular human experience or time in human history, but as a law-constructing narrative, a narrative kept alive by law itself. Law by its own account saves us from "unbridled passion and atrocious crimes" by asserting its jurisdiction over us, and by demanding our acquiescence. This imperialistic tendency of law is exemplified in the famous opinion of Judge Baldwin in *United States v. Holmes.*

Holmes was a sailor tried for murder, who had saved his own life by throwing some passengers overboard from an overcrowded, leaking lifeboat. Baldwin faced the question of whether Holmes's action could be justified. The claim was made that Holmes was essentially in a state of nature when he found himself adrift at sea on the verge of starvation. Baldwin refused to honor this claim and asserted that

> the law of nature forms part of the municipal law; and in a proper case . . . homicide is justifiable, not because the municipal law is subverted by the law of nature, but because no rule of municipal law makes homicide, in such cases, criminal. It is . . . the law of the land . . . that regulates the social duties of men . . . everywhere. Everywhere are civilized men under its protection, everywhere, subject to its authority.

Law "everywhere," law, the indispensable ingredient of our social lives, thus explains and seeks to justify both its imperialism and its own violent nature.

It is precisely the ability of law's words to turn themselves into violent deeds, and to do so on a regular basis, that distinguishes law from philosophy or literary criticism and commands yet another crossing of disciplinary boundaries. All too often students take for granted what is essential in any legal act, the social organization and structure that turns word into deed, that takes the judicial declaration of rights and duties and turns it into effective action. As Cover puts it,

> the system guarantees the judge massive amounts of force. . . . It guarantees . . . a relatively faithful adherence to the word of the judge in the deeds carried out against the prisoner. . . . I think it is unquestionably the case in the United States that most prisoners walk into prison because they know they will be dragged or beaten into prison if they did not walk. . . . The experience of the prisoner is, from the outset, an experience of being violently dominated, and it is colored from the beginning by the fear of being violently treated.

As a teacher of law one also, then, must be a teacher of the sociology of law. Teaching law to undergraduates means helping them see the sociological connections between law's words and rhetoric, especially the way it portrays violence outside its boundaries, and the pain and death in which it deals.

One begins by showing how law itself speaks about violence, where law's violence is made visible, and where it is kept in the shadows. In reading law, one typically finds a vivid portrait of the violence of offenders, of those like Holmes who defy law's jurisdiction. At the same time, one encounters virtual silence about the violence done by or in the name of the law. One looks in vain for even an imaginative account of what it is like to be sentenced, incarcerated, or executed in the name of the law.

Nowhere is this absence more conspicuous or more telling than in the case of *Francis v. Resweber*. Willie Francis committed murder and was, as punishment, sentenced to be executed for his crime. As the court recounts the facts, "Francis was prepared for execution and on May 3, 1946 . . . was placed in the official electric chair of the State of Louisiana. . . . The executioner threw the switch but, presumably because of some mechanical difficulty, death did not result." The case came to the Supreme Court of the United States when Willie Francis sought to prevent the carrying out of a "second" execution. He argued that subjecting him to such a procedure would be both a denial of due process and a form of cruel and unusual punishment.

Justice Reed, writing for the majority, carefully scrutinized the behavior of the state officials who had participated in the first "execution" and concluded that they had carried out their duties in a "careful and humane manner." He then held that the Constitution permitted what he called "necessary suffering" incident even to the most humane techniques of capital punishment; and he suggested that the fact of the first attempt at electrocution would not "add an element of cruelty to a subsequent execution." For Reed it was critical that there was no "purpose to inflict unnecessary pain" on Willie Francis; the state was simply attempting to carry out the order of the trial court.

The state could not, in Reed's view, be held accountable for what he described as "an unforeseeable accident [that] prevented the prompt consummation of the sentence." It is as if, for Reed, the issue was whether the state itself would be punished by being deprived of a second chance to execute Willie Francis. As a result, he worked hard to understand and describe the actions and intentions of state officials, and he conjured up a picture of diligent, even compassionate executioners frustrated by an accident "for which no man is to blame."

And what of Willie Francis? He hardly even appears in Reed's opinion. We learn little about him except that he was a "colored citizen of Louisiana." His absence initially seems quite unremarkable to students perhaps already conditioned by claims about law's distanced objectivity—by claims that law attends to rules, not persons. Braced subsequently by Cover's essay, however, they reconsider what it means to render Francis virtually invisible in the course of deciding his fate.

Reed does tell us that preparation for a second execution attempt placed no undue psychological strain on Francis, and that he was an "unfortunate victim of this accident" who, during the first effort to electrocute him, suffered "the identical amount of mental anguish and physical pain [as in] any other occurrence, such as . . . a fire in the cell block." But the issue for Francis, of course, was not just the pain that he had already suffered; it was as much the anguish of contemplating the state's second effort to end his life and the pain he would experience when the state, with the Supreme Court's blessing, electrocuted him for the second time.

Indeed, so remote was that pain from the Court's consideration that it was only in a footnote, late in the dissenting opinion of Justice Burton, that any reference was made to what the first, unsuccessful execution attempt did to Willie Francis. There we are told that his "lips puffed out and he groaned and jumped so that the chair came off the floor." Yet this material, taken from affidavits by witnesses to the first electrocution, was included by Burton not for its constitutional significance but simply to point out what he called "conflict of testimony."

Francis illustrates for my students Cover's argument that, in the business of doing law,

> the perpetrator and victim of organized violence . . . undergo achingly disparate significant experiences. For the perpetrator, the pain and fear are remote, unreal, and largely unshared. They are, therefore, almost never made part of the interpretive artifact, such as the judicial opinion. On the other hand, for those who impose the violence, the justification is important, real and carefully cultivated. Conversely, for the victim,

the justification for the violence recedes in reality and significance in proportion to the overwhelming reality of the pain and fear that is suffered.

I ask students to understand the perspective and position of those most concerned with justification, and how that concern may not be shared equally by all participants in the doing of law's business. Here again I can express my endorsement of, and discomfort with, Tocqueville's understanding of the powerful way that law is learned when one comes in contact with the "spirit of the judges." I can present what is almost always left out when law professors teach lawyer's law: the law as it is seen and experienced by the death-row inmate, the welfare mother, Mrs. Palsgraf, or the homeless person living on the street. My students and I can explore what law would be like if we built legal theory from those experiences; we can also explore the way law's connection to moral judgment and political argument would change if those voices were made part of the conversation.

In the end, it turns out that the law teacher in a liberal arts college is out of place not just because he does not teach in the places where *real* law is taught. To teach law in the liberal arts is also to be outside of—or in unusual juxtaposition with—traditional disciplinary activities. It involves more than just another interdisciplinary venture, though it certainly draws on a variety of disciplines. Thinking about law on the other side of the boundary marked off by professional education means finding the place where moral philosophy (with its arguments about the right and the good), literary theory (with its understandings of the meanings and uses of language), and political science (with its understandings of the nature of social organization and of the harsh face of power) come together; and it means claiming that place as the space of law.

In that space I can show undergraduates the way moral and political philosophy and language itself take on greater seriousness than they do at any other place in our lives. The study of law can be more than a technical, lawyerly activity. In the rare moments when it is done right, it focuses the mind, stretches imagination, and brings students close to an understanding of the way thought and argument get translated into social action. Here the teaching of law truly crosses boundaries and finds its real home in the liberal arts. Here the authority to interpret *Palsgraf, Yania* and other cases, and to make Mrs. Palsgraf and Willie Francis part of the conversation about law, does not derive from the institutional authority of the law school. It derives from the moral engagement, insistent curiosity and sympathetic imagination that the liberal arts call forth.

I am grateful for the intellectual companionship and generosity of Thomas Kearns with whom I have shared many of the challenges and experiences described in this essay. I'd also like to acknowledge the helpful comments and suggestions made by Lawrence Douglas, George Kateb, Peter Pouncey, Stephanie Sandler and Susan Silbey.

Evolving Science for a Dynamic Earth

Tekla Harms
Assistant Professor of Geology

Visitors to any mid-continent national park—to as far west as the Rockies, Glacier and the Grand Canyon in particular—may encounter a geologic history of that park describing a vast shallow sea that covered the region hundreds of millions of years ago, in which were deposited the sedimentary strata dramatically exposed in the landscape today. Worldwide sea level has changed, and changed significantly, over geologic time. Today we live in a period of very low sea-level stand, although it is higher than it was just a few thousand years ago. There may be a number of causes for these profound changes in global sea level. The process remains an enigma that fascinates many; but, with apologies to those earth scientists who research it, the subject leaves me a little sleepy. Like glaciation and erosion, sea-level change is a process *imposed upon* the earth's surface by outside agents such as climate.

I am fascinated by a very different set of processes. Inherent in its internal make-up, because of its unique combination of composition, energy and structure, the earth has the capacity to *change itself from within*. The solid earth is in a state of dynamic equilibrium, which means that, within certain physical limits, the earth can and does change its own architecture. It is neither static nor inert, adjectives that are just a nuance away from dull and dead. Continents migrate about the globe, mountain belts rise, ocean basins open and are destroyed, and the deep rocky interior of the earth constantly churns. (Modification of topography, or the redistribution of water and ice at the surface of the planet, are superficial changes by comparison.) Tangible evidence of the earth's dynamic activity on the North American continent encompasses earthquakes along the Pacific coast, the eruption of Mount St. Helens, and the very existence of the Cordilleran mountains to the west and the older Appalachians to the east. The outer layer of the earth is driven to reorganize and to rebuild because a mechanism for constant but balanced change is intrinsic to the earth's constitution. I do not mean to romanticize or to anthropomorphize the earth. These processes are entirely mechanical. Nevertheless, to me no field of inquiry is more compelling than that which looks into the driving mechanisms and geological consequences of a very active earth.

Earth Dynamics and Plate Tectonics

OUR PLANET HAS a cold, rigid outer skin—the *lithosphere*—that is essentially floating on the deeper portions of the earth, where the temperature is high enough to make rock weak. In that underlying domain, the *asthenosphere,* rock is not molten but flows readily. It has properties very much like silly putty (which is sold in packages labeled "the real solid liquid").

The earth is steadily dissipating heat from its interior to the surface. That heat has two sources. One is primitive, created from potential energy released during the gravitational collapse of matter that formed the planet. The larger source is the radioactive decay of unstable isotopes. These isotopes form a minuscule fraction of the composition of the earth but are abundant enough to make the planet a significant heat producer. By far the most efficient means of heat dissipation in rock is convection. This occurs in a pot of water on the stove, where water heated along the burner rises and displaces cold surface water that sinks to replace the rising current and become warmed in turn. The water conveys heat from the burner to the air above. The earth is able to take advantage of convection within the non-molten but fluid asthenosphere. Hot rock rises from great depth in the earth, carrying heat with it. At or near the surface, heat is then delivered to the atmosphere. Asthenospheric rock that has lost heat in this manner and thereby increased its density will sink back to depth and acquire another "load" of heat.

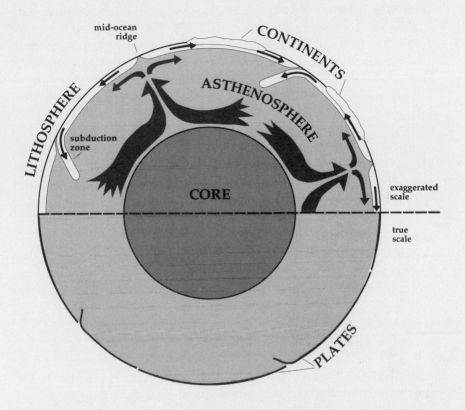

At the earth's surface, the convective mechanism for heat dissipation is expressed through a system of interrelated dynamic processes called *plate tectonics*. Hot asthenosphere rises to the surface of the earth and breaches it in long linear belts that lie within the oceans and encircle the globe. These are the *mid-ocean ridges*. The "plates" in plate tectonics are the very large-scale fragments of the rigid outer lithosphere shell, segmented by mid-ocean ridges. Hot asthenospheric rock gives up its heat at these ridges by sudden quenching, and welds itself to the edges of the lithospheric plates through which it has risen. The constant flow of rising asthenosphere shoulders these surface plates aside to make room for more, driving them apart and creating new ocean lithosphere simply by cooling at the diverging edges. This growth of ocean lithosphere must be compensated by the disposal of equal amounts. On the opposite sides of oceanic plates, in equally long linear belts known as *subduction zones,* old, thoroughly cooled and dense ocean lithosphere sinks back into the asthenosphere and is absorbed, completing the convection cycle. The oceans' floors are the cold surface limbs of convection cells that start in, and return to, the hot lower asthenosphere. Oceanic lithosphere is nothing more than a chilled, rigid skin on the recycling asthenosphere. With respect to the lithosphere's relative thickness, this analogy holds; it has an average thickness of 100 kilometers, which is only 1.6 percent of the earth's radius.

In the earth's fractured lithospheric shell a number of plates diverge, converge, or slide past each other as they go through the convection system. There is no *a priori* order to the geometry of plates or the directions they travel; plate interactions, and the nature of plate boundaries, are changeable. This has created nearly infinite variability in the configuration of oceans around the globe over the course of geologic time. New oceans can develop where a new asthenospheric current rises, and old oceans can be consumed in subduction zones. The dynamic nature of the earth lies in the vast wanderings of these plates around the surface of the globe, powered by the earth's internal heat engine.

Continental Dynamics

CONTINENTS ARE STOREHOUSES of the lightest material of the earth, the elemental froth that gravity differentiated from the bulk of the developing planet. As such, they are distinct in composition from the underlying asthenosphere and from the ocean floors around them, which are essentially solidified asthenosphere. (It is not an arbitrary arrangement that continents are above sea level and the ocean floor below. Less dense, the continents float higher on the fluid asthenosphere than ocean lithosphere does.) Due to their low density, continents do not participate in the convective overturn that drives plate tectonics; they are too buoyant to subduct, and they do not grow by the addition of material rising from the asthenosphere. Continents are simply carried as passengers embedded in larger plates. The motion of a plate, driven by processes occurring at mid-ocean ridges and subduction zones, causes any continent it carries to "drift." North America lies on a plate that has its eastern boundary in the center of the Atlantic. With the rest of the plate, the continent is moving west as upwelling and cooling asthenosphere widens the Atlantic Ocean floor.

Dynamic change observed in continents is a *byproduct* of plate tectonics, occurring for the most part only where continents lie at a plate edge. In contrast to North America's eastern continental margin, its western margin is geologically active because it lies along the western rim of the North American plate. Earthquakes along the San Andreas fault—the plate boundary—occur as the Pacific plate slides along the edge of North America. Where plates diverge, at a site of upwelling asthenosphere and new ocean growth, continents can be split apart. Dividing what once was a "supercontinent" that geologists call *Pangea,* South America was formed by rifting from Africa, and North America from Europe, at the birth of the Atlantic Ocean. As the ocean basin grew, the continents' margins were shielded behind newly-formed oceanic lithosphere that moved them away from the active plate boundary. Their Atlantic coastal outlines can still be fit back together like pieces in a jigsaw puzzle. By a similar process, a new ocean is now opening along the narrow Red Sea that eventually will separate Africa entirely from the Middle East and Asia.

On the other hand, when ocean basins are consumed by subduction, continents collide. Fifty million years ago, India rode as an island continent within its predominately oceanic plate. Intervening ocean lithosphere was subsequently subducted to the north, drawing the continent into what was then the southern coastal margin of Tibet. Today the Indian Ocean plate continues to travel north, growing at a mid-ocean ridge south of India. The plate propels India deeper and deeper into Asia, bulldozing the Himalayas up before it. In fact, many of the world's mountain belts are the accordion-like result of continents crumpling as they collide. Dynamic changes in the lithosphere arise from the *horizontal* motion of the relatively thin plates; but when continents interact in the process, the motion can be translated into *vertical* displacements that seem prodigious in a human reference frame, piling the continental crust into mountainous topography. To me, the most fascinating aspect of the dynamics of continents is the growth of these mountain belts.

Although continents are not directly a part of plate tectonic convection, their geologic history—shaped by the motions of the plates—can be read as a secondary source for a partial history of the earth's plate tectonics. Paradoxically, the archive that contains the best primary record of plate tectonics, the ocean lithosphere, is consumed by the process itself. Ocean lithosphere is reprocessed through the asthenosphere by the convective cycle at a very fast rate with respect to the age of the earth. The oldest existing ocean lithosphere represents only the latest five percent of the

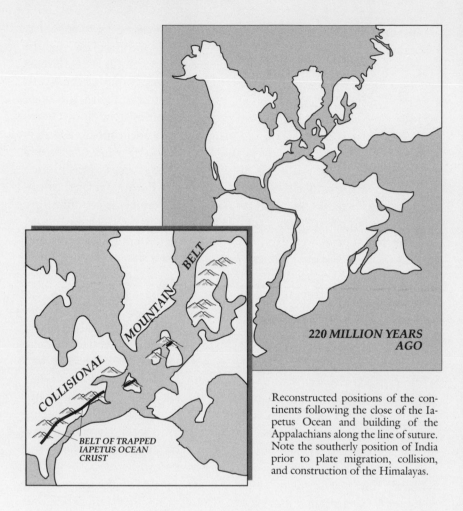

**220 MILLION YEARS
AGO**

Reconstructed positions of the continents following the close of the Iapetus Ocean and building of the Appalachians along the line of suture. Note the southerly position of India prior to plate migration, collision, and construction of the Himalayas.

earth's history. Mid-ocean ridges and subduction zones that were active during most of geologic time have been extinguished. Continents, then, become the fundamental source for understanding the full scope and history of the process. For example, the Appalachians of eastern North America and the Caledonides of the British Isles and Scandinavia—which were a single, continuous mountain chain prior to the opening of the Atlantic Ocean—formed as a result of continental collision that sutured Eurasia and Africa to North America to build Pangea, the supercontinent.

We must infer from this that the collision closed an ocean that preceded the modern Atlantic. All that is left of that earlier ocean is a narrow belt of ocean-type crust, distinct in composition from adjacent parts of the continent, trapped within the Appalachians. (This belt passes through New England just west of Amherst, Massachusetts. Boston lies on continental crust that was part of Eurasia prior to the collision and was left behind in North America when the Atlantic opened along a somewhat different line.) The precursor of the Atlantic, the *Iapetus* Ocean, must have been produced by upwelling asthenosphere then consumed by subduction —a plate cycle for which we have no other record than that in the now dispersed continents and their mountain belts.

The New Paradigm

WHEN I STAND in front of my class in plate tectonics today my own undergraduate introduction to the paradigm is still clear to me. It was, after all, not long ago. Nevertheless, plate tectonic theory was just beginning to circulate through the general geologic community. In my introductory Physical Geology course I was taught *both* the most widely accepted model at that time for the dynamic behavior of continents, *geosynclinal theory,* and what was then understood of plate tectonics, as two equally viable, alternative interpretations.

The new paradigm of plate tectonics had developed from data gathered during and after the second World War, when technological advances and new defense initiatives led to the first scientific exploration of the ocean floor. Until then, the world's oceans were geologically unknown. In spite or perhaps because of that vacuum, most geologists considered ocean basins to be insignificant to the study of continental dynamics. Plate tectonics, however, described the production and consumption of ocean lithosphere as the main characteristic of the earth's dynamics, a process that secondarily drives many other geologic systems, including change in the continental crust. In this way, it offered a radically new and exciting perspective. A framework of theory was emerging that integrated the subdisciplines of earth science and linked processes and observations which had previously appeared to be independent. As the first truly unifying theory in the history of geosciences, the development of the plate tectonic paradigm was a *bona fide* scientific revolution.

The momentum of the new theory was tremendous. Lightbulbs were going on at a phenomenal rate as new data were reported and old data were brilliantly reinterpreted. My undergraduate Physical Geology course may indeed have been the last time a syllabus incorporating both plate tectonics and geosynclines was taught. Unacceptably *ad hoc* by comparison, geosynclinal theory became one of many old hypotheses that were quickly swept aside. It had been based on the observation that the world's mountain belts occur where the thickest known sedimentary deposits have previously accumulated. Broad linear domains where layer after layer of sands and muds collected and lithified—in sequences reaching over half the total thickness of typical continental crust—subsequently become deformed and uplifted by mountain-building processes. It had been deduced from this that those trough-like zones of continental crust were inherently weak. They were "geosynclines." According to theory, geosynclines would subside profoundly, acting as catchment basins, until they reached a point of instability that would trigger a paroxysm of upheaval and produce a mountain belt. That is as comprehensive an explanation of the mysterious activating mechanism of the geosynclinal process as could be given to me as an undergraduate! At about that time, oceanic exploration determined that continental margins characteristically are flanked by thick aprons of sediment. The sediment, delivered by rivers flowing to the edge of the continent, is built up from the deep ocean floor to the continental shelf. It was promptly recognized that geosynclines are nothing more than continental margins. Over the course of geologic time, because of their location, continental margin deposits are likely to become involved in the continental collisions that result from plate migrations. The relationship between thick margin sequences and mountain building has been compared to an automobile bumper and a car accident. Geosynclinal theory held the bumper responsible for causing the damage. Plate tectonic theory has made it clear that thick sedimentary sequences do not inherently produce mountain belts; they are just inherently in the place where collisions occur.

Dynamics of a Paradigm

PLATE TECTONICS both acts upon and is expressed through the ocean crust. It was as a result of ocean floor research that the paradigm was formulated. Soon after the development of the basic plate tectonic model, however, work that meant to establish the applicability of plate tectonics to the interpretation of continental geology began. Geologists sought direct evidence for various facets of the model in the rock record. For example, the collisional nature of the Appalachians was perceived at this time. After this and many other widely varied investigations, the resounding consensus was that plate tectonics *is* the fundamental principle underlying continental dynamics.

During that period, scientists did not actively look for contradictions between plate tectonic theory and evidence in continental rocks. Discrepancies were overlooked or underplayed. Yet discrepancies exist; and since the late 1970s, many geoscientists have been trying to amend the theory of plate tectonics to accommodate those anomalies. There has been a subtle shift of research objectives from an effort to substantiate plate dynamics to a more objective test of the strengths and weaknesses of the model. It was at this crossroads that I began my research as a graduate student.

While continental collision has provided a compelling model for the development of the Appalachian, Alpine, Himalayan, and Ural mountain belts, the Cordilleran mountains of western North America—where I conduct my own research—are more difficult to explain by this process. There was no continent in the Pacific realm that could have collided with western North America to form the Cordillera at the appropriate time; the positions of the continents during that period have been fairly well determined. The well-publicized new theory of *suspect terranes* helps to resolve the paradox. Within the Cordilleran mountains there are domains —terranes—some as large as medium-sized states, where the geologic history recorded in the rocks does not correlate in any way with that of adjacent parts of the continent. Many terranes have the character of volcanic islands similar to the Aleutians or to Hawaii. These terranes could not have occupied their present positions within continental western North America at the time they were formed and their discordant histories were recorded. Their initial position with respect to North America is therefore "suspect." The terranes' histories suggest that plate motion brought them some distance, potentially great, from their original locations. Carried on a subducting ocean plate, they were swept against and accreted to North America's Pacific margin. (Similarly, this may be the distant forecast for Hawaii, which is now being carried toward the north

Asian coast.) Riding over the subduction zone, North America acted as a giant chisel, scraping off and accumulating the high-standing islands of the down-going plate. *Accretion* is another, incompletely understood agent of mountain building that brings greater complexity into our understanding of plate motion, collision, and continental dynamics.

I conduct my research in a suspect terrane in the northern Cordillera of British Columbia. It consists of a suite of rocks that were formed along with the chilled asthenosphere that makes up the deep ocean floors. This terrane now sits as an isolated, sheet-like body on top of ancient continental strata. The plate tectonic rubric says that when denser, cold ocean lithosphere meets lighter material of a continent at a subduction zone, the oceanic lithosphere accommodatingly slides down. How, then, did this oceanic terrane come to be *on top* of the continent? Did the poorly understood process of accretion have something to do with it? The mechanism of subduction needs re-examination. It isn't that plate tectonic theory is fundamentally flawed, but rather that our understanding of it—and in particular its interaction with continents—needs to be more sophisticated.

When I was just beginning to study geology, I saw one generally accepted theory for mountain building and continental dynamics replaced by one for global tectonics. By my senior year I essentially had to learn Physical Geology again in its newly conceived form. Subsequently, attitudes toward *that* theory matured. As I started my graduate work, I found myself among scientists who were reinterpreting plate tectonics based on complexities in the geologic histories of continents and their mountain belts. The course and timing of this personal initiation to geology has left me with a sharply felt appreciation of the axiom that no scientific theory is ever "right," at least not in the sense of being complete or definitive.

In the course of scientific investigation or experimentation, observations are gathered. They are the certainties or "truth" in science. The creativity in science lies in deducing an explanation for the observations —one that rationalizes the physical world. Analyses do not simply add up to a unique conclusion. Science seeks the best possible approximation to the data at hand. "Good" theories, those that advance understanding, incorporate more observations than the theories they replace. They generally cannot accommodate even all the known observations, much less those that are still to be made; the capacity to be improved, amended, or even replaced exists in any hypothesis. As a case in point, the correlation between mountain belts and thick sedimentary sequences is undeniably true. It is an observation; it is rock-solid data. Geosynclinal theory and plate tectonics are both hypotheses that seek to explain mountain-building processes using that observation. New data that contradict the geosynclinal model and are consistent with plate tectonics have made the latter the better theory. But it is one that should evolve and be improved upon as well.

Valuable theories are distinguished by the breadth of phenomena they embrace. They also are predictive. They will suggest previously unrecognized relationships between phenomena that can subsequently be investigated, and so they provide their own built-in test and give direction to further research. The plate tectonic paradigm initially explained the observed "fit" of the Atlantic continents by the growth of that ocean basin through asthenosphere upwelling at a mid-ocean ridge. As a logical corollary, the model also predicted that rock of the Atlantic ocean floor would be hottest along the topographic mid-ocean ridge, coldest approaching the continental margins, and incrementally cooler in between. Subsequent ocean science expeditions proved this to be true and reinforced plate tectonics.

It is the backbone of science to run this iteration, the proving-out of a theory from prediction to test and analysis. By this scientists substantiate the applicability of a model and its consistency with the widest possible body of observation. But it is equally important to study with great care those observations that a theory *fails* to incorporate, or phenomena it does not explain. While it may seem counterproductive, this is where advances begin. Each theory raises its own challenge. The venerable game of poking holes in someone else's model, done with professionalism, is not trivial negativism or competitiveness; it is what presses science forward. Progress is most swiftly made when ideas have, so to speak, the shortest half-lives. Rapid advancement of this kind was the source of great excitement when the plate tectonic revolution occurred. In turn, we should be scrutinizing rather then enshrining plate tectonics. Since the most complete record of earth dynamics lies in the continents, and the most complex data lie in their mountains, those belts are excellent places to analyze inconsistencies in our present plate tectonic model and to improve it. Like all sciences, when geology is healthy it is undergoing change and reorganization. Geology today is as dynamic as the earth it studies.

Teaching Earth Science—Aiming for a Moving Target

AS THE FIELD OF SCIENCE is steadily evolving, and if, in fact, you actively participate in changing the science you teach, what and how *can* you teach? How can you prepare students for a future in which some— or many—of the models you teach may no longer be useful? Teaching only what is guaranteed to endure would be to teach little more than a dry list of observations and data. In fact, students who took a traditional introductory geology course prior to the advent of plate tectonics, in the absence of a unifying theory, may remember it as the tedious and seemingly pointless assimilation of rock and fossil names and the events of various epochs. Granite, gabbro, greywacke—Eocene, Oligocene, Miocene: knowledge of what those terms refer to certainly isn't harmful and undoubtedly can enhance an appreciation of the earth we live on. But surely we can give students a broader way of looking at the earth and at science.

As educators, geologists have, in plate tectonics, a marvelous if incomplete framework in which to explore and integrate characteristics of the earth and its materials. Plate tectonics is an outline within which data and observations yield intellectual rewards. A student who learns the distinguishing attributes of a granite, gabbro or greywacke, holds the key to interpreting the plate tectonic settings in which they formed. Each new student who begins to see a coherent pattern in the earth's activity reignites the excitement of the early days of plate tectonics.

The conundrum is that a greywacke will still be a greywacke, whether we interpret it as accumulating in a geosyncline or a continental margin. Observations are timeless, while the unifying theory that gives them significance in the mind is—at least in part—certain to change. One should not overemphasize models; but an excess of data becomes unintelligible. I consider this trade-off with each lecture I prepare. Perhaps it is not so much a matter of teaching one or the other but of making certain that students learn both *about* theories and *about* data. They should respect data and observation as the measure against which theory is tested and either stands or fails. They should realize that hypotheses can be transitory and that, while geology helps us understand the earth, its concepts are not fixed.

Short of staging another scientific revolution during the course of each undergraduate's education—like the one I had the questionable fortune to experience—I think the best way to bring students who major in geology to terms with the dynamic nature of earth science is to have them participate in changing it. Each successive course introduces them to more data by providing a format, commonly laboratory exercise, in which to make the observations needed to develop interpretations. A repertoire of observations equips students to think critically about hypotheses and assumptions presented to them in class and challenges them to begin to formulate their own. It is the strength of the major as an educational format that it is not only, or even primarily, professional training. It is the means by which students learn a method for developing ideas and solutions, and become accustomed to the changes in frame of reference that will characterize their futures. This culminates in senior research. By formulating and testing a new geologic hypothesis, seniors test their own problem-solving methodology. They take that skill from the laboratory— where limitations of the classroom often necessitate that steps be demonstrated, problems be presented, or that a body of data be constrained for them—and use it under their own direction.

Students who work with me in British Columbia for their senior research projects help piece together the geologic history of the suspect terrane that I study. One student recently documented that an area of the terrane was deformed as if it had been involved in collision or accretion well before the time the terrane is known to have arrived at the margin of North America. The student's project was geologically successful: she was able to recognize and assemble critical data and formulate an objective interpretation of the character and timing of the deformation. Still, in the end she also confronted the larger and harder issue that there is no place for her conclusion in the present model of Cordilleran development. We recognize no plate tectonic mechanism for deformation of this sort within an ocean basin. Troubling as this disparity was for her, it makes her work a success of another kind. It is one of those inconsistencies that will eventually improve our understanding of the processes that built the Cordillera. Through her work, the limitations of present plate tectonic theory as it applies to mountain building became clearer to her, and to the geologic community.

I do not mean to foster irreverence for models in general or for plate tectonics in particular, but I do like a healthy independence from accepted wisdom. When theories are clearly understood to be interpretations, the search for where theory falls short, and thereby, how it can be improved, will have more vitality and creativity. Students who recognize and are comfortable with this will be well prepared to propose new theories of their own and to drive scientific advance.

With impressive symmetry, teaching has helped me remain alert to the uncertainties in tectonic theory for my *own* research. Students collaborate —without being aware of it—by the questions they ask, because they do not know the constraints of prevailing scientific opinion. Providing an explanation to an agile mind keeps me in touch with the weak points in the geologic models I use. All teachers know that sinking realization when a student's capacity to ask well-directed questions exceeds their own capacity to give cogent answers. Their questions identify for me what I am satisfied with, and what still dissatisfies me, in my own discipline. Students shake my complacency with present theory, and that is the starting point for new avenues of discovery.

Ancient History and Ancient Morals

Peter R. Pouncey
Professor of Classics

One of the first pleasures of embarking on the study of ancient history is the discovery of how uncluttered the ground is, in terms of the evidence to be garnered on almost any problem or period. The terrain around the Mediterranean is still soaked in the echoes and memories of large figures and events, but when you try to round out the stories and complete them, the voices falter or become intermittent. The actual deposits left in the ground or in libraries are, in sum, relatively small; dots in the text to indicate missing folios of manuscript, eroded or defaced inscriptions, truncated sculptures, and shards of pots—it amounts to a rather poignant record of fragments. Anyone who has stood at a remote classical site (Bassae or Paestum, say) and heard nothing but the din of cicadas has a living sense of the *emptiness* of history, and knows how mysteriously deep human silence runs over time. To some, this spareness is frustrating; but, as I say, I find it pleasurable. The thinness of the evidence puts all inquiring minds on the same footing: they all have the same clues to work with—what is the most to be gleaned from these scattered pieces, and into what pattern of plausibility, if any, can they be assembled? I like the sense of probing a mystery in recovering the past, and I like the sense of mystery that still remains, whatever small shafts of light have been thrown into this or that corner, when one's best efforts have been spent. The work of history should be humble in this regard. A poem by George Seferis, called "The King of Asine," spells this out well. Asine is a name that appears just once, without any associations, in the *Iliad,* in the catalogue of ships. Three millennia pass, and an archaeological dig is conducted on the site of ancient Asine in the Peloponnese; from the shaded azure water off shore, "breast of a slain peacock," the poet scans the citadel of Asine, and contemplates its King, whose gold sepulchral mask survives.

> The King of Asine an emptiness beneath the mask. . . .
> And the poet lingers, looks at the stones and asks himself:
> Do they still exist, then,
> Among these broken lines, edges, points, hollows, curves,
> Do they still exist
> Here at the meeting place of rain, wind, ruin,
> Do they exist, the movement of the face,
> The form and fashion of the tenderness
> Of those who so strangely have dwindled in our life . . . ?"
> (Warner's translation)

We do not want to become too wistful or mystical about the work of history; it is, often literally, a more down-to-earth sort of business, at one level closer to "criminal detection" kinds of mystery than to mysticism—though even here, when it is done well, a surprising sense of revelation can result. To do it well, you want a proper, gumshoe skepticism about the evidence you have found; you want to weigh the worth of each piece of evidence before you use it, biting it for authenticity before inserting it into the puzzle. Little by little a new picture emerges; as you look at it, you may learn something you didn't know.

A character from the 7th century B.C. will, I think, make this process clear. Pheidon of Argos is almost as vestigial a figure as the King of Asine; he is so precariously located in history that, as a scholar has remarked, his appeal lies in being assignable to any of three centuries. But we will locate him in the 7th century, because he fits best there—and because the 7th century *needs* Pheidon. Here is a cluster of facts and references, which amount pretty much to the sum of relevant knowledge about Pheidon (with a couple of choices made, and a few textual confusions willfully smoothed).

1. Hoplite armor (heavy infantry), according to archaeological findings, may date from the last half of the 8th century.

2. Aristotle's *Politics* says Pheidon changed from being king to tyrant.

3. Pausanias, using the Olympic victor lists, dates a victory of Argos over Sparta to 669, at the battle of Hysiae.

4. Unfortunately, the same Pausanias says that Pheidon of Argos was brought in by Pisa in the *eighth* Olympiad, to take control of the Games from Elis. That takes us all the way back to 748. But could that be a manuscript error—eighth for twenty-eighth? The change is not large in terms of numerical notation; and something like it seems to be confirmed by the Augustan geographer Strabo, who says Pisa first took over the Games after the twenty-sixth Olympiad (676).

5. Herodotus says Pheidon instituted a system of measures for the Peloponnesians, and this is confirmed by Strabo; Aristotle makes it clear that Athens also used the same system prior to Solon (594).

6. Pheidon of Argos instituted coinage for the island of Aegina, and dedicated in the temple of Hera at Argos the old iron spits the Aeginetans had used up to then (a fragment of Heracleides of Pontus). We have found the spits in the temple!

What do we make of this information, and how does it fit with anything else we know of the period? Pheidon is clearly one big Argive; he establishes a larger reach for Argos than it will have for a long time, if ever again—across the Peloponnese to Olympia, and out into the Saronic Gulf to Aegina. Given other temporal associations, it makes sense to attribute Argos's victory over Sparta to Pheidon as well—it is a victory that runs very much against later "form." But why can't he do it all as King? What is the force of Aristotle's note (2) that he became a tyrant? The important thing here is Aristotle's distinction that a king is a figure with constitutional restraints, usually in the form of an aristocratic council whose advice he must seek as a kind of *primus inter pares;* we see it operating normally in the *Iliad*. A tyrant has thrown over these traditional restraints. But now the big question: if he can do without the support of his peers, who is supporting him?

A little contextual history. A long dark age separates the heroic age, which has cast so strong a spell over the human imagination through succeeding millennia, from "real" history. What intervened is referred to as the Dorian invasion. Hordes of doubtful provenance, probably from the north and northwest, descended through Greece, leaving new strands of ethnicity, religion and mythology, and claiming strong bastions along the way, especially in the ancient states of the Peloponnese. Greece was not well equipped to support the new population; it is, as a Patrick White character observes, a country of bare bones. Everywhere the rock breaks through, pouring the inhabitants off the slopes toward the sea. After a restless sleep of 250 years, around 750 B.C., the Greeks woke up to a mean world of land hunger and social unrest. They looked back with intense longing to a golden age of settled feudal values, large meals and prizes, and honor. They had to get moving. Surplus populations were siphoned off in widespread colonial movements, westward to Sicily and Italy, and eastward to the Black Sea. Colonization opens up possibilities of trade, and trade creates new classes. The old feudal order is threatened still more.

My thesis is that by the time Pheidon changed his stripes from king to tyrant, there is a strong, emergent class, ambitious and resourceful, engaged in trade. The class is still politically disfranchised; it has no vote because it has no land, which, in ancient cultures, may be inalienable. Aristocratic landowners cling to ancient prerogatives and try to sustain their feudal control. But Pheidon has scented the wind of change, and appeals to the emerging class. The fact that he institutes new weight measures and new coinage (5 and 6, above) caters directly to a mercantile class. You do not need coinage or standardized weights if you are living on your own estates, but you do if you are seeking to exchange commodities; merchants need established standards of exchange to do business. It may also indicate mercantile power, that Pheidon is able to establish his influence on the island of Aegina. That takes shipping, and merchants have ships. Farmers do not like taking to the sea (read the poet Hesiod on this). I would go further with Andrewes, whom this interpretation follows, and argue that the reason Pheidon is militarily unstoppable in Greece (3 and 4, above) is that he has equipped his supporters as Greece's first really formidable hoplite infantry force. Hoplite armor is expensive, and economically is gauged by the Athenian Solon some 80 years later as appropriate for a middle class; also, hoplite warfare takes concerted, carefully regimented training, of the kind that polo-playing nobles do not lend themselves to. By the end of the century Sparta will have seized the hegemony of the Peloponnese by converting its entire male population into a hoplite fighting force. Perhaps it learned its first lesson in this direction from its defeat by Pheidon at the battle of Hysiae (1 and 3).

Whether true or false, this interpretation changes Pheidon from a historical will-o'-the-wisp into an important figure with a specific social context. It makes him, in fact, the leading figure of a crucial trend in Greece —the eruption of tyrannies throughout the Greek world over the course of the next century, in nearby Corinth, Sicyon, Megara, and Athens. When we examine those tyrannies in the light of subsequent history, we see that their function was exactly that we have attributed to Pheidon— to smash the ancient feudal structure, and serve as a painful interstitial phase preparing the way for more broadly based constitutional forms of government. In the case of Athens, the Pisistratid tyranny in the 6th century was the precursor of a full-fledged democracy.

So much then for Pheidon: we have glued six shards of evidence together to form a very small, perhaps misshapen pot, on which he appears at last as a figure with a background. Every historian does something like this, though seldom, especially in modern history, will one have only six pieces of evidence to relate to each other. Not to enjoy this kind of pattern-building is not to be a historian. I always recommend students who show an aptitude for this work to test their powers of argument and inference with ancient history first—not because the orderly mind should start at the beginning, but because you have command of the field, and the chance to test the reliability of your own taste, judgment and hunches, earlier than in periods with more complex and crowded layers of evidence. At least for the historian, if not for those who lived it, it was a simpler time.

BUT THERE IS ANOTHER work of history, which has increasingly enticed, or entrapped me, since my own undergraduate years. It is the work of historiography, which is, in Hayden White's term, a kind of Metahistory. If you are a classical historian, you realize that you are not the first to attempt to make sense of events, to round out the story. It has been told many times before. What is this impulse to reclaim the past, to tell or retell the story? And what do you hope to achieve by telling it? These are questions with different answers for different writers, but they are worth pondering for a lifetime.

There are several paradoxes and several assumptions that I find moving in the impulse to reclaim the past, or to perpetuate the present against inroads of the future. On the one hand, we believe that time is irreversible; we keep being told that we cannot put the clock back, cannot recall the home-run pitch, cannot undo the unhappy decision that led to our defeat. On the other hand, we are conscious of the reach of the past into our present lives—in the sins and genes of our fathers, in our own character flaws, in the traditions we inherit that seem to give ballast and solemnity to our lives but also drag us back like sea-anchors when we would sail free. Above all, the past extends to us in the structures of language and thought by which we try to make sense of our present world. With this inherent tension, we should not be surprised if the effort to reclaim the past, to make it real again, is going to meet frustration; like Orpheus trying to bring Eurydice back into the light, the more we turn to embrace her, the more she slips from us. Or rather, what we are left holding is something else, often something thin and unsensuous.

Faced with these limitations, I have chosen to concentrate on the great literary works of the ancient historians. I use the word literary not to demean them—quite the contrary. They write with an intense control of detail and nuance, and command of rhetorical theory—rhetorical understanding so lost in the twentieth century, I am afraid, as to be almost unintelligible. What has rhetoric to do with history? It has this to do with it: these writers are bound together by the assumption that one can *learn* from the past, or, inversely, for a more significant formulation, that *the past has moral lessons to teach us*. The literary works of ancient history are moral works. That explains the intense control of the narration: the historian is intent upon having the reader in posterity *persuaded*, by episode, anecdote and gesture, by speech, argument and nuance, of the right moral lesson. Narrative is always a kind of argument. Rhetoric is the art of persuasion, by which the audience is led to *believe* the argument. (One might add, by the way, that this shows a progression from epic. Epic and history share the same muse, Clio. Epic's role is to celebrate heroes, to offer them a kind of immortality, even though they will die. But prose historians have discovered that the past is not so unequivocally worth celebration: there are things to applaud, but things to deplore as well. The moral instruction of history seeks to play, like Justice herself, this balanced role).

Let us take an obvious instance of a historian arguing a case, making use of rhetoric. The following is an example from Pericles' Funeral Oration, in Thucydides (2.36.1–3):

Ἄρξομαι δ' ἀπὸ τῶν προγόνων πρῶτον· δίκαιον γὰρ αὐτοῖς καὶ
πρέπον δὲ ἅμα ἐν τῷ τοιῷδε τὴν τιμὴν ταύτην τῆς μνήμης δι-
΄δοσθαι. τὴν γὰρ χώραν αἰεὶ οἱ αὐτοὶ <u>οἰκοῦντες</u> διαδοχῇ τῶν
ἐπιγιγνομένων μέχρι τοῦδε ἐλευθέραν δι' ἀρετὴν <u>παρέδοσαν.</u>
καὶ ἐκεῖνοί τε ἄξιοι ἐπαίνου καὶ ἔτι μᾶλλον οἱ πατέρες ἡμῶν·
<u>κτησάμενοι</u> γὰρ πρὸς οἷς ἐδέξαντο ὅσην ἔχομεν ἀρχὴν οὐκ
ἀπόνως ἡμῖν τοῖς νῦν <u>προσκατέλιπον.</u> τὰ δὲ πλείω αὐτῆς αὐτοὶ
ἡμεῖς οἵδε οἱ νῦν ἔτι ὄντες μάλιστα ἐν τῇ καθεστηκυίᾳ ἡλικίᾳ
<u>ἐπηυξήσαμεν,</u> καὶ τὴν πόλιν τοῖς πᾶσι <u>παρεσκευάσαμεν</u> καὶ ἐς
πόλεμον καὶ ἐς εἰρήνην αὐταρκεστάτην.

You don't need a translation for the point I want to make, but here is a
very literal one. The verb forms have been underlined in both versions.

I will begin with our forefathers first; for it is right and fitting to pay
them this tribute of memory on such an occasion. For continually <u>in-
habiting</u> this land, in a succession of generations to the present, <u>they
handed it down</u> free through their courage. They deserve praise and still
more do our fathers. For in addition to what they received, <u>having
acquired</u> an empire of the size we now hold, <u>they left it behind</u> for us,
not without toil. And we ourselves of this generation, who are mostly
in our established years, <u>have increased</u> it, and <u>have equipped</u> the city in
all respects as most self-sufficient for peace and war.

What we have here is a progression of generations—forefathers, fathers
and us—and of empire extended. In the Greek the three periods (in the
classicist's trade, called *tricola*) that narrate this progression are built
around a participle and a main verb for the forefathers and fathers, and
two large main verbs for the present, thus:

> *oikountes. . . . paredosan*
> *ktēsamenoi. . . . proskatelipon*
> *epēuxēsamen. . . . pareskeuasamen.*

Look what has happened. The first stage of the progression gives us a
three-syllable participle and a four-syllable main verb. The second stage
gives us a four-syllable participle and a five-syllable main verb. The third

stage gives us two main verbs, the first five syllables, and the second a whopping six. A fair question is, Who in God's name is counting? The answer is that it is not a matter of counting syllables as one hears them being delivered, but that the words register *with growing weight* on the listener's ear as the periods proceed. The empire expands from one generation to the next, so the diction reporting the growth expands with it. The ear receives the correct impression of mounting achievement.

This is a clear case of a historian using rhetorical technique, but it does not surprise us, because it occurs in the course of a speech. It does not stop there. Rhetorical theory and practice imbue narratives as well as speeches. Sometimes writers also use a particular *topos,* or commonplace, to shape the tone of a whole scene. One might imagine that this use of "set" devices would stultify the writing, but that is not necessarily so; there is plenty of room for false bombast and derivative banality (what the ancients referred to as "frigidity"), but plenty of room for flexible and imaginative writing, too.

Here are three passages from three different genres (history, speech, biography), and three different periods, all of them using the same *topos.* We will discuss it at the end.

1. The first passage comes from Xenophon's *Hellenica,* a historical work that continued Thucydides' unfinished study of the Peloponnesian war from 411, and then followed Greek fortunes down to 362, the battle of Mantinea. Xenophon, like Plato, was a disciple of Socrates. He wrote philosophical as well as historical texts. He was an admirer of the Spartans, and to young students of Greek, who encounter him early, he seems to have imbibed a measure of Sparta's unliterary stodginess. But Xenophon is smarter and more adventurous than he appears at first glance. Theramenes' final stand against the Thirty in 404, recorded in this passage, is riveting, because it conveys a sense of the inexorability of tyranny having its way. From what we know of him, we would not have expected Theramenes to have exposed himself so fatally; as Athenian general and politician, he had stepped nimbly through the troubled transitions in Athens in the last decade of the war. It is conceivable that at the end he misread the tide: it would turn soon, in a matter of months, against the Thirty, but not at this moment. I prefer to believe myself, as Xenophon clearly does, that, for all the shrewd political calculations in the past, Theramenes was grounded on principle, and reached a point—disastrous for him—when he had to assert it.

Xen. Hell. 2.3.50-5

When he [Theramenes] had finished his speech and the Council was clearly in an uproar [*epithorubēsasa*] of approval for it, Critias realized that if he were to allow them to vote on the man, he would be acquitted. He could not live with this conclusion, so, after approaching the Thirty and discussing the matter, he went out and told his picked men to take their stand conspicuously with their daggers at the railings of the Council-chamber. He then returned to the Council himself, and said: "Gentlemen, I consider it the duty of a responsible political leader, who sees his friends being deceived, to refuse to allow it to happen. And that is what I am going to do. And these men standing here tell me they will not permit it, if we intend to release a man who is so obviously damaging the oligarchy. It is written in the new laws that none of those on the list of Three Thousand can be put to death without your vote, whereas, for those who are not on the list, the Thirty has the authority to sentence to death. I therefore," he said, "strike this man Theramenes from the list, since we are all agreed on it. And now," he said, "we sentence him to death." At that Theramenes leapt up to the altar, and said: "And I, gentlemen," he said, "call on the most sacred powers of law, that it should not be in Critias' power to erase either myself or any of you that he chooses, but that judgment on you and on me should be according to the law which this body wrote. And by the gods," he said, "I am well aware that this altar will avail me nothing, but I want to prove that these men are not only without justice to men, but without reverence for the gods as well. But my worthy friends," he said, "I shall be surprised at you, if you are not prepared to help yourselves, since you must be fully aware that my name is no more easily erasable than any of yours."

Thereupon the herald of the Thirty dispatched the Commission of Eleven against Theramenes. They entered with their assistants under the command of Satyrus, the boldest and most shameless of them, and Critias said: "We hand over to you," he said, "this man Theramenes, who has been condemned according to the law. Take him and conduct him to the appropriate place, and do what is necessary." When he had said this, Satyrus dragged Theramenes from the altar, and his henchmen helped him, while Theramenes, as was natural, invoked gods and men to witness what was happening. But the Council kept silent, seeing characters like Satyrus at the railings and the front of the chamber full of guards.

2. The second piece could make a strong claim to be the most famous passage of the greatest speech of the most celebrated orator in antiquity.

It is taken from Demosthenes' speech "On the Crown," which was delivered in 330 B.C. A civic crown had been voted to Demosthenes for his services to the state, but opposition from his rival Aeschines (we have *his* speech, too) made the award controversial and soured the moment. The first words of this passage in Greek (*Hespera men gar ēn*) are cited by "Longinus" *On the Sublime* as a prime instance of his theme. Their rhythm has a dying fall, exactly matching in content and resonance the twilight of Athens which the speaker describes. In the spring of 338, eight years earlier, Philip of Macedon, efficient and ebullient, descended through central Greece to make his hegemony final over the exhausted great powers of the past. Demosthenes had backed an Athenian alliance with Thebes to stay the flood, but the result was a foregone conclusion—the end of both Theban and Athenian independence. It is unusual to have a speech dwell so carefully on an earlier speech, but it does so to evoke strong emotions of dignity in defeat. We can imagine in what sad and emotionally charged silence his audience listened. By then speeches were all Athens had left.

Dem. 19.169–73:
It was evening when the messenger arrived to tell the Executive Committee of the Council that Elateia had been taken. They were in the middle of dinner, but immediately got up and had the Agora cleared of its market stalls, and the straw partitions burnt; and they sent for the generals and the trumpeter. The whole city was in tumult (*thorubou*). On the following day, at dawn, the President summoned the Council to its chamber, while the rest of you all proceeded to the Assembly. In fact, the whole people was already seated there, before the Council had finished its business or fixed the agenda. Finally the Council arrived and reported what they had been told, and introduced the messenger, who spoke himself. And then the herald asked, "Who wishes to speak?" But no one came forward. He asked the question several times, but no one stood up to speak, although all the generals and all the orators were present, and their country was calling for someone to speak and save it. (For the voice which the herald proclaims according to the law we rightly consider the common voice of our country). And yet if the call was simply for people who wanted the city to be saved, then all of you and the whole population of Athens would have stood up and marched to the rostrum: for I know that you all wanted her saved. And if the call had been simply for wealthy people, then the three hundred patrons would have stood up. And if it had been for

both these qualities, for patriotism and munificence combined, then those benefactors who subsequently gave such great largesse would have stood up: for they acted out of patriotism and munificence. But that day and that hour were calling, I think, not merely for a patriotic and wealthy man, but for one who had attended to events from the beginning, and had calculated correctly why Philip was acting in this way, and what he wanted; for anyone who was ignorant of all this or failed to examine it in depth was unlikely to know what must be done and unlikely to be able to counsel you. But on that day I proved to be the man, and coming forward I spoke to you. . . .

3. The third passage comes from Plutarch's *Life of Alexander*—one of his *Parallel Lives* of notable Greeks and Romans, written early in the 2nd century A.D. Alexander was paired with Julius Caesar in this collection, two prime conquerors. For a Greek subject of the Roman empire, a small political point is probably being scored by this principle of matching heroes—behind "parallel" lies parity of Greeks with Romans. At the same time, there may be a small notion of cyclical time—similar circumstances recur over the ages, and similar characters arise to meet them. Plutarch came from Chaeronea, where Alexander shared in his father's final victory over the Greeks in the August of 338 BC. Alexander also later annihilated the neighboring city of Thebes. Plutarch may well have been inclined to shade his account towards disparagement. In the structure and emphasis of his essay, we can see him suggesting an overall reading of the young King's career as a cautionary progression, in which noble character is corrupted by excess, the conqueror is conquered by his own failings, the hellenizer is barbarized, and Alexander, after gaining the whole world, is seen to suffer the loss of his own soul. The story of his killing his best friend Cleitus occurs at a pivotal point of this decline; I know of no more powerfully narrated anecdote in the classical corpus.

Plutarch, *Alexander* 50–51:
Not long afterwards, the incident with Cleitus occurred, which, to a casual view, might seem a more uncontrolled act of savagery than the Philotas affair. But if we take into account the nature of the occasion and the provocation, we find that the King's actions were not done by calculation, but under some cloud of fatality; his own anger and drunkenness played directly on Cleitus' temperament. This is the way it happened. Some people had arrived from the coast bringing fresh fruit for the King from Greece. He was delighted at its

fresh beauty and wanted to show and share it with Cleitus, so he sent for him. Cleitus was making a sacrifice at the time, but left it and came at once. And three of the sheep that had already been sprinkled with the libation wandered after him. When the King heard of this, he consulted his seers Aristander and Cleomantis the Spartan. They said that it was a grievous omen, so he gave orders for sacrifices to be offered for Cleitus without delay. (Two days before this, he had himself had a disturbing dream: Cleitus appeared sitting with the sons of Parmenio in black robes, and all of them dead). On this occasion, Cleitus never finished his sacrifice, but went immediately to the banquet, while the King sacrificed to the Dioscuri.

In the immature drinking bout that developed, some poems were sung to embarrass and ridicule Greek commanders, who had recently been defeated by the barbarians. The veteran officers were insulted and full of abuse for the poet and the singer, while Alexander and his party were enjoying themselves and telling the singer to continue. Then Cleitus, who was already drunk, and by temperament passionate and stubborn, became extremely angry, and said it was not right for Macedonians to be insulted in an audience of barbarians, who were their enemies; they were far better people, even if they had been unlucky. Alexander replied that Cleitus was indulging in special pleading, dressing cowardice up as misfortune. Then Cleitus stood up and said "But this was the cowardice that saved you from Spithridates' sword, when you turned your divine back to him; and it's thanks to Macedonian blood and wounds like this that you have grown so great, and can disown Philip and attach yourself to Ammon."

Alexander was stung by this, and said, "Do you think you will get off free resisting us like this all the time and sowing dissent like a rotten seed among the Macedonians?" "We don't get away even now," Cleitus replied, "but pay too high a price for all our labors. In fact, we bless those who have died already, before they ever had to see Macedonians beaten with the rods of Medes, and begging Persians for an audience with their King."

So Cleitus made free with his denunciations, and Alexander's group stood up to him and returned his insults, while older heads tried to control the uproar (*thorubou*). Then Alexander turned to Xenodochus of Cardia and Artemius of Colophon and said, "Don't true Greeks seem to you to walk among the Macedonians, like demigods among brute beasts?" But Cleitus would not let go, but told Alexander if he had something to say, to spit it out for all to hear, or else not to invite free men to dinner who spoke their minds freely, but instead to live with his barbarian slaves, who would bow down before his white robe and Persian girdle. At this, Alexander could not contain his rage, and pelted him with an apple on the table, and started looking for his sword. But one of his bodyguards, Aristophanes, had got there first and removed it, while others surrounded him and begged him to stop. Then he leapt up and called in Macedonian for his special Guard—a sign of a major disturbance—(*thorubou*) and ordered the trumpeter to sound the alarm, and punched him when he hesitated. Meanwhile his friends had with difficulty manhandled Cleitus out of the hall, still refusing to give way.

But he broke in again through another door, and in his headstrong and contemptuous way chanted the line from Euripides' *Andromache,* "Alas, how badly things are done in Greece."

Then Alexander grabbed a spear from one of his guards and rushed to meet Cleitus as he was pulling the curtain back from the door—and runs him through. He fell with a roar and a groan, and immediately the anger left Alexander. He came to himself, and saw his friends standing speechless, and first tried to pull the spear out of the body, and dash it into his own throat, but his guards seized his hands and forcibly carried him to his chamber.

THREE PASSAGES SPANNING almost 500 years, and many distinctive features in each of them, which we could linger over. In the Xenophon piece, for example, we note the almost artificial repetition of "he said," when both Critias and his victim Theramenes are speaking; the effect is to give emphasis and deliberation to the individual lines, to make the reader go slow and attend to them: each utterance stands alone and weighs heavy. In the Plutarch passage, we note the eccentric present tense at "runs him through," which the translation awkwardly retains. It is the only present tense in the passage. This is a frequent practice in both Greek and Latin—you make a verb graphic and immediate, by bringing it, against the grain of narrative, into the present. Damon Runyan, of course, does it the other way round. The Greek verb in question, *dielaunei,* has been used only once before in the work—it is what Cleitus does to Spithridates, to save Alexander's life.

But the point of putting the three passages down side by side is not to pick at their individual differences, but to show how they share common ground. I have already said they make use of a common topos; in a moment we will look at it directly. One obvious aspect of these dramatic, emotionally charged pieces is that they are all intent on the important Greek notion of freedom of speech *(parrēsia)*. In the case of Theramenes and Cleitus, this is explicit—they both get into trouble by speaking out, and the behavior of a tyrant is most clear in repressing them. In the case of Demosthenes, this is strongly implicit in the scene he so carefully sets: after what happened at Elatea, it is clear that Athenian freedom is over. Democracy meets to debate its fate, but no one at the outset has anything to say; Philip of Macedon has stolen their voice. But then the true patriotic orator comes forward, and the process of democratic life goes on, at least for the moment. Demosthenes deliberately portrays himself as heroic in his speaking, like the other two. But what of the topos, the commonplace that binds all three passages together? It is the device of conjuring up a scene of noise or uproar *(thorubos)* and bringing it to a charged silence: the pain of the drama is felt in the hush. Words, of course, break silence —it is a particularly skillful rhetorical inversion to remember that silence can often be more dramatic than words, and to put that thought to use. In Longinus, the silence of Ajax is seen to be another instance of the Sublime.

It is clear from such instances that history, in its narrative, makes use of rhetoric, the art and techniques of persuasion, to teach its lessons. But are not at least the facts of history, if they are to remain trustworthy facts, surely immune from this kind of manipulation? Not necessarily. Let us take as an example, the familiar story of the birth of Cyrus, which is basically a version of the story of Oedipus. In Herodotus we are told that Astyages, King of the Medes, has bad dreams about his daughter Mandane, and fears future trouble from her children. Instead of marrying her to a Mede, he puts her out of harm's way by choosing an inferior Persian for her husband. She produces a child Cyrus, and Astyages tells his chief of security, Harpagus, to take the child and kill it. Harpagus finds the assignment repugnant and hands the infant to one of Astyages's shepherds to be exposed to death in a remote wilderness. The shepherd's wife is called Kuno, which means Bitch (prostitute?), who happens to have gone into labor with their own child when her husband was summoned by Harpagus for his delegated chore. "They were worried about each other, he because of his wife's confinement, and she because Harpagus had sent for her husband out of the blue." He returns with the baby royally bedecked in funeral clothes, and his wife, whose child, it happens, was stillborn, persuades him to substitute the living for the dead. Their own child will be assured a royal funeral, and the authorities will be none the wiser. Cyrus, the half-caste Mede-Persian, is then raised by the shepherd and his wife, turns out to have natural charisma and gifts of leadership, courts the disfranchised Persians, and eventually establishes the Persian Empire. The rest, as they say, is history.

The story is borrowed by Livy for the raising of Romulus and Remus, leading to the foundation of Rome. There are some calculated differences. There is again a paranoid king, and shepherds again save the day. But the fact that it is not one child but twins is something Livy will work with (the historical theme of fraternal strife is important from the outset); and the added detail that the twins were suckled by a wolf, until human relief was at hand, may be etiologically linked to the name (Bitch) of the shepherd's wife in Herodotus. There are many versions of these stories. Otto Rank, in his great essay, *The Myth of the Birth of the Hero*, counts nineteen of them, including Moses, Jesus of Nazareth, and Lohengrin. He takes them all as versions of the Oedipus story and accounts for them, in Freudian terms, as "supplanting" myths. They are at least that.

But it is worth taking one moment to note what sort of function this kind of story has within a work of history. It is important to realize that all of Livy's readers would have known the Herodotus version; it is not a little piece of plagiarism, which he hoped to sneak by them. In fact, far from resenting a "borrowed" account of their founding, they would have regarded it as enriched by its associations with the earlier event, and by the skillful variations which the historian works on the theme. I believe the story, when it appears in a historical work, serves as a kind of composite image. It signals first a *dynastic shift*. One generation succeeding another in a regular progression does not call for this kind of myth; but when Persians take the place of Medes, or Romans of Latins, or the New Testament of the Old, the myth brings a special focus and color to the transition. Secondly, the strong attraction of the myth consists at least in part in its view of the working of destiny: the new order is *fated* to have its way. A new power is born and will sweep away the old. The old may dream of the threat and take every precaution to stave off the new, but it will not succeed. A powerful king may try to kill a defenseless infant, but a king is powerless before fate, which will arrange for the baby to survive through other agencies, and grow up to fulfill his destiny.

You may concede that the coloring of events with mythical images in this way, to give moral force to a story, might be permissible in accounting for an ancient city's foundation, which is buried in the mists of time. But is it appropriate in describing a historical period for which we actually have sources? We should be wary of this sort of distinction—the mythical consciousness of a society plays every bit as great a role in its knowledge of itself as its historical documents do. In fact, the myths shape the documents, and the writers correctly proceed as though there was no discontinuity between the two.

A pair of examples from a "historical" period will serve to make the point. Conveniently, they both convey, not the beginning, but the end of a dynasty. In Herodotus, the mad and tyannical King of the Persians Cambyses forms a passion for his sister and marries her (contrary to Persian custom, though not Egyptian); but he falls into a rage and kills her by kicking her when she is pregnant. In Tacitus' *Annals,* Nero kills his wife Poppaea, whom he passionately loves, by falling into a rage and kicking her when she is pregnant. What are we to make of this? Is there a tendency for paranoid tyrants to dispose of their wives by kicking? Two initial points: 1) note once more that all of Tacitus' readers will know the story of Cambyses; and 2) we are not talking of mythical periods—Cambyses died less than 50 years before Herodotus was born, and Tacitus was about 12 when Nero killed Poppaea. There is evidence that Tacitus has willfully brought the two stories into line: he discounts alternative versions which mention poisoning. Why? Because he does not believe that the actual circumstances of Poppaea's death are as important as the moral considerations to be associated with it. To emphasize the latter, he borrows all the associations of the Cambyses story, which depicts the depths power can reach when corrupted to an ultimate nadir. Cambyses shows his total lack of control by killing what he loves best; he shows his total lack of human feeling by killing what is most vulnerable (a pregnant woman); and most importantly, at this nadir of degeneration he brings his dynasty to an end by killing his unborn heir. The dynasty of Cyrus reaches its end with Cambyses, and the Julio-Claudian dynasty reaches its end with Nero. Unpacking the force of the image in this rather literal way, we see what induced Tacitus to make use of it. History may not repeat itself, but it seems historians do.

Modern historians, who wish us to draw morals from the past, tailor their evidence, too. In his *Eminent Victorians,* Lytton Strachey is eager to impress on his contemporaries the hypocrisy and raw ambition that lay at the heart of Victorian rectitude and order. Cardinal Manning, the worldly and successful Catholic prelate, is a fine archetype of his thesis. He is energetic and influential with political figures, but his heart is consumed, not with Christian charity, but with hatred and jealousy of the saintly John Henry Newman. Newman is a scholar and runs deep; Manning is shallow. Newman is gentle and quiet; Manning is politically aggressive and manipulates others. Needless to say, Manning is intent on baffling and defeating Newman. Newman ardently desires to have a Catholic house founded at Oxford. Manning, using his minion Monsignor Talbot in Rome, ensures that the plan is thwarted. Talbot encourages Manning's views of Newman as a dangerous figure and writes from Rome that "His spirit must be crushed!"

In this context, Strachey narrates a sad visit by Newman to his old parish at Littlemore outside Oxford, where he had spent the happiest years of his life in almost monastic retreat, and where he had finally been converted to the Catholic faith:

> At about this time the Curate of Littlemore had a singular experience. As he was passing by the Church he noticed an old man, very poorly dressed in an old grey coat with the collar turned up, leaning over the lynch gate, in floods of tears. He was apparently in great trouble, and his hat was pulled down over his eyes, as if he wished to hide his features. For a moment, however, he turned towards the Curate, who was suddenly struck by something familiar in the face. Could it be—? A photograph hung over the Curate's mantelpiece of the man who had made Littlemore famous by his sojourn there more than twenty years ago; he had never seen the original; but now, was it possible—? He looked again, and he could no longer doubt. It was Dr. Newman. He sprang forward, with proffers of assistance. Could he be of any use? "Oh no, no!" was the reply. "Oh, no, no!" But the Curate felt he could not turn away, and leave so eminent a character in such distress. "Was it not Dr. Newman he had the honor of addressing?" he asked, with all the respect and sympathy at his command. Was there nothing to be done? But the old man hardly seemed to understand what was being said to him. "Oh, no, no!" he repeated, with the tears streaming down his face. "Oh, no, no!"

End of chapter, and end of Newman.

We have the source from which Strachey drew this passage. It is taken from Wilfrid Ward's *Life of Cardinal Newman:*

> I was passing by the Church at Littlemore when I observed a man very poorly dressed leaning over the lynch gate crying. He was to all appearance in great trouble. He was dressed in an old great coat with the collar turned up and his hat pulled down over his face as if he wished to hide his features. As he turned towards me I thought it was a face I had seen before. The thought instantly flashed through my mind it was Dr. Newman. I had never seen him, but I remember Mr. Crawley had got a photo of Dr. Newman. I went and told Mr. Crawley I thought Dr. Newman was in the village, but he said I must be mistaken, it could not be. I asked him to let me see the photo, which he did. I then told him I was sure it was [he]. Mr. Crawley wished me to have another look at him. I went and met him in the churchyard. He was walking with Mr. St. John. I made bold to ask him if he was not an old friend of Mr. Crawley's, because if he was I felt sure Mr. Crawley would be very pleased to see him; as he was a great invalid and not able to get out himself, would he please go and see Mr. Crawley. He instantly burst out crying and said "Oh no, oh no!" Mr. St. John begged him to go, but he said "I cannot." Mr. St. John asked him then to send his name, but he said "Oh no!" At last Mr. St. John said, "You may tell Mr. Crawley Dr. Newman is here." I did so, and Mr. Crawley sent his compliments, begged him to come and see him which he did and had a long chat with him. After that he went and saw several of the old people in the village.

If this were a class, we would spend a fair amount of time analyzing the differences between these accounts. They are more fundamental than they might seem. Strachey's version is an elaboration of the topos "You can never go home." All the physical details seem to emphasize Newman's basic homelessness—he is utterly bereft, lost in his grief, unable to understand sympathy even when extended directly to him. The Ward version actually amounts to the opposite of this: it turns out you *can* go home. The sad physical details give way to a realization that Newman is not alone—his friend Mr. St. John is with him throughout, and ultimately he is persuaded to renew his contacts with older friends.

What are we to make of Strachey's changes? We must understand that they put a rhetorical topos to work to make a different point: they offer a vivid pictorial conclusion of great pathos to Monsignor Talbot's insistence that "His spirit must be crushed!" The poignant picture at the church gate shows that Manning and his minion had their way with Newman. Ward's biography would not disagree with this conclusion; it makes it clear that about this time Newman lapsed into a profound depression. Whatever the truth about the particular incident, Strachey's reading of the whole context seems to me absolutely accurate.

By the examples in this essay I have tried to show that there is a rhetoric in historical narrative, which often uses events as almost poetic images, with strong moral associations. As Quintilian, the Roman rhetorician of the first century A.D., observes, History is close to poetry. The writer of history reads lessons in the past, which have urgent meanings for posterity, and uses a wealth of technique to convey them. In this way, the past is made to reach out to persuade future generations of their own connection to it, and of a moral force behind the drift of events. I see my work as a historiographer not as trying to catch the past out in its inconsistencies, but as probing the art with which it offers a version of itself, and then seeing exactly where I can accept my own connection with it. And this is what I try to do with my classes. Looking out from my middle-aged viewpoint on those young faces, some of them eager, some of them bored, but most of them with only short histories of their own, what I wish for my students is this: to read these narratives with intensity and sympathy, and then to engage with the rhetoric, reflect hard on the judgments it offers, and work out what they will accept, what they will leave behind, or what alternative judgments they will pass on their own. If they are successful, they will have what we all should want: they will be deepened by connections with the past, but in a way that does not hold them back, but releases them, from a stronger base of understanding, to dare brave new departures for themselves.

Unrequired Passions: Learning Foreign Languages

Jay Caplan
Associate Professor of Romance Languages

Marie-Hélène Huet
Professor of Romance Languages

I.   The Language of Need

IN A RARELY-DISCUSSED PASSAGE of the Second Discourse on the *Origine et fondements de l'inégalité parmi les hommes* [1754], Jean-Jacques Rousseau submitted that, before the formation of social groups, children developed their own languages: "L'Enfant, ayant tous ses besoins à expliquer, et par conséquent, plus de choses à dire à la Mère, que la Mère à l'Enfant, c'est lui qui doit faire les plus grands frais de l'invention . . . et la langue qu'il emploie doit être en partie son ouvrage" [Pléiade, III, 147]. ("The child having all his needs to explain and consequently more things to say to the mother than the mother to the child, it is the child who must make the greatest efforts of invention, and . . . the language he uses must be in great part his own work." In an implicit reversal of the commonplace notion of a "mother tongue," Rousseau imagined that languages (note the plural) were taught by individual children to their mothers, only later to be forgotten, once the children had grown up and adopted the solitary, nomadic existence of prehistoric times. This curious idea was quickly forgotten by Rousseau and his commentators, but it deserves reconsideration today, as we try to understand what it means for young adults to learn foreign languages.

According to conventional belief, children learn language from their parents, and through language they also acquire the rules and social conventions of their culture. Language, in this view, enables children to become social beings, capable of negotiating the discrepancy between total fulfillment of their desires and the equally imperious demands of social order. Yet in Rousseau's imaginary languages, children spontaneously invent whatever words they require to state their needs; when they experience needs, they create words that are perfectly suited to their expression. With this language, the children construct a narrow and entirely subjective view of the world: a world without convention or tradition, knowledge or belief; a timeless world, without past or future. It is the language of a world prior to the advent of history. The language that each child invents has no relationship to any possible desire for knowledge of the world, responding to the urgency of need, rather than to the dormant curiosity of the mind. It is a language expressly conceived for the perfectly complementary relationship between mother and infant. In the undisturbed intimacy of this dual relationship, words never meet interference, there is no room for misrepresentation, no possibility of misunderstanding. In fact, there is no word that does not directly and unproblematically relate to a felt need. Before that necessary and perfectly natural moment when mother and child separate, they communicate in a language that has all the immediacy and transparency of the language to which Rousseau aspired: a language that speaks directly to the soul, a language still uncontaminated by the vanity of social relations, a language whose words concern nothing more or less than needs and the means to their satisfaction. It cannot betray the speaker's meaning, as a language adapted to a multiplicity of speakers necessarily must, for this language is tailored to the child's desires. Its words cannot be misunderstood by the mother, since they are meant for her alone (she knows no other), and she alone has all the answers to the demands that her child expresses. It is therefore not surprising, indeed it is quite natural, that such a language would quickly be lost to mankind, and never be shared by a community.

It could not fit two individuals in exactly the same way, and it certainly would not lend itself to more complex social relations or a broader conception of social requirements. This language presumably had no name for anything, however simple or concrete, that lay beyond the horizon of a dependent infant. According to Rousseau, in these pre-social times, needs and desires coincided perfectly; all wishes could be granted. It was a language of unmediated happiness.

Paradoxical as it may appear, in the process of learning a foreign language, students reinvest in these new patterns and sounds some of the creative energy that fueled Rousseau's primitive and lost languages. Students borrow, transform, and reinvent foreign sounds to express a complex set of needs. They often do so in joyous disregard for all existing grammatical structures and all present and prospective interlocutors (whether the latter are empowered to grade them or not); they enjoy a freedom of words, a jubilatory play with sounds still free of social or historical connotations. At first glance, of course, this description of language learning seems far removed from class experience. Not only do students actually learn from an authority figure, but they do so in organized and controlled conditions: with regular class meetings, language laboratory assignments, and a strict schedule of homework and examinations. Yet for all the grammatical strictures and syntactical obligations that the process entails, it is when learning a foreign language that students come closest to that privileged, hypothetical moment when children invented languages to express their immediate needs and taught these tongues to their mothers.

In the first place, foreign languages have no historical dimension for students; as in Rousseau, they do not evoke anything in the students' personal past, nor do they carry reminiscences of earlier moments of linguistic subjection, when children are made to obey the laws of their mother tongue and culture. In this way, foreign languages are remarkably free of personal memories. They have an innocence about them, such that they appear in the classroom as if they had never previously existed; they are free, as it were, to be used for the very first time in the first classroom of French 1.

The process that follows students' initial submersion in this sea of incomprehensible words and sounds is a phenomenon that can best be described by the word *appropriation*. Appropriation has little to do with the more familiar concept of learning, even if appropriation will eventually lead the student to master all the necessary conventions of a foreign language. Appropriation is a way of taking hold of these new forms and sounds and making them *one's own,* with an almost wanton disregard for what the words are supposed to "mean," or how they are meant to be "used." Not that a student who says, "Bonjour, comment allez-vous?" on the first day of class is indifferent to the explicit meaning and social conventions underlying these words. It is just that the pleasure of using them —a fascination with sounds, and repeated attempts to make them familiar and tame them—has really little, if anything, to do with the desire to be socially and verbally correct when greeting a person in French.

An introductory course in a foreign language is, above all, an opportunity for students to discover an innocent language, a language only remotely connected to another country and its inhabitants. By appropriating these words and mastering their pronunciation, students reinvent the language *as their own.* Individual responses to a given class are so varied as to elude systematic analysis. However, it is clear that each student, through a process of selection that remains mysterious, chooses among the masses of new sounds and structures those that will best fit his or her individual, half-acknowledged needs. Thus some students will revel endlessly in a form of verbal jubilation, in the utter pleasure of playing with new sounds. They will develop an almost obsessive need to master these sounds, to achieve the perfect accent, eager only to speak, and almost indifferent to meaning or use: as if the communicative function of language were secondary to the gratification to be derived from making new sounds. Some students, we are told, have no "ear" for foreign languages, even though they may be very talented musicians. Yet a student's success at reproducing a native accent may have less basis in physiological limitations than in the psychological conflict that language learning entails. It may stem rather from the ambivalence that students feel towards, on the one hand, the prodigious freedom granted by new linguistic forms, and on the other, the extreme rigidity of the rules that must be assimilated, an ambivalent process reminiscent of learning one's own mother tongue, and one that must be overcome for appropriation to be successful.

At any rate, learning takes place not by repetition but by appropriation. It is somewhat disheartening for a language teacher to see a student faultlessly complete a three-page exercise on the subjunctive, and then completely fail to use the subjunctive appropriately in the course of a conversation. For such a student, the case is clear: no appropriation has taken place. The subjunctive has not yet entered the personal language that he or she has constructed from foreign patterns and words. In fact, as long as such an appropriation fails to take place, no subjunctive will ever find its place in the student's individual practice of the language, even if the desire for a good grade and a little courteous consideration for the teacher are enough to get the student through an endless series of exercises. The reverse also happens. Students may be so delighted by an unusual construction, adverb, or tense, that they constantly invent opportunities for using it, independently of any relevance to context or practical results. Thus words are learned and invented, structures memorized and forgotten; new forms spring up, new sounds are forged, and the foreign language class starts to sound like a new Babel. The lonely teacher then has to fend off the proliferating forms of an individually created language that resembles French, and yet is unfit for any form of serious communication, an idiom that is so dear to its new speakers that they will not relinquish its use without a formidable struggle. This is the moment when students, having successfully overcome their initial shyness at speaking, are only too eager to say anything, to speak their own personal brand of French, whether or not anyone else likes or even understands it. At such times, grammar is forgotten and useless. In this language entirely fueled by individual, asocial (or presocial) impulses, there is no place for listeners. For at these moments when students speak, without hesitation and with a touching eagerness, they are often barely comprehensible to the teacher. So that momentarily, at least, the student-teacher relationship undergoes a Rousseauist reversal, as the teacher struggles to understand this confusion of foreign tongues. Of course, by worrying about understanding and communication, the teacher may be missing a point that is most clearly made later on, in "conversation" classes. Here students emphatically demonstrate that what matters for them is less the exchange of ideas or information, than the pleasure of speaking, the pure verbal satisfaction of speaking a chosen language rather than the mother tongue, an idiom where all identities seem possible, all avenues open.

These observations constitute a compelling argument against the widely held belief that students learn foreign languages for purely practical reasons. Doubtless, for some of them, training in a foreign language will be a valuable addition to their dossiers when they apply to graduate or professional schools; and many more will use the language as tourists. A few years ago, a major effort was launched, with important backing from publishing houses, to develop "business language courses" aimed directly at the productive application of foreign languages, and meant to give students all the skills needed to do business in another language (from transactions as small as opening a bank account to ambitious deals involving international corporations). The most interesting fact about these business language courses is how little success they had in terms of enrollment. The reason for their relative lack of success is not that they were poorly designed or ill adapted to their goals, but that they relied entirely on the premise that students take foreign language courses for practical purposes. We can no longer cling to this persistent myth. In a recent conversation class at Amherst, the students were given a list of topics meant to focus discussion on a set of issues relevant to contemporary French society. The range of topics was wide enough to accommodate all tastes: art, cinema, sports, politics, student life, *etc*. All topics were met with polite interest, and no more. For students learning French are only remotely interested in the specific features of a country that for them has one, and only one distinctive characteristic: that of being a place where the language they have been having such a wonderful time inventing is spoken. Or so they think.

Sooner or later, the time of reckoning arrives, when some form of a trade-off takes place. At that point, students partially abandon their own personal, creative form of French—the chosen language that has given them a brand new opportunity to define themselves as speaking subjects —in order to assimilate the official, exterior language with its pre-existing structures and strict rules, a language of limited phonetic opportunities. This trade-off usually takes place, and often very successfully, at the time when appropriation of a foreign language is tested outside the classroom, in situations where the language is needed to communicate with other people. At that time, which usually corresponds to a student's first extended stay in France, Russia, Spain, or Japan, they also may become interested in speaking about topics that in the classroom had been of no more than "academic" interest. In fact, learning correct German, or Italian, or Chinese, may be the ultimate form of appropriation: the language I have just created has then become yours as well, it has become legitimate. Students who successfully negotiate this step will never have any difficulty speaking French in a francophone country, no matter how incorrect their accent, or how fanciful their grammar. They will view the foreign country as a privileged location for linguistic self-expression: the same feeling of inebriating freedom all travelers experience upon arriving in a foreign country, between the time they clear customs and their first encounter with a taxi driver. This brief but wonderful moment when everything seems possible, when a linguistic and social heritage no longer seems to determine one's identity and fate, when the mysterious possibilities of a new language open up all doors. That moment lasts, of course, until the first argument over the taxi fare, when reality intrudes rudely into the dream, and business French comes back to haunt those who have eschewed its practicality.

II. Foreign Affairs

WHEN ENOUGH SUCCESSFUL APPROPRIATION has taken place, students are ready for literary texts. Since most students have been resisting all efforts to *teach* them the foreign language (by producing a personal version of French close enough to the normative form so that the teacher can understand it *and* give them an acceptable grade), moving into literature is no small step. For now the student's hybrid idiom, born of a personal myth, and free of all political, socio-economic and regional associations, must encounter a language steeped in cultural associations of all kinds.

The entrance of the Author bears comparison with what psychoanalysts have described as the discovery of the Name of the Father: that moment when the child learns that its binary relationship to the mother must be expanded to include another term, and social rules must be recognized and accepted through the acquisition of language. At this moment, language enables the student to make an ordered entrance into a common linguistic society. Due to centuries of canonical prejudice, most of the authors that beginning students of French first read are white men who have lived in metropolitan France. However, with both decolonization and the resurgence of the women's movement, a less unified picture of the French language and its literatures has emerged. French no longer appears as a monolith, but as a multiplicity of fragmented forms, in a dialogue of rich world discourses, sometimes at odds with each other, in a liberated use of the French language by people who have used it in varying ways during the course of a tumultuous history. French is no longer the sole preserve of Corneille or Victor Hugo: it also belongs to a Kabyl writer fighting for freedom in North Africa; it is the troubling voice of a Maryse Condé, reflecting on her fragmented identity as a Caribbean woman and seeking to come to terms with her African ancestry in French, her mother tongue.

These multiple voices will help the students find their own places in the language they have been building. While encountering variations in the literary canon, as well as in grammar and vocabulary, students will come to realize that the French language is not just the language of clarity, law and order, but also the language of colonization, and the language of national liberation and reconstruction. Amid these heterogeneous voices, students can make themselves at home, in a cultural-linguistic identity of their own choosing. Obviously they will never read a French literary text like a native speaker, but they can turn that apparent handicap into an advantage. At first, for example, they will not associate Flaubert's legendary "Mme. Bovary, c'est moi," with anything but a particularly satisfying phonetic sequence. Yet in so doing, they will have access to a "poetic" experience of the language that in a sense is much closer to Flaubert's than is that of his French readers, for whom the possibility of hearing these words as sound rather than meaning has been foreclosed. For our students, the image of the embattled author of *Madame Bovary* fades away in the immediate enjoyment of an exceptionally successful utterance. Likewise, the experience of teaching literature in French to students who have just invented their own versions of the language will bear only the remotest connection to teaching that literature to students who share essentially the same linguistic heritage as the authors. In the first place, the author's stature hardly makes a dent in the new-found linguistic identity of these readers. No weighty tradition imposes respect for Racine, passion for Baudelaire, or a sense of awe before Mallarmé. Students are unmoved by Romantic appeals, unruffled by the symbolist's tortured syntax, oblivious to the star system that until recently has dictated the French literary canon. They do not wish to know better, nor should they. From their perspective, the French author is just someone who happened to write in the personal language they have recently invented. In fact, the pleasure they derive from the literary text is so closely bound up with the pleasure of using that personal idiom, that students will resist any attempt to facilitate more complex expression of ideas by having part of the discussion in English, or to read the texts in translation to ensure better understanding of the ideas. Any such suggestions on the teacher's part will usually be met with bland refusal or an intense disappointment.

We may best appreciate what it means for a student to read a foreign text by considering the use of foreign quotations in Edgar Allan Poe's *The Murders in the Rue Morgue.*[1] This famous short story, doubtless the first modern version of the detective story, takes place in Paris, where the detective C. Auguste Dupin uses his formidable analytic powers to solve a horrible and seemingly inexplicable crime. It is also, as we shall see, a story about what foreign languages are, about what makes languages foreign. A double murder has been committed in the rue Morgue, and one of the major clues that will lead Dupin to elucidate the mystery is the identity of the mysterious language spoken by a murderer who has been overheard but not seen. Dupin quickly finds the solution to this linguistic puzzle, and presents it as follows: "But in regard to the shrill voice, the peculiarity is—not that [the witnesses] disagreed—but that, while an Italian, an Englishman, a Spaniard, a Hollander, and a Frenchman attempted to describe it, each one spoke of it as that *of a foreigner.* Each is sure that it was not the voice of one of his own countrymen. Each likens it—not to the voice of an individual of any nation with whose language he is conversant—but the converse. The Frenchman supposes it the voice of a Spaniard, and might have distinguished some words *'had he been acquainted with the Spanish.'* The Dutchman maintains it to have been that of a Frenchman; but we find it stated that *'not understanding French this witness was examined through an interpreter.'* The Englishman thinks it the voice of a German, and *'does not understand German.'* The Spaniard 'is sure' that it was that of an Englishman, but 'judges by the intonation' altogether, *'as he has no knowledge of the English.'* The Italian believes it the voice of a Russian, but *'has never conversed with a native of Russia'* " (authors' emphases). This voice, "foreign in tone to the ears of many nations and devoid of all distinct or intelligible syllabification," will lead Dupin to identify the murder as an "alien to humanity," one of the prodigious orangutans that so fascinated nineteenth-century naturalists.

We may infer from Dupin's astute reading of the witnesses' reports that a foreign tongue, for those who do not yet speak it, is a language that brings them back, confusedly but surely, to a primitive and forgotten past. The witnesses give various names to this linguistic missing link, doubtless

---

[1] Some of the following comments are the indirect result of a Kenan Colloquium I co-taught with Andrew Parker on "Margins of Literature." I wish to thank both Andrew Parker and the class for furthering my reading of E. A. Poe. —*M. H. Huet.*

an ironic salute to the efforts of nineteenth-century linguists to identify the Indo-European roots of all Western languages; they all recognize it as the tongue they do not speak, but would surely understand if they knew the language. There is no uncertainty in the witnesses' reports: the language is *familiar* enough to be identified without hesitation as the very language one does not speak. But how can one recognize what one does not know? Or is knowledge also the recognition, immediate and certain, of what is foreign to us; and what is a foreign language, if not an idiom we are always just on the verge of understanding—one we can identify without knowing it, one that we can name, albeit erroneously?

Dupin, on the other hand, understands immediately that what characterizes the language these witnesses heard is, precisely, that it defies understanding, that no names will ever make it any less strange. No translation will ever make it accessible to us, so remote is the past it conveys. That all the witnesses should find this language so familiar, and yet completely unintelligible, close enough to be named, and yet hermetically sealed to understanding—these qualities suggest a common and remote ancestry. The language lies dormant in the collective memory of the species, not only because it is so ancient but also because it is in the nature of language to change and evolve, to adjust and adapt. These sounds from a distant past, prior even to Rousseau's speculative tongue, are recognized by Dupin for the simple reason summarized in a Latin line he was fond of citing:

Perdidit antiquum litera prima sonum.

Dupin has not heard the language spoken, he has only read about it in the newspaper accounts of the witnesses' reports. Knowledge of the theories of evolution (including the evolution of languages) thus provides a partial solution to the enigma of the Rue Morgue. However, we are told that the true source of Dupin's superior analytic capabilities lies precisely in the same "exertion of the intellect" that enables him to win at draughts, a game he considers more intellectually demanding than chess: "Deprived of ordinary resources, the analyst throws himself into the spirit of his opponent, identifies himself therewith, and not infrequently sees thus, at a glance, the sole methods (sometimes indeed absurdly simple ones) by which he may seduce into error or hurry into miscalculation." The talents that he applies to the solution of a crime are quite similar to those that are needed in order to learn a foreign language. By throwing oneself into the spirit of one's "opponent," an imaginary speaker of French, or Spanish, or Greek, one appropriates a new and different structure of thought, and successfully learns a language. But is proper identification with this language enough to recall the past, reconcile past and present, and to name the criminal as well? In short, is knowledge of what is essentially *foreign* also sufficient to understand chaos and crime, and to restore law and order? So one might believe, after Dupin, having confounded the police with his masterful analysis, secures freedom for the sailor/owner of the orangutan, as well as a peaceful and harmless existence for the animal in the Paris *Jardin des Plantes*.

Yet despite all the detective's linguistic *savoir-faire,* he and his companion, the narrator, do not believe that languages can successfully be translated. Quotations in Latin and French are scattered throughout the text, and we are frequently reminded that there is no satisfactory way of translating them: either because there is no corresponding meaning ("Many individuals have been examined in relation to this most extraordinary affair. [The word *affairs* has not yet, in France, that levity of import which it conveys with us.]"), or because some words simply resist adequate translation ("I have said that the whims of my friend were manifold, and that *je les ménageais:*—for this phrase there is no English equivalent.") Of course, one could find many acceptable ways of translating *je les ménageais:* "I indulged them, showed consideration for them, humored them," *etc.* But aside from the fact that none of them really does the trick (the notion of "indulgence," for example, carries the inappropriate suggestion of yielding to a weakness), no translation will ever convey the semantic relationship between the verb *ménager* (to spare, show consideration, or save) and the noun *ménage* (household, couple), as in the expression (usually left untranslated) *ménage à trois.* Before rushing, however, to the conclusion that, due to the peculiarities of French *moeurs,* certain words are best left in their language, the English-speaking reader may be chagrined by Poe's admonition that *affaire* has never taken on the "levity" of its English cognate: in other words, that in French *affaires,* business never mixes with pleasure.

Surely an important step forward in language pedagogy was made when the idea of learning a language by translating it ("*Gallia divisa est in partes tres,*") was finally abandoned. Of course, something may have been lost in the process of giving up translation. When students are called upon to show that they have grasped all the details of a sentence, by translating it into English, they invariably fail to take all the words of the sentence into consideration. Instead they choose to convey a general impression they have of the sentence, by rendering it loosely (although often correctly) in English. In so doing they express their sense that a foreign language is not a conversion of one's mother tongue into different words or rhythms. For the elements of one's own language have no equivalents or duplicates in a foreign language. What is at stake in a foreign language class is the acquisition and reappropriation of a mode of expression that, to a surprising extent, can be tailored to fit one's needs and desires. For this reason, the foreign language will always to some degree be a mythical language, an imaginary treasure of sounds and syllables, a language of infinite possibilities.

In contrast to the imaginary richness of foreign languages, translations usually do not fare well. Either they seemingly fail to convey something more or less definable in the original text, or they exceed or distort it. Anglo-American readers have often attributed the unmitigated admiration of French readers for Poe's tales to the magnificence of Baudelaire's translation, a reaction ostensibly compounded by the translator's own prestige as a poet; they find French admiration for Poe's verses, such as "The Raven," utterly baffling (Aldous Huxley could explain it only by arguing that the French have no ear for English prosody). In any case, Baudelaire had nothing but praise for the *Tales of Mystery and Imagination,* and was largely responsible for its great success among symbolist writers. Yet for all its elegance, Baudelaire's glorious translation necessarily erases the singular mystery of all the French words scattered throughout Poe's text. In Edgar Allan Poe's tales, these expressions stand alone; alien, untranslatable, they take on an individual glow. They add to the story more than their dictionary meanings, for they convey a sense of adventure, a foreignness, as it were, which Baudelaire's French prose is destined to erase. The note, *"en français dans le texte,"* completely fails to register the uncanniness of the word *outré,* for example—as in "something excessively *outré.*" For is not the fact that *outré* is untranslatable, or should not be translated, precisely what makes its meaning so *outré?* What is more *outré* than to have no equivalent, and to say so? *Outré* (literally pointing to that which is "beyond") will always be more *outré* in a non-French context, because of the suggestion that it defies translation. Yet in French, it is barely excessive. Or again, Dupin remarks: "I observed that the shutters of the fourth story were of a peculiar kind called by Parisian carpenters *ferrades* —a kind rarely employed at the present day, but frequently seen upon very old mansions at Lyons and Bordeaux." The word *ferrade,* rarely used in modern French, maintains an opacity in Poe's text that can be measured only in relation to another language. Similarly, the reading of foreign texts is always for students something more than for native speakers, more similar to an adventure into a closed system, whose alterity and complexity (and sometimes also its beauty) can be measured only in its own terms.

Thus one should resist translations as much as possible, as students instinctively do, even when they are asked to translate. Their understanding of the French classics will always be a surprise to those who grew up with them, and who have become so familiar with the patina of received meanings that have been inscribed on their syntax and sounds. Foreign students are quick to perceive what has escaped native speakers, enmeshed as we are since infancy in the familiar rhythms of our own tongue. But for our students, no noun is familiar, no verse is taken for granted, no metaphor is anything but a surprise. When they read these texts as if they were being read for the first time, we can imagine the innocence of that moment when Rimbaud's *Illuminations* were read by their first readers. On the other hand, since students do not expect a genre, a style, or particular themes, they soon become formidable judges as well as remarkable analysts, no matter how slow and painful their first encounter may be. Then again, such an experience teaches us that all literature should be read as if it had been written in a foreign language: in a language reappropriated by the poet or novelist to their specific needs, in response to their desires, as the writers, in their creative imagination, also assumed the role of Rousseau's first infants.

The learning of a foreign language is thus both more and less than the simple acquisition of new skills. This fact will always be a source of irritation to those who advocate the learning of a second language for purely practical purposes. One does not *acquire* a foreign language as a simple mathematical addition to one's own linguistic system. It is not as if, in an exotic version of vocabulary building, one could simply store up a few additional sounds and syllables, to give more varied expression to a known feeling or familiar concept. The disproportion between the enormous quantity of mental energy spent in the learning of a foreign language and the practical results of this new knowledge should suffice to discourage those who believe that knowing French enables one to snub a *maitre d',* read a train schedule, or successfully argue with a Parisian cab driver (a feat most Parisians would not attempt). There are, of course, good and practical reasons for knowing Arabic, Chinese, French, German, Russian or any foreign language: it promotes understanding, it facilitates relationships between countries, not to mention relationships within these increasingly multilingual United States. It encourages one to appreciate differences, to try out new mental structures: to discover, for example, that there are linguistic forms, and cultures, where the subject does not always come first. Learning foreign languages lends flexibility to the mind.

Still all these reasons fall short of acknowledging what takes place when a language is "appropriated," not just as a skill and means of communication, but also as a chosen language, as the vehicle of unspoken needs, as an opportunity for creation, and for recreation of oneself. This purely creative activity, exercised within loose networks of rules and with words that are free of personal memories, allows for a rediscovery, a re-creation. Nothing less can justify the sacrifice of long hours, the willingness to forgo all past knowledge, and to pretend, several hours a week, that one is learning how to speak again, learning how to know and to express all knowledge for the first time, pretending that one has a chance to rewrite at least some of the past.

To those who like to think of learning a foreign language as a more or less businesslike proposition, we can say, quoting Poe (himself quoting Molière) that they "put us in mind of Monsieur Jourdain's calling for his *robe de chambre—pour mieux entendre la musique.*" [2]

---

[2] Loosely translated: calling for his dressing gown—in order to hear the music better.

The Laboratory Study of Childhood Disorders

Lisa Raskin
Associate Professor of Psychology and Neuroscience

LISA SCHULE HAD TROUBLE thinking of herself as a scientist, yet she thought she might go to medical school. I guess she really wanted the "Doctor" part and not the chemistry and math. I first met her in my lecture class, a big class with ninety students. She was very sharp, practically jumping out of her seat with questions. The subject of the course was the biology of psychiatric disorders, and it thoroughly engaged her.

A couple of years later she came to me about doing a psychology honors thesis in my lab. By then she had given up her ideas about medicine and switched to law. She had shied away from most science courses, feeling defeated by scientific and quantitative reasoning. Yet she wanted to do a thesis in my physiological psychology lab; she still cared.

Someone told me she thought I wouldn't take her seriously because she wanted to go to law school, not medical school. I told her I wanted what she wished for herself (secretly, I wanted her to lick her fears so she could go to whichever school she preferred).

Lisa worked assiduously in my lab for a year. She learned to formulate hypotheses, to test and challenge her assumptions, to eliminate bias in her observations. In short, she learned the scientific method. She worked harder, thought more seriously, and cared more deeply than most students I've known. At the end of the year my colleagues and I in the neuroscience program met to give out the departmental prize for research. Someone (not I) suggested that the prize go not to a neuroscience student but to a psychology major, Lisa Schule. I almost wept. My Lisa got the neuroscience prize for scientific research.

The honors program, for me, is one of the greatest joys of teaching at Amherst. It gives me a chance to work one-on-one with a student, to help him or her develop skills in the laboratory, to read scientific literature critically and, finally, to think like a behavioral scientist. Students are not taught facts, they are taught a method of investigation. They learn to form clear and logical hypotheses, to gather data appropriately, and to evaluate it. In time, students like Lisa Schule, who begin a project under my close supervision, can become so independent in the lab (and in their thinking) that I begin to look at them as young colleagues. Our weekly honors meetings become true dialectics on how the project should proceed.

For the past eleven years, research in my lab has focused on the psychiatric disorders of childhood. Lisa Schule's thesis was about the biological basis of the Attention Deficit Disorder of Childhood (ADD).

My particular bias leads me to believe that many explanations and cures for behavior disorders can be found in the chemistry of the brain. The field of biological psychiatry has revolutionized psychiatry in the past twenty years. Illnesses that we previously thought stemmed exclusively from poor parenting may, we now know, occur in part because of brain dysfunction. Two examples of illnesses that probably occur because of an aberration in brain chemistry are schizophrenia and manic depression; and the list is getting longer all the time. A recent study published by the 1974 Amherst graduate, Dr. Alan Zametkin of the National Institute for Mental Health, has, in fact, highlighted the brain abnormalities which may be associated with ADD.

Children who suffer with ADD often find it impossible to pay attention. They are typically hyperactive and impulsive. The disorder can be diagnosed as early as age three or four, although behavior problems are often not picked up until school age. It is much more common in boys than in girls. The disorder varies in its severity: some children have trouble paying attention, yet are not hypermotoric; some show attentional and hyperactivity problems, and others (at least half of the children diagnosed) show a conduct disorder along with their problems of attention. The last group obviously presents the greatest problem at home and in the classroom. Looking at a clinic one can tell if such an ADD child has been there: whatever isn't bolted down may be overturned! ADD children, at their worst, can seriously disrupt a classroom; they are verbally impulsive and may taunt and tease classmates. Many need close supervision (we had a case of a child who, when his mother left him alone, drank bleach). When the disorder becomes severe, teachers and parents can be overwhelmed.

There is no question that environmental factors are important in both the origin and management of this disorder. However, to believe that this disorder is, in all cases, a reaction to environment is, I think, to believe a myth. Subjecting the study of ADD to the scientific method has told us something vital: some of these children cannot help themselves. They do not behave badly on purpose; they cannot control their impulses. ADD children probably have a brain dysfunction. In my lab at Amherst, I have been working over the years with honors students like Lisa Schule to try to understand the brain mechanisms that underlie ADD.

For years, a major problem in understanding the disorder was refining a diagnosis (it is a problem in all psychiatric research). There was a myth that at least one fifth of the school-age population had ADD or a hyperactivity problem. Estimates of the prevalence of this disorder have ranged from three to twenty percent. That alone should give us pause; the difference between three and twenty percent is considerable and represents a difference of millions of children. ADD, or "hyperactivity" as it is sometimes called, had become a diagnostic wastebasket—a term used to label children who were aggressive, oppositional, bored, or maybe just different. Yet just because the diagnosis has been over-used doesn't mean that a serious deficit in attention and an inability to control impulses and activity is not a real problem in some children. Over the past ten or fifteen years, researchers and clinicians have been working hard to refine the diagnosis of ADD so that children can be treated appropriately.

Appropriate diagnosis is important not only for treatment, but also for understanding the brain correlates which may underlie a disorder. Researchers have a better chance of comparing their subject populations if those populations are homogeneous. Recent investigation into the biological correlates of ADD, in which a diagnosis has been made carefully and rigorously, suggests that it may be associated with a dysfunction in certain brain chemicals called "neurotransmitters" which transmit information from one brain or nerve cell to another. On the basis of clinical studies, Dr. Paul Wender at the University of Utah Medical Center and Dr. Bennett Shaywitz at the Yale School of Medicine have proposed that the neurotransmitters which are dysfunctional in ADD are dopamine and norepinephrine.

The cell bodies of dopamine and norepinephrine neurons are located in the midbrain and brainstem, the oldest parts of the brain in terms of evolution. Yet processes from these cell bodies extend into areas thought to be involved in emotion (the limbic system), motor (the basal ganglia), and newer brain areas such as those concerned with higher thought processes (the frontal cortex); consequently, a disorder or "imbalance" in these chemicals could affect a wide range of behavior.

Dr. Shaywitz and his associates, years ago, introduced an animal model to study the role that dopamine systems have in ADD. They found that when laboratory animals had dopamine deficiencies around the time of their birth, they were hyperactive and showed learning deficiencies. In my lab at Amherst, I have worked with Lisa Schule and other honors students to push these investigations forward. We have found that when dopamine levels are low early in life, animals are not only hyperactive; they show perseverative behaviors, spend a lot of time "off task," and are more easily distracted than other animals. They have great difficulty solving complex mazes. The results of Lisa Schule's thesis investigation suggested that male animals were more vulnerable to changes in levels of dopamine than were female animals. While we would not extrapolate these results to a human condition, this behavioral profile is akin to children with ADD. We hope that these results will offer insight into future clinical research.

Evidence from clinical work already strongly implicates dopamine in motor disorders. It has been established that Parkinson's disease, a motor disorder characterized by tremor, postural rigidity, and a shuffling gait, is associated with a marked loss in the dopamine cells in an area of the brain called the substantia nigra. The most effective treatment of Parkinson's discovered so far is the drug L-Dopa—a chemical that can enter the brain and be converted into dopamine. Without L-Dopa, many Parkinson's patients would not be able to move. Parkinson's disease is associated with the degeneration of specific nuclei containing dopamine neurons, which indicates a strong link between that neurotransmitter and motor function.

In fact, the link between dopamine cells and Parkinsonian symptoms goes further. Recently, some physicians have attempted to reverse the neuro-degenerative process of Parkinson's by grafting dopamine cells from an individual's own adrenal gland (on top of the kidney) into his substantia nigra. It has been discovered in work with animals that the brain is immunologically privileged and will not reject foreign tissue; cells from body tissue, and even from another brain (a controversial proposal, using human fetal brain tissue) can be transplanted into a host brain. The first brain-grafting studies in which substantia nigra dopamine cells were grafted were performed on laboratory animals and met with remarkable success. Animals with damage in their substantia nigra showed motor disorders, and brain grafts of dopamine cells into these substantia nigra reversed the disorder.

Brain grafting for the treatment of Parkinson's disease in people was first performed in Sweden and met with mixed results. More recently, doctors in Mexico have reported greater success. The process by which behavioral recovery occurs with brain grafts is not clearly understood. Surgery is risky and the results have been equivocal. Success with brain grafts would be a milestone in the treatment of Parkinson's. Replacement of dopamine cells would be a more effective treatment than L-Dopa, a drug to which many individuals become resistant.

Drs. Wender and Shaywitz suggest that children with ADD may also have a deficiency in dopamine function. Although ADD children do not show Parkinsonian symptoms, an important point is made: the effects produced by a neurochemical deficiency in a developing brain may be different from those produced by the same deficiency in an adult brain. Around the turn of the century, in fact, the pandemic of Von Economo's encephalitis left many adults with Parkinsonian symptoms while it left children with symptoms resembling ADD.

There is also reason to believe that dopamine may play a role in attentional mechanisms. This notion comes from the work on the biology of schizophrenia, a profound thought disorder that is characterized at times by delusions (believing oneself to be, for example, John Kennedy or Napoleon), and loose associations and hallucinations (which in some cases take the form of voices telling the individual that he is bad or that he should hurt someone else). Some schizophrenic individuals also report that they feel bombarded with stimulation—hyperattentive, as if they cannot filter out sensations. These thoughts and sensations are uncontrollable. What causes schizophrenia? No one knows. For years it was believed that it developed exclusively from pathogenic family interactions. Such behavior was seen to result from early psychic trauma, severe stress, or dysfunctional families. While studies have shown that these factors are related to the emergence of schizophrenia, increasing evidence implicates a genetic predisposition for the disease.

Schizophrenia has been particularly difficult to treat. Historically, symptoms were attenuated by any number of harrowing techniques including drilling holes in the individual's skull to release evil spirits, inducing hypoglycemic shock with insulin injections, and even psychosurgery —removing parts of the brain known to be associated with personality, such as the frontal lobes. Over the past thirty or so years, research has led to a more humane and effective way of treating this disorder: drugs that bind to the dopamine receptor and block it are the most effective agents in attenuating schizophrenic symptoms. This fact adds to the growing body of research supporting a dopamine theory of schizophrenia. Although the details have not been worked out, schizophrenia is thought to be associated with an excess in functional dopamine in areas such as the frontal cortex. An aberration in frontal cortical areas of the brain could explain the severe thought disorders that characterize the disease. That schizophrenia is associated with increased sensory stimulation and "hypervigilance," and dopamine is associated with schizophrenia, suggests that this neurotransmitter may be important in attentional mechanisms. One note about the side effects of drugs that block dopamine receptors: they must be used with caution. Any drug that decreases dopamine can produce motor side effects, some of which resemble Parkinson's disease.

It is simplistic but tempting to look at the role of dopamine in the following way: excessive levels are associated with enhanced sensory responsiveness (schizophrenic symptoms), and low levels are associated with problems in paying attention (ADD) and motor abnormalities (Parkinson's in adults, and hyperactivity in children). This is, of course, an oversimplification of how the brain works. For one thing, a difference in levels of neurotransmitters may not be the only brain abnormality associated with psychiatric disorders. Intracellular and intercellular mechanisms of neurons that contain these neurotransmitters are also important. Also, dopamine is not the only neurotransmitter in the brain. It is one of six or seven chemicals identified so far that are considered to be neurotransmitters (that is, they function as communicators between neurons). There are hundreds, maybe thousands, of chemicals that are candidates for this title. In fact, one theory holds that dopamine may not influence behavior directly, but instead influences other neurotransmitters which directly affect behavior. In trying to understand the biological bases of ADD, my students also ask this bigger question concerning dopamine's function in the brain and its influence on behavior.

The most effective way to treat ADD is to administer stimulants, drugs that increase levels of dopamine and another neurotransmitter in the brain —one that was mentioned earlier, norepinephrine. Drugs such as amphetamine (Dexedrine) or methylphenidate (Ritalin) seem to help children pay attention and focus on the task at hand. It is not surprising, given the theory that low functional dopamine may be associated with attentional problems, that drugs which increase dopamine levels improve attention. Do children taking Dexedrine or Ritalin—drugs which increase levels of dopamine—begin to show, then, schizophrenic symptoms? In theory they could. In fact, a "differential diagnosis" for schizophrenia— that is, a possibility which must be eliminated before a diagnosis is made —is amphetamine addiction. Adults who self-administer and abuse amphetamines begin to show schizophrenic symptoms such as hallucinations, paranoia, and delusions. (This, too, supports a dopamine theory of schizophrenia). But children who are prescribed Dexedrine or Ritalin do not show this response, because their dosage is smaller and they are taken off medication every night.

That is not to say that there are no side effects resulting from administration of stimulants in the treatment of ADD. Some children develop tics and obsessive-compulsive behaviors. Dr. Judith Rapoport at the National Institute of Mental Health has shown, however, that careful prescription and follow-up can significantly decrease side effects from stimulant medication. While controversy remains about side effects of the drugs, and whether they produce long-lasting improvements in ADD, most clinicians will say that, in serious cases, it is better to medicate than not, as long as the medication is carefully supervised.

The treatment of ADD with drugs that increase levels of dopamine and norepinephrine does not provide enough evidence for us to claim that the disorder is caused by a deficit in these neurotransmitters. However, it is a finding which adds to the many other results from clinical studies and basic research suggesting that dopamine in particular may play a role in this serious childhood disorder. Honors students in my lab continue to pursue these questions.

A footnote on Lisa Schule: she is currently in law school and finding it easy. She says the training that her thesis gave her, in analytic thinking and the testing of hypotheses, prepared her well.

EAR TRAINING

William H. Pritchard
Professor of English

THE CRITIC WILLIAM EMPSON once said that he did not know how much of his mind T. S. Eliot had invented. In setting out to write about myself as a teacher in Amherst classrooms, the only proper place to begin is with an earlier self in those same classrooms, forty or so years ago, when my mind—such as it is—was invented. The inventors were essentially three in number—Theodore Baird and G. Armour Craig, both professors of English at the college, and their colleague Reuben Brower who had an effect on me at Amherst but even more when he became a teacher and I a graduate student at Harvard. I encountered Armour Craig in the fall of Freshman year when I took the required Composition course, conceived by Theodore Baird some years previously and—by 1949—having come fully into its own as a brilliantly original approach to writing as an activity. That activity, performed by us three times each week—in short responses to difficult, sometimes impossible questions about thinking, meaning, knowing, and other essential human pastimes—was my introduction to serious intellectual inquiry. Having graduated from high school, I had already become an expert in solemnity, but the Amherst English inquiry, as it was conducted in the questions asked us and in the professor's response to our papers, was invariably playful, therefore puzzling to us. By the end of term if not earlier, we began to suspect that language was something other than the mirror of reality; that—in a phrase of Joseph Conrad's I would come to later on—words are, among other things, "the great foes of reality"; and that the way we went about marshaling our words into sentences, "composing" reality, could be both a matter for despair and for hopefulness, but was nothing less than central to what we did every day.

Freshman Composition was valuable to me partly as a deterrent to flatulence. Since among other things the course was an elementary education in irony, it was salutary for a young achiever whose high school valedictory address three months previously was titled "Health" and stressed the importance of all of us staying healthy. In the extended activity of writing as practiced in English I (thirty-three times the first term) we—teacher and students—looked at what we had written, at what could or couldn't be said in a sentence. The course took no notice of literature; that noticing occurred the following year in the Sophomore "Introduction to Literature," another staff course, this one mainly the creation of Reuben Brower. English 21–22 had the effect, whether intended or not, of helping us regain some of the confidence we might have lost the previous year, since Brower and his staffmates had what looked to be a useful vocabulary for talking about what went on in poems and stories and novels. That vocabulary, which featured such terms as tone, attitude, dramatic situation, was derived from Brower's study with I. A. Richards, author of the extraordinarily influential *Practical Criticism*. In Sophomore English, and in the Humanities 6 course Brower subsequently introduced at Harvard (in which I did my first teaching), we engaged in collaborative reading carried on in both a leisurely and a sharply-focussed manner. Just as Freshman Composition consisted in examining the particular essays, paragraphs, and sentences we students had produced, so the literature course never wandered for long from its intent consideration of the words on the page—of the individual poem or stanza or line or word that momentarily engaged us.

The words on the page—well, yes; but what I remember most about my Amherst English teachers is the way they took words off the page and brought them to life through the speaking voice. Baird reading aloud a soliloquy from *Hamlet* in a rather self-consciously loud, deliberately unactorish way, yet one that was scrupulously observant of the syntax and sense of the lines; Craig beginning his consideration of Milton's poetry with an extended reading out of "Lycidas" ("Yet once more, O ye laurels, and once more/ Ye myrtles brown, with ivy never sere"); Brower imitating the finicky, weary cadences of the lady in T. S. Eliot's "Portrait of a Lady":

> So intimate, this Chopin, that I think his soul
> Should be resurrected only among friends
> Some two or three, who will not touch the bloom
> That is rubbed and questioned in the concert room.

Behind such performances—the insistence that in the beginning, first of all, the poem needed to be *heard,* realized in the manner through which it was read aloud—was the example of Frost ("Now I'm gonna *say* a few poems for ya"). It was the same Frost who remembered hearing Brower, when he was a student at Amherst, read aloud in class a 16th-century poem by an otherwise forgotten poet, Richard Edwards, which began "In going to my naked bed as one that would have slept." "Goodness sake, the way his voice fell into those lines, the natural way he did that very difficult poem," said Frost years after the event.

This primacy of the speaking voice, this insistence on getting the tone right—of (in Frost's own words) seizing the special "posture" needed to deliver it correctly—informed, in ways I surely wasn't conscious of at the time, my "approach" to literature and eventually my dealings with it in the classroom. Nor was I conscious that Frost's discovery, so he truly thought it, of the primacy of voice in poetry was the cornerstone of what theorizing he did about the act and the art of reading. He put these thoughts powerfully and succinctly in a letter written home from England in February of 1914:

> *The ear does it.* The ear is the only true writer and the only true reader. I have known people who could read without hearing the sentence sounds and they were the fastest readers. Eye readers we call them. They can get the meaning by glances. But they are bad readers because they miss the best part of what a good writer puts into his work.

My education at Amherst—that part of it conducted within the English department, both in the composition and the literature course, and in their successors—was essentially a training in ear reading, whether the bit of writing under scrutiny was (as it often was) a lyric of Frost's, or the opening of Henry James's *Portrait of a Lady* ("Under certain circumstances there are few hours in life more agreeable than the hour dedicated to the ceremony known as afternoon tea"), or one of the unwittingly fatuous sentences I turned out in my papers. Do you want to sound like *that?* was the direct or implied question we were invited to put to our own prose, while practice in listening to Frost and James brought the awareness that other designs, other ways of sounding, were possible, at least within reach of our ears.

Despite my introduction to ear-reading, I graduated from Amherst a philosophy major, with the intention of becoming a teacher of that discipline. Accordingly, I spent a year listening to some very good eye-readers in the Columbia University department of philosophy. Unlike Frost's eye-readers, who speedily picked up the meaning by glances, these professors were hardnosed teasers-out of the sense of passages in Locke or Kant or Whitehead. But outside of class I was reading Kenneth Burke's *A Grammar of Motives,* in which Burke performed "dramatistic" readings of and listenings to the philosophers, showing how their sentences talked to each other and made for a "life" in their words analogous to that found in poetry or fiction. Burke's subversive demonstrations of how philosophic meaning was as much a creation of language, of voice even, as was "literary" meaning, pushed me out of the formal study of philosophy and into literature. Subsequent work quickly showed me, however, that the academic study of literature could be every bit as "eye"-oriented as traditional academic philosophy. With the important exception of Brower, by then teaching at Harvard (the institution to which I transferred), professors of literature were either scholars or historians of ideas, English literature being conceived of as a matter of sources and influences, traditions and literary movements. Reading, it was assumed, was something everybody did on their own time and presumably was perfectly capable of doing. Were we not, after all, in graduate school and at Fair Harvard to boot?

Whether or not Harvard English was right or wrong in its procedures and assumptions, "we"—the Amherst people studying literature there, a substantial number—were up to something rather different. Insofar as we conceived of our purpose in criticizing and teaching literature, it was something clearly distinct from the way Harvard laid out the map of literature and placed individual figures and groups on that map. Most of us in the "Amherst contingent" (we were sometimes referred to as such) didn't think of ourselves as scholars, or even as potential writers of books. There was rather—and I think in contrast to many of our peers from other institutions—an eagerness to get into the classroom and instruct others about the kinds of literary discoveries we were making. While our peers were busily contriving to get a first article published (so it seemed to us, perhaps paranoically), we contrived to ignore the whole matter of publication, even though it might be necessary to move our professional careers into orbit.

If my own career didn't exactly get into orbit, it began to assume a direction when, suddenly and unforgettably, a call came in December of 1957 from the then chairman of the Amherst English department, Benjamin DeMott, asking me how I'd like to come down for an interview with the president and the department, with the likely outcome of an appointment at the college. For someone who had carried around with him since undergraduate days the notion of teaching at a small college like Amherst, this was a heady and risky invitation—for now it was to be not just "like" Amherst but the very thing itself. How fitting it was that, in preparation for my interview with President Charles W. Cole, the only piece of advice I received was a simple, memorable injunction from Theodore Baird: "Speak up!" I was, in other words, to announce myself at the outset as a young man with a voice, someone who was going to be heard. I must have spoken up at least enough to convince the department and president of my adequacy; later, when it came time for the tenure decision to be made, I was again smiled upon and became—in one colleague's word—a "keeper." Except for terms spent on sabbatical leave I've been teaching at this college since the fall of 1958.

SO MUCH, THEN, FOR AUTOBIOGRAPHY: there follows an attempt to say what I've been doing in the classroom during the past three decades. Along with describing one or two pedagogical clarities or discoveries, I need also to name what I'm "against"—approaches to teaching, to literature, to students, that seem to me markedly unhelpful toward, sometimes destructive of, good reading and writing. My examples are taken from courses I've taught over the past few years: period ones in Romantic and Modern British poetry; seminars in literary criticism and in 17th-century poetry; larger lecture courses in Reading Fiction and Modern Satiric Fiction; and the introductory course, Writing About Reading, which I teach every fall.

Recently a secondary school teacher of English asked me what I ex-

pected or hoped my students would "know" about poetry, about literature, when they came to college as first-year students. My response was,
after thinking about it for a while, that students need not necessarily know
anything in particular—need own nothing except, in Yeats' phrase, their
blind stupefied hearts. Less melodramatically, let them own an ear open
to the soundings of words; let them also own feelings not wholly dedicated to immediate suppression in favor of preparing for law or medical
school exams. What then do they need, to read with some success the
following lines from Shakespeare's *Antony and Cleopatra* in which Cleopatra eulogizes her dead lover:

> For his bounty,
> There was no winter in't: an autumn 'twas
> That grew the more by reaping: his delights
> Were dolphin-like, they show'd his back above
> The elements they lived in: in his livery
> Walk'd crown and crownets: realms and islands were
> As plates dropp'd from his pocket.

In asking a class of first-year students what's going on in this sequence
I don't expect they will immediately begin talking about the difference it
makes that the lines are enjambed; that the sentence units run over the
lines and create an impassioned—and vividly metaphorical—utterance
quite different from, say, a speech in *Romeo and Juliet*. My main concern
has to do rather with the quality of feeling these lines about Antony
project or express through the extraordinary language Shakespeare gives
Cleopatra. But of course that quality of feeling can be approached only by
readers who listen to the pace and cadence of the verse instead of merely
moving their eyes across the lines.

For a moment, suppose we forget that poetry is written in feet and
lines, thereby presenting special challenges to the reader who is attempting
to tune in. One of the hoariest prejudices or assumptions among my
students is that it takes a special talent or faculty to read poetry well,
whereas everybody is pretty much equal before prose. (My fiction courses
are much more heavily enrolled in than the poetry ones.) In fact, as I try
to show them, such is not the case. Consider the ending of one of Hemingway's early stories, "Indian Camp," in which the young Nick Adams
witnesses his father-doctor's makeshift Caesarian operation on an Indian

woman, the operation undertaken with "a jacknife and nine-foot, tapered gut leaders." During this operation the woman's husband slits his throat, and as Nick and his father return home in their boat the following dialogue between them concludes the story:

> "Why did he kill himself, Daddy?"
> "I don't know, Nick. He couldn't stand things, I guess."
> "Do many men kill themselves, Daddy?"
> "Not very many, Nick."
> "Is dying hard, Daddy?"
> "No, I think it's pretty easy, Nick. It all depends."
>
> They were seated in the boat, Nick in the stern, his father rowing. The sun was coming up over the hills. A bass jumped, making a circle in the water. Nick trailed his hand in the water. It felt warm in the sharp chill of the morning.
>
> In the early morning on the lake sitting in the stern of the boat with his father rowing he felt quite sure that he would never die.

This lovely moment in Hemingway's work is especially vulnerable, in its delicate poise, to unlovely attempts by interpreters of the story concerned to tell us what it Really Means: one of them has called "Indian Camp" "the story of a boy coming into contact with violence and evil," while another has informed us that, at the story's end, Nick has "rejected his father and retreated from reality."

With Shakespeare's figurative and tonal richness everywhere evident ("For his bounty/There was no winter in't"), it would be a travesty to say that in praising Antony lavishly Cleopatra has "retreated from reality" or has exaggerated his virtues through the enlargements of metaphor. These would be unfortunate attempts to "understand" Shakespeare's language by reducing it to formula and pretending that the characters made up their own speeches. With Hemingway, who—unlike Shakespeare—leaves out rather than puts in, aggressive and all-too-confident ways of understanding (such as are offered by the critics above) get in the way of good reading. They do so by providing crude and hasty ways for us to avoid what we should be engaged in; namely, with *listening* to the rhythms and manner of presentation, the "feel" of the scene. "A bass jumped, making a circle in the water . . . It felt warm in the sharp chill of the morning": how could anyone who really listens to those sentences want to go on and talk about rejection of the father or retreating from reality? Why would they not want instead to talk about the beautiful sequence Hemingway has created here, from the father rowing, to the sun coming up over the hills, to the jumping bass, to Nick trailing his hand in the water and feeling it "warm in the sharp chill of the morning." Why would they not want to engage with what Frost says all poetry is about—"Performance and prowess and feats of association." "Why don't critics talk about those things"? Frost went on to ask. "What a feat it was to turn that that way, and what a feat it was to remember that, to be reminded of that by this. Why don't they talk about that?"

"They" don't—and here I mean by "they" many secondary school and college teachers of literature, as well as professional critics—because they are looking for literature to provide kinds of stabilities, the moral and psychological certainties writers like Shakespeare and Hemingway are concerned to undermine, or at least to ignore. When students of mine begin sentences telling me that in such a poem Keats or Emily Dickinson says that . . . , or how, in "Sunday Morning," Wallace Stevens believes that . . . , or how Shakespeare thinks that . . . —such sentences are tip-offs to a conception of literature as the repository of messages, opinions and beliefs about life held by the writer and conveyed (doubtless in excellent language) to readers ready to be instructed. And if the teacher or critic has a strong agenda, the poem or story may be enlisted as an ally in furthering the cause. Or perhaps it is simply that teachers confronting a class and critics trying to get their essay written are reluctant to live with the instabilities and fluidities that imaginative writing like Shakespeare's or Hemingway's presents us with. "Did Shakespeare think anything at all," T. S. Eliot once asked somewhat mischievously. "He was preoccupied with turning human actions into poetry," added Eliot. And it was Eliot also who remarked that Henry James had a mind so fine "no idea could violate it." Such challenges were aimed at disconcerting readers eager to extract ideas or beliefs from the work of notable artists; Eliot reminds us that these artists will not be reduced to the pedagogical or analytical needs of those who talk and write about their art.

ONE OF OUR BEST CRITICS and teachers of poetry, Helen Vendler, wrote recently of her teacher at Harvard, I. A. Richards (who years previously had been Brower's teacher at Cambridge), that he was the only professor she encountered there who—as she put it to herself at the time—"taught poetry":

> My other teachers rarely talked in detail about poems they had assigned: they talked about history, or politics, or theology, or literary movements, or archetypes—but not about those radiant and annihilating complexes of words that seemed to me to be crying out for attention, so inexplicable was their power and so compelling their effect.

My experience at Harvard tallies with Vendler's, though with Brower's and other Amherst voices in my head I didn't feel the need, as she did, to seek out Richards. But Vendler's speaking of poetry's "complexes of words" as both "radiant and annihilating" should give us interesting pause. Annihilating of what? Perhaps Richards's own writing provides a clue, if we remember what he once said about the final moment from *Antony and Cleopatra* when Octavius Caesar gazes down at the dead Cleopatra and observes that

> She looks like sleep,
> As she would catch another Antony
> In her strong toil of grace.

After quoting once more the final line—"In her strong toil of grace"— Richards asked "Where in terms of what entries in what possible dictionary, do the meanings here of *toil* and *grace* come to rest?" This is a question not to be answered by neat measurement, and one provoked, I think, by the way a particular complex of words, used by a master of language, can be "annihilating" of boundaries and limits as defined by the dictionary, or by the teacher intent on fixing a character or the play within some "meaningful" scheme of his own.

Most Amherst students who elect to take a poetry course with me expect that we will be centrally concerned with "complexes of words" as they are laid into lines and stanzas. But when fiction rather than poetry is the subject, such an assumption about focus is less common. In Modern Satiric Fiction we read many books during the semester—about one a week—so that there isn't time to pay the kind of respectful and detailed attention to language one can afford a lyric by Hardy or Yeats. Does that mean that attention must, initially or ultimately, be turned somewhere else than toward language? There are different ways to view this issue, and one critic (Marvin Mudrick) whose major interest was in fiction rather than poetry, has warned us that "In the beginning of poetry is the word; in the beginning of fiction is the event." Mudrick argues that the words of a work of fiction needn't be so precise and special as the words of a poem, and that fiction's words should not arrogate to themselves too much precision or "radiance" (Vendler's word). Perhaps so; yet the characters and events in a novel are perceived—are constructed by the reader —only through language. If some novelists, Dreiser say, or Dostoyevsky, ask to be considered in terms other than for their "precise and special use of words," there are others, James or Proust or John Updike, who as far as I can see stake everything on their "verbal complexes," on their styles.

In any case, I find that students in my fiction class are often puzzled as to what, in their papers, they should be writing about. I remember vividly how one member of the class who had done poorly on his first essay came to talk to me about this matter: what did I, in the famous word, "want"? I may have been somewhat evasive, but finally he asked, point blank, "You mean you want us to write about the language"? Remaining calm, I said that this didn't seem a bad idea to me; sure, why not try writing about the writing, rather than about the truth, or American society, or male-female relationships. No doubt the student left my office figuring that he'd pegged me as one of those aesthetes interested in technique rather than substance. What he didn't know, and what I couldn't tell him at that point, was that "technique" is more mysterious and even "annihilating" of clearly marked boundaries and dictionary definitions than he might have thought. Once more Eliot provides the useful formulation: "We cannot say at what point technique begins or where it ends."

Writing well about writing—whether that writing is poetry, drama, or fiction—means that the student must be helped to listen well; so, in a recent term of Reading Fiction, I invited the class which had just completed works by Dickens, Trollope and George Eliot (the latter two items were fairly short, and I assigned only half of Dickens's *Pickwick Papers*) to see what would happen if they practiced some of Frost's "ear-reading" with respect to a particular sequence from one of these writers. They were to select a passage, quote it at least in part (such focus localizes attention to individual sentences) and then—in a deliberately vague question I often resort to—try to describe their "interest" in the sequence or passage. One student quoted some sentences from Eliot's short novel, "Amos Barton," in which the clergyman's wife Milly is introduced: "a lovely woman— Mrs. Amos Barton: a large, fair, gentle Madonna, with thick, close chestnut curls beside her well-rounded cheeks, and with large, tender, shortsighted eyes." The student felt, rightly, that such language contrasted rather sharply with Eliot's comic and satirical presentations of other characters—most notably, the Rev. Amos Barton himself—in previous chapters. Where on earth, asked the student, did "this gentle Madonna" with her "placid elegance and sense of distinction" come from?

> Is she perhaps instead a divine being descended directly from the heavens? Somehow it is too much to swallow without choking a bit. Are we to believe that the sly wit so skillfully exhibited on the preceding pages can perform such an abrupt about face?

He went on to quote more of Eliot's picture of Milly as possessing the "Soothing, unspeakable charm of gentle womanhood; which supersedes all acquisitions, all accomplishments . . . You would even perhaps have been rather scandalized if she had descended from the serene dignity of *being* to the assiduous unrest of *doing*."

All this, the student felt, was too much. Was it possible, he wondered, that Eliot, "a highly intelligent and sensitive woman in a society dominated by the male sex," felt contempt for the "regard" in which women were held? Could indeed the description of Milly be understood as "a parody of the skewed, romantic, Christian notion of the 'ideal woman' current at the time"? Could Eliot, in going so far as to write the following sentence—"Happy the man, you would have thought, whose eye will rest on her in the pauses of his fireside reading"—be deliberately mocking the conception of woman as pure and sacrosanct, a conception given much currency by male poets and novelists?

Whether his speculations and inferences are wholly correct or need to be adjusted and qualified, needn't concern us here, though they were of concern when we discussed his paper in class. The point is that the student gave us something to argue about, and did so by beginning with George Eliot's "technique": with matters of voice, diction, and intonation— words brought off the page and to life in an imagined utterance. We can't say where technique begins or where it ends, proof of which statement is there in the student's move from small, local matters of hearing and noticing, to speculations about male and female in 19th-century England—large matters indeed. But the respect paid to Eliot's art is both evident and admirable. This is an "English" paper, a piece of literary criticism rather than a sociological or political argument.

One further example of how practice in listening to, in constructing and describing the "sound" of a particular novelistic moment may lead to results that couldn't otherwise have been achieved. The climactic chapter of Jane Austen's *Persuasion* is one in which the heroine, Anne Elliott, and her lover-husband to be, Captain Wentworth, become fully aware of their love for one another. Anne is engaged in conversation with a mutual friend of hers and Wentworth's, Captain Harville, while Wentworth sits nearby, writing a letter, but in fact eavesdropping on the conversation. Anne and Harville get into a friendly argument about the differences between men and women, and which sex has the stronger capacity for feeling, for "loving longest" especially "when existence or when hope has gone." (Anne and Wentworth, through her decision, were separated years previously and she has never ceased to grieve for him.) Anne claims the privilege for women, but Harville, somewhat teasingly reminds her that "all histories are against you, all stories, prose and verse." He tells her that

> "I do not think I ever opened a book in my life which had not some-thing to say upon woman's inconstancy. Songs and proverbs, all talk of woman's fickleness. But perhaps you will say, these were all written by men."
>
> "Perhaps I shall.—Yes, yes, if you please no reference to examples in books. Men have had every advantage in telling their own story. . . . I will not allow books to prove any thing."

Since throughout this particular book Anne has been characterized as a very serious reader, exceptionally responsive to fiction and poetry, her forbidding any reference to books has a sharp ring to it. The discussion continues with her own voice gradually becoming firmer and more poign-ant as, without ever mentioning his name, she indirectly confesses to the ever more attentive Wentworth the faithfulness and durability of her love for him.

In the exercise I gave my students I said that this passage in *Persuasion* could be studied for what it might reveal about Jane Austen's attitude toward the sexes. But, I suggested, it might be studied—at least *read*—

for something else, and I asked them to try to describe that something. I had in mind the way, as Anne assumes the ascendancy and moves toward a quite glowing affirmation of her love, she responds to Harville's polite admission that, since the evidence he alludes to comes from books which were all written by men, she is justified in denying their authority as foolproof indication of female inconstancy: "But perhaps you will say, these were all written by men." Then, with no narrative indication of how Anne says them (vigorously, teasingly, scornfully, determinedly?) we are given her three words back at Harville: "Perhaps I shall—." My point was that in this wonderful moment Austen is inviting, indeed compelling individual readers to do something, to "hear" these three words in a particular way—or at least to entertain some different ways in which they might be spoken. Whether the reader opts for calm certainty on Anne's part or a sudden seizing of the reins as the opportunity presents itself; whether she makes a humorous, eye-twinkling riposte to Harville or settles into a righteous affirmation of her claim's virtue—the three words need to be heard as rendered other than in a monotone. It is a moment in a dramatic sequence, in a conversation that has a before and after; it is progressive; it issues in something beyond itself. Returning to Frost once more: "The ear does it; the ear is the only true writer and the only true reader." My mildly polemical point in the exercise was that a reader interested only in what Jane Austen "thinks" about the sexes (in fact she thinks lots of things, contradictory ones even) is engaged in eye-reading merely, and is losing the best part of the experience of art.

"I'd no more set out in pursuit of the truth than I would in pursuit of a living unless mounted on my prejudices."

—Robert Frost

KINGSLEY AMIS, ONE OF THE MOST entertaining novelists currently at work, once said with regard to a question of English usage: "I sometimes feel I have shifted a good way to the right in this matter over the years, but I feel no less often that (as in other matters) I have stayed more or less where I was while nearly everybody else has shifted to the left." There are a number of matters involving teaching, colleagues, students, and curriculum, where Amis's observation strikes home to me. Some are trivial; others perhaps less so. For instance: I still call students by their last name (Miss Jones, Mr. Smith) in class; still give a two-hour final examination in my courses. I dislike catalogue descriptions by colleagues that go on for too long, or use "critique" as a verb ("students will critique each other's papers") or show an over-fondness for words like "problematizing." I look with a wary eye on courses that appear to have a political agenda with a view to replacing presumably unexamined student prejudices with "correct" left-liberal ones—though sometimes I think the left-liberal ones are correct. (It will of course be pointed out to me that the claim to have no political agenda is but another sort of political agenda. My withers are unwrung.) Although my department offers serious courses in film, I would prefer that students chose to study Shakespeare or Romantic poetry first, just as I want them to read and study literature before they take a course in literary theory, if they ever do. And at a time when the cry is for "opening up" what is termed the literary "canon" so as to include within it (or substitute for it) works by recently discovered or rediscovered female and minority, non-Western, non-white-male writers, my interest is in going deeper into the canon as currently perceived. Or rather, in exposing students to the canonical works few of them are even acquainted with.

Some years back I had occasion, in a required course for English majors, to ask the class what it thought of this notion of opening up the canon; to a man and woman they replied that it seemed like a fine idea. I then threw out some names of well-known works and authors from the unopened canon—Marvell's "Horatian Ode," Wordsworth's "Resolution and Independence," Samuel Johnson, John Henry Newman, Anthony Trollope, Bernard Shaw. Not just the majority but virtually the entire class of intelligent and articulate Amherst College students had no sense at all of these writers and their work. Admittedly this fact isn't about to impress teachers dedicated to opening things up. But it brought home to me that, in these days of "pluralistic" (to use the dignified word for it) approaches to the teaching of English—days in which, more or less, anything goes—that it might be adventurous to teach the canon. Accordingly over the past few years I have offered old-fashioned "period" courses in English poetry from Spenser to Pope, or Wordsworth to Tennyson, and I plan to offer further ones involving 18th and 19th-century British novelists and prose writers. In an important sense this is a selfish act on my part, since I'm serving my own need to explore further an already established list of writers and to share my discoveries with an audience. (It is easy, by the way, to forget how important students are in providing ears—sometimes responsive ones—for talk about writers, Marvell or Wordsworth or Samuel Johnson, on whom you'd have trouble focussing the conversation at a dinner or cocktail party.)

How much does my resistance to some of today's going concerns have to do with being one of the tiny number of Amherst graduates who currently teach on its faculty? (There are four extant, three of us in our late fifties.) I do know that I'm strongly prejudiced against the notion that education at Amherst has improved over the past few decades as a result of gradual liberation from a required curriculum—The New Curriculum. Those who delight in Amherst's current pluralism have been known to characterize the learning atmosphere of that old New Curriculum as an "intellectual boot camp." On the other hand, nobody has suggested that the U.S. Marines were not well-trained, and there is a case to be made for the kind of learning that, sometimes, went on in Amherst between 1946 and 1966. Still, the teacher-alumnus must also distrust his own affection for an undergraduate experience he may well be idealizing. The last two lines of Randall Jarrell's "In Those Days" put the case with proper ambiguousness—"And yet after so long, one thinks/ In those days everything was better." "One thinks" that everything was better back then, when in fact things were, perhaps not worse, but certainly different. And to a nostalgic eye like my own, the very fact of difference, of something that was once and is now retrievable only in memory and imagination, imperceptibly elides itself from "different" into "better."

An unskeptical eye may also view the profession of English studies in rather more glamorous colors than are appropriate to the case. A useful critic of such glamorizing, Richard Poirier, has written of what he calls the "illusions" under which many academics labor—

> the illusion, first, of the necessity, and second of the enormous importance of literary studies. These illusions, shared in some degree by anyone occupationally involved, are difficult but necessary to resist. They intrude themselves because the study is confused with the subject, and teaching confused with the thing taught, the teacher, very often, with the author, whom he is "making available" to the young and to himself. It's a heady experience, after all, to have a direct line to Shakespeare, especially when it's assumed there's only one.

The warning is worth heeding, and yet—as Poirier himself admits—anyone who teaches English has to share such illusions "in some degree." Who knows when a line of poetry, read aloud in the classroom or to oneself in one's dormitory room, may come home to roost? More than once I've received testimony from a student about how—fifteen, twenty years after the fact—something Yeats wrote in a poem (a poem read sophomore year at Amherst) suddenly made sense. There is a poignant moment in Saul Bellow's *Seize the Day* when its hapless protagonist, Tommy Wilhelm, on the edge of failure and disaster, recalls involuntarily some words from a Shakespeare sonnet—"love that well which thou must leave ere long." Wilhelm begins to think about his college days and "the one course that now made sense"—"Literature I":

> The textbook was Lieder and Lovett's *British Poetry and Prose,* a black heavy book with thin pages. Did I read that? he asked himself. Yes, he had read it and there was one accomplishment at least he could recall with pleasure. He had read "Yet once more O ye laurels." How pure this was to say! It was beautiful.
> Sunk though he be beneath the wat'ry floor . . .

For all his clunkishness, Wilhelm has got it right, and the rightness involves his listening to a voice—Shakespeare's or Milton's or his own buried one—that suddenly surfaces with something momentous. Here, it seems to me, "the enormous importance of literary studies" (Poirier's words) becomes not illusory, but real and inescapable.

"Teaching what we do"—my "doing" in this essay may well sound too simple and schematic in its dwelling rather exclusively on matters of voice and listening as my focus in the classroom and in the papers I ask students to write. I might have gone on at some length about the mutually enhancing relationship I feel between the teaching I do in class and the writing I do outside of it. Or, if it were not an impossibly self-regarding occupation, I could have written about my teaching style as a humorous one. "If it isn't any fun, don't do it," D. H. Lawrence once advised; as I grow older I grow less interested in classes where there's no laughter. "Humor is the most engaging form of cowardice," was Frost's inventive definition, and it's clear to me that, with the exception of one or two transcendent geniuses like Milton or Wordsworth, few poets and novelists live without engaging us in humorous ways (in fact the poetic behavior of both Milton and Wordsworth can be the occasion for a good deal of fun in the classroom). So the teacher—and the student as well—needs to speak back to the work in a comparably fresh and enlivening manner. The most awkward moment in any class term is that first meeting, in which any pronouncement, no matter how outrageous, is likely to be met with total, if not totally respectful, silence. To make that silence come to life is part of the fun and point of any academic term. One of my best recent students wrote me a note at the end of a semester, saying that her sister was planning to take a course of mine in the fall, and that she had advised her sister to read the books carefully, write honestly on the papers, and listen hard for my jokes. If it's true that "the ear really does it," then her final bit of advice was a particularly good one.

ACHIEVING PLACE: TEACHING SOCIAL STRATIFICATION TO TOMORROW'S ELITE

Jan E. Dizard
Professor of Sociology

LIKE MANY UNDERGRADUATES in the late 1950s and early '60s, I was drawn to sociology because it, more than any other discipline, offered ways of talking about societies in flux. Even though sociology was then dominated by scholars who were intent on analyzing the manifold ways societies maintain stability and continuity from one generation to the next, their concern for order could not obscure the rich and voluminous literature on the sources of conflict, disruption, and pressures for change that I encountered in assigned readings. It was these centrifugal tendencies, the ways societies come unhinged, that intrigued me then and intrigue me today.

Part of this fascination grew out of a desire to spur change. I entered college confident that reason carefully applied to problems could improve society, perhaps even perfect it. I was intending a career in science, but when physical chemistry made me into a precipitate I gravitated to sociology, carrying along the conviction that science, including social science, would in time unlock all the mysteries of the universe. Irrationality and unpredictability were anathema and I wanted to find out where they came from and how they might be eliminated. The systematic study of social organization promised just such an opportunity.

Two distinct forces propelled me. The most obvious and general of these was the fact that our brief moment of national celebration was rapidly drawing to a close as I entered college in the fall of 1958. Blacks in the South were stirring, and by the end of my sophomore year a handful of young black students sitting in at a Woolworth lunch counter had electrified northern campuses. While civil rights opened up debate on domestic affairs, the discovery of strontium 90 in milk supplies, the result of weapons testing, brought the Cold War to our dining tables and gave rise to a peace movement that would grow by leaps and bounds over the next ten years. Though I had no way of knowing all that these stirrings portended, change and experimentation were in the air.

Change also, as it happened, was in my blood. I was the child of left-wing activists. Obviously, this contributed to my fascination with the idea of change, particularly change that moves society in the direction of greater equality. But I also learned a deep respect for the power of theory. My parents were quite young when the traditional left reached the height of its reputability and influence. Later, however, during my childhood years, my parents were on the defensive. Throughout my youth, the fear of job loss or jail terms hung over the household. No matter; my parents and their friends had explanations for what was happening. Though powerless to alter the direction of things, they could appear to be in charge of their own fate because they had a compelling account of what was going on.

I grew up immersed in conversation about the forces behind events, the ways economic interests governed action, and the ways consciousness was shaped by social class. When I encountered sociological versions of these left-wing themes, it was like rediscovering an old friend. The sociology I was reading brought freshness and vitality to arguments that were otherwise destined to go stale. Social structure, including but not limited to class inequalities, struck me as an immensely powerful idea. Locate people structurally and it is then relatively easy to explain their behavior. Sociology held out the prospect not only of decoding the world, but—to paraphrase Marx—of providing some of the tools needed to change it.

Would that it were so simple.

I.   Structure, Consciousness, and Choice

IN MY EARLY DETERMINIST ZEAL, I was prepared to see spontaneity and unpredictability as signs of theoretical inadequacy. The more we learned, the less we would be surprised. My studies soon disabused me of this naive, mechanical view. But ultimately the turning point was more spiritual than scholarly. B. F. Skinner and Carl Rogers came to campus to debate. I went to the debate a partisan of Skinner's views: human behavior is determined; all that's left to us is to figure out the determinants and then devise ways of manipulating them to achieve the desired behavioral results. I left shaken to my roots. Rogers had devastated Skinner's (and my) determinism, showing it to be not only dangerous but foolish. Contingency, accident, the unexpected—these, Rogers argued, are irreducible features of psychic and social life. (The elemental truth of his claim is now compressed in the popular bumper sticker: SHIT HAPPENS.)

Were it not for the timing of this upheaval in my own thinking, I might have abandoned the effort and sought another vocation. But academic sociology at this moment was entering a period of similar ferment. Critics like C. Wright Mills were sharply questioning the scientific pretensions of sociology, especially the lopsided emphasis on structural factors as determinants of behavior. Moreover, the stirrings of the new left were creating opportunities for fresh readings of social theory, Marx included. The crude determinism of both official Marxism and the conventional sociology of that day was in retreat. Emerging in its place was a style of sociology far more attentive to the ways that structural determinants weakened or even deflected individuals' interpretations of, and responses to, social pressures.

Not that social structure is meaningless, a paper tiger. It is just that the effects of social structure are not experienced or understood by everyone in the same ways. The fact that workers share a common fate does not mean that they all attach the same meaning to that fate, or even that they recognize their commonalities. Moreover, though social structure compels behavior consistent with itself, behavior can run ahead of structural "permission"—if only because humans can extrapolate, predict, anticipate, and wish. Put another way, societies never quite get the kinds of people they prefer. Despite all the forces impinging on the individual, despite all the inducements to conform to social norms and expectations, individuals are refractory—not everyone all of the time, but enough of us to rob structure of its certainties. History, then, is the outcome of complex interactions between the unexpected and the more predictable influences of social structure.

In this light, social structure is not something that is "out there," independent of the human beings who happen to be alive at that moment. It is not like gravity, which will work its way whether we like it or not or are even aware of its power. More nearly, social structure is a creature of our imagination: it is the totality of culturally loaded and intrinsically subjective judgments which, taken together, form the patterns of constraint we collectively impose upon ourselves. But since they are self-imposed, we are able to change these constraints or even refuse to abide by them.

When the refusal is entirely personal, we think of deviance. When the refusal is broad-based, we encounter social movements ranging in scope from protests to revolutions. Social structure, then, is the product of constant, largely implicit negotiation. Norms are continually being tested; people jockey for position, and choices are repeatedly made about what behavior to sanction and what actions to tolerate or encourage. The power of the group over the individual is great, even daunting; but it is not all-encompassing.

Attempts to cast social structure as a purely independent variable, as if it had an existence independent of the participants, largely emulate the natural sciences. But it is one thing when scientists explain the behavior of genes or atoms by ascribing to them certain properties that are said to account for their behavior. Genes and atoms are presumed to have no say in the matter: they have no intentionality; they are exactly as they appear.[1] It is quite another thing to account for human behavior. We do

---

[1] This view, too, is subject to sharp critique. Atoms are exactly as we choose to define them. Even now, despite electron microscopes and other powerful devices, we have to infer their structure. It may well be the case that atoms have many characteristics of which we remain unaware—either because we haven't the theory that posits those characteristics or because our instruments, theory-driven as they are, don't allow us to see all that is conceivably there. This way of looking at science dissolves entirely the notion of an objective reality—what's "out there" is what we choose to acknowledge and name. Scientific facts are, in this view, cultural contrivances that permit us to shape the elements of our natural setting into purposes that suit our needs and self-understandings. See Bruno Latour and Steve Woolgar, *Laboratory Life: The Construction of Scientific Facts,* Princeton: Princeton University Press, (1986).

have intentionality and motive: we are rarely what we appear to be. To be sure, forces located in our subconscious, or in the decisions of others remote from us, may drive us this way or that. But it is ultimately what we make of these imperatives, not simply the imperatives themselves, that analysts need to take into account.

For example, the coming of the Great Depression created an array of urgent structural imperatives—the need for reforms in the banking industry, the need for workers to defend their livelihoods, and the need for state-funded welfare programs, to name only a few obvious initiatives. Indeed, the depression provoked these changes, but by no means automatically. There were no foregone conclusions, precisely because there was no single monolithic reality to which people were responding. To make matters more complex, a number of European societies had enacted such reforms, and more besides, without the spur of the depression. One might reasonably deduce from this that "structural imperatives" are not very imperative, however much they may be structural.[2]

We can say at most that social structure shapes the broad parameters within which individuals act. If, for example, no structural forces propel workers and employers along a collision course, the history of industrializing societies would be far different from what it is. If we add that, within these broad parameters, social action depends upon the myriad ways that individuals experience structure and interpret that experience, then we have built in the necessary indeterminacy that respect for the historical record demands.

---

[2] This particular debate over the origins of the welfare state, whether it flows from the need to rationalize capitalism or from the autonomous desires of state authorities to maintain the polity, is more than simply an arid debate among scholars whose discipline does not yet provide a commonly agreed-upon set of principles. With the conservative assault on welfarist assumptions that has characterized our current period, the argument takes on much larger implications. For a sampling of the debate, see the exchange between Jill Quadagno and Theda Skocpol. Jill Quadagno, "Welfare Capitalism and the Social Security Act of 1935," *American Sociological Review,* 49 (Oct., 1984), pp. 632–647; Theda Skocpol and Edwin Amenta, "Did Capitalists Shape Social Security?" *American Sociological Review,* 50 (Aug., 1985), pp. 572–575; and Quadagno's rejoinder, "Two Models of Welfare State Development: Reply to Skocpol and Amenta," following the Skocpol/Amenta essay, pp. 575–578. Fred Block's collection of essays, *Revising State Theory,* Philadelphia: Temple University Press, (1987), provides a comprehensive overview of the contending theories. Though he offers no formulation that will likely settle the matter, his approach is fresh and sensible.

In the final analysis, structure is only what we deduce from observing the countless interactions that take place among the individuals who comprise a society. Structure is continually being constructed, remodeled, and—to follow the metaphor—occasionally demolished by the actions we take. If structure really does set parameters for action, it is equally and reciprocally the case that action defines structure. Only by studying the action itself, as well as the symbolic understandings that individuals give to their action, can we hope to account for why people behave as they do.[3]

Under the pressures of graduate school, broad reflections such as these are relegated to late-night discussions among graduate students. During the day, in courses and at research institutes, more narrow concerns dominate. The trick is to keep one's own agenda alive while concentrating on the immediate tasks at hand. In the broadest sense, I was becoming an expert in what is now known as the problem of social reproduction—how societies reproduce themselves—and the circumstances in which social reproduction falters. I pursued this in two overlapping areas of research: the unique difficulties of reproducing hierarchy in democratic cultures, with particular reference to racial and ethnic hierarchy; and the changing role of the family in the process of cultural transmission.

While my research necessarily remained narrowly focussed, my teaching allowed me more freedom to convey the excitement I felt in trying to describe how determinist forces interact with contingency to produce a social order that is orderly and predictable, yet capable of stunning change. Nowhere is the tension between order and change clearer than it is in the area of social stratification. Even in the most stable societies, inequalities give rise to all sorts of jockeying for position; and those who are frustrated in their bids for mobility are a ripe audience for those who would attack the existing order. For this reason, if no other, societies devote considerable resources, material and ideological, to buttressing the

---

[3] This argument has been made from a variety of epistemological positions, ranging from phenomenological and hermeneutical traditions flowing from the work of Husserl and Schutz as well as from behaviorist influences of academic psychology. Examples of the former are Aaron V. Cicourel and Peter Berger. The most prominent exponent of the latter is George C. Homans. For an excellent summary of several of the major figures who regularly contend over these matters, see Richard J. Bernstein's *The Reconstruction of Social and Political Theory,* Philadelphia: The University of Pennsylvania Press, (1978).

status quo. From the beginning, my teaching has focussed on this phenomenon—on the ways in which hierarchy gets renewed from one generation to the next.

II.   Reproducing Hierarchy in the Classroom

IN MY EARLY YEARS of teaching, first at the University of California, Berkeley, and then at Amherst, I did not need to persuade anyone that modern societies were rife with tensions and conflicts over stratification. Elites were in disarray. Students who, just a few years earlier, would have accepted a normal progression into the ranks of the elite instead were suspicious of such progressions and sharply critical of the nation's leaders. Activism, commitment to change, and an insistence that there be some correspondence between what they read for courses and what they were reading in the newspapers—these were deeply felt needs among large numbers of students at Amherst and across the nation. As the status quo came under critical scrutiny, sociology enrollments surged.[4] For someone preoccupied with how societies reproduce or fail to reproduce hierarchy, the timing of a career could not have been better.

Systems of stratification create "winners" and "losers." In the early years of my teaching, the nation's attention was largely focussed on the "losers" —the men and women who had to settle for lousy jobs and reconcile themselves to lives of hardship and deprivation. Students had little difficulty deploring poverty and racism but they were troubled by the resignation, the tacit acceptance, that most studies of the poor and downtrodden reveal.[5] In the face of personal disorganization, passivity,

---

[4] There is a pattern worth noting here. Sociology as a distinctive enterprise emerged amid the chaos of the industrial and democratic revolutions that, together, were making a shambles of venerable features of social life. In much the same way, sociology's fortunes seem to ebb and flow with the swings between stability and change. Under conditions of stability and social calm, sociology enrollments decline. But when taken-for-granted features of social life suddenly appear problematic, interest in sociology rises.

[5] I recall one finding that was particularly disturbing to students. Studies of attitudes toward welfare and welfare recipients have regularly shown that welfare recipients themselves have some of the harshest and most condemnatory attitudes toward those who receive welfare. In effect they say, "My need is legitimate but people on welfare are generally lazy, good-for-nothing cheats."

and self-blame, it is temptingly easy to move from pity to contempt, from decrying victimization to blaming the victim. The challenge is to help students—students whose own experiences are with a world largely eager to encourage and respond to them—understand how people can be ground down and left little choice but become complicitous in their own troubles.

Over the years, no text has been more useful in spurring vigorous discussion about the fate of the underdog and the ways in which the "losers" are led to believe that in fact they deserve to lose, than Richard Sennett's and Jonathan Cobb's *The Hidden Injuries of Class*.[6] Sennett and Cobb show how schools teach working-class children that they are inadequate and how, as they grow up, the expanding array of contacts with the larger society, through employers, professionals, and the police, to name only a few intersections, corroborate their self-doubts. They also show how people are taught to feel that those above them in the social hierarchy are superior precisely because they seem to know things about them that they do not know about themselves.

Working-class children enter school at a disadvantage and the schools, instead of trying to overcome the disadvantage, end up more often than not confirming it. By purporting to measure performances objectively, the schools leave youngsters little recourse but to accept the judgment of those who are culturally charged with knowing these things. Thus, the lower classes are made to feel responsible for their own condition. With no one else to blame, they turn on themselves, in the process behaving in ways that help perpetuate their condition. Losing becomes a self-fulfilling prophecy that buttresses everyone's sense that the system is working fairly, and that the losers appear to have asked for it.

Discussions in class are agitated as students grapple with long-cherished notions of equality, fairness, and personal responsibility. It is troubling to see that the deck is stacked, that parents, schools, and employers are involved in a complex and largely unstated collusion to keep losers

---

[6] New York: Knopf, (1972). This book is still assigned in college courses across the country, but there are now a number of studies that have gone well beyond Sennett and Cobb. For a sampling of this more recent literature, see Paul E. Willis, *Learning to Labor,* Aldershot, England: Gower (1977); Henry A. Giroux, "Theories of Reproduction and Resistance in the New Sociology of Education," *Harvard Educational Review* 53 (August 1983):257–293; and Jay MacLeod, *Ain't No Makin' It: Leveled Aspirations in a Low-Income Neighborhood,* Boulder, Colo.: Westview Press, (1987).

losing. Moreover, it is never long before a student observes that if this is true, then the deck must also be stacked to keep winners winning. Silence commonly greets this observation as its implications sink in.

At this point, I often ask students to characterize the social hierarchy as they understand it and to locate themselves and their families in the hierarchy. Nearly all students describe the hierarchy as either pyramidal or diamond-shaped, and they locate themselves somewhere between the middle and the middle of the top third of the figure. Their sense of the general contours of hierarchy is reasonably accurate, but most students are wide of the mark in locating themselves. Though there is some variation from year to year, roughly a half to two-thirds of Amherst students come from families whose income places them securely at the very top, among the wealthiest five to ten percent of all American families. By contrast, just over ten percent of Amherst's students are drawn from the bottom half of society, ranked by income.[7]

For years, I used their error as an example of how society blunts and distorts perceptions of hierarchy, the better to sustain it. To be sure, there are more innocuous things involved. Many parents do not convey detailed or accurate financial information to their children because they feel it is not information to which children need be privy. More importantly, since our residential patterns tend to produce broadly homogeneous neighborhoods (and thus schools), young people grow up with only the dimmest sense of the range of incomes and life styles that characterize the broader society. But when most people place themselves in an undefined middle, for whatever reasons, the likelihood of a challenge to the extant hierarchy is seriously diminished. Thus, in intended and unintended ways, hierarchy gets insulated from scrutiny and challenge.

The process is a subtle one, more subtle than I had appreciated until a

---

[7] These figures are taken from the annual survey of incoming freshman. A little over fifty percent of members of the Class of 1991 reported that their parents earned $75,000 or more. This places them comfortably among the wealthiest ten percent of all American families. Amherst College is by no means unusual in this regard. The most affluent twenty percent of America's families supply well over half of the enrollment in the nation's select colleges and universities. For a summary of trends in income and wealth distribution for the last decade or so, as well as a provocative assessment of the political implications of the rapid increase in inequality that has occurred since 1980, see Kevin Phillips, *The Politics of Rich and Poor: Wealth and the American Electorate in the Reagan Aftermath,* New York, Random House (1990).

student told the class how she had deduced where her family should be placed. "I thought we were in the middle," she observed, "because we are clearly not poor but whenever something comes up, all my parents talk about is how there isn't enough money."

Suddenly it was clear why so many Americans—not just college students—think of America and themselves as "middle class." For all but an extraordinarily small number of American families, there is never enough money to meet every need, much less a whim or two. Even among the comfortably affluent, those in the $75–$100,000 range, ends are met by reliance on credit and various jugglings among the competing claims on the monthly paycheck. So even affluent youngsters hear conversations about money that are not *formally* different from conversations that might be overheard around the kitchen table in the home of a factory worker making a third or less than a third of an affluent family's income. Obviously, the ends each family is trying to meet are substantively quite different; but that is a separate matter. On the evidence available to them, young people sensibly conclude that they are in the middle. They don't have to be hoodwinked by some conspiratorial elite into affirming the myth of America as a middle-class society.

But we do need to be convinced that both losers and winners have been fairly chosen. If the deck is stacked against losers, how can winners believe they deserve their winnings? It is at this moment, precisely, that we can begin to discuss the full intricacies of the reproduction of hierarchy, and the ways in which crucially sustaining fictions are made to seem real. Here, also, we can begin to sense what happens when sustaining fictions cease being persuasive. It is not only that losers might stop accepting their fate; as importantly, winners might lose confidence in their abilities or lose interest in the competition altogether.[8] If both winners and losers arrive at these doubts more or less simultaneously, the society is headed for crisis and change.

For a time in the late '60s and early '70s it appeared as though that was exactly what would happen. The poor, especially the black poor, were

---

[8] This is a common affliction of many in our society and, when it is severe, comprises one of the classic paths to clinical depression: plummeting self-esteem, sudden, inexplicable fears of inadequacy and incompetence, and, of course, thoughts of suicide. In popular psychology, these feelings have been captured by the catchy phrase, "mid-life crisis."

mobilizing, and their leaders explicitly rejected even the merest hint that poverty was the outcome of a fair contest. And many of society's winners —especially upper-middle-class college students—did not want to continue playing in a rigged game. The upsurge of feminism that began in the late '60s added another dimension to the discrediting of hierarchy. White males were being shown how their achievements and rewards were tainted to the core. The notion that they deserved admission to good schools, and the access to prestigious occupations that good schooling assured them, was hard to sustain in the face of irrefutable evidence that the field had been cleared of significant competition before the contest even began. Self-doubt and disorientation suddenly became common among students who, only a few years earlier, would have gone along confident that their accomplishments were testimony to the essential fairness of things.[9]

No society can long tolerate persistent doubts about the legitimacy of its hierarchy. Even in times of calm, insuring this confidence is no easy task, especially in a liberal society like ours which proclaims equality as a goal but nonetheless is predicated upon institutions that produce a remarkably constant hierarchy.[10] Those at the top, no longer able to reassure

---

[9] Perversely, the same self-doubts may now be afflicting blacks who are entering formerly all-white domains. The continuing controversy over affirmative action and quotas almost certainly keeps some blacks off guard, never sure that they have really earned admission, the grade, or the promotion. This is worse than the psychological burden an earlier generation of "tokens" faced, if only because "tokens" knew why they were where they were and they could reasonably persuade themselves that they could, at whatever toll to themselves, pave the way for future generations of blacks. This may have more than a minor role to play in what some have come to regard as the self-segregation of blacks on campuses across the country. In the face of persistent self-doubts, it is all too clear why black students might want to seek the comfort of their fellows. Ambiguity, like misery, loves company. For a provocative discussion of contemporary black students on largely white campuses, see Shelby Steele, "The Recoloring of Campus Life: Student Racism, Academic Pluralism, and the End of a Dream," *Harper's* (February, 1989):47–55.

[10] The differences between Western European societies and the U.S. in terms of how wealth and income are distributed (before taxes), and how much movement there is up or down in the occupational hierarchy from one generation to the next, are negligible. For all the self-congratulatory talk about the encrusted class relations of Europe and the free flow of opportunity-seekers in the New World, the fact is that the differences are nil. See Frank Parkin, *Class Inequality &*

156   TEACHING WHAT WE DO

themselves of divine appointment, have to base their standing on claims of having earned it. This, arguably, is the reason we celebrate entrepreneurial risk, and fret about the high stress to which we subject our executives and professionals; it may also be a reaction to the long history of middle-class depictions of the hoi polloi as a carefree, sexually active, irresponsible lot.

In order to make our elites comfortable with their status and power, in other words, we have to construct a culture of work and sacrifice surrounding them as they wend their way to the top. Much of the stressful work associated with colleges like Amherst has less to do with learning (and may in fact get in the way of learning) than it has to do with maintaining the cultural expectations of sacrifice and of being tested.[11] Only if one has been subjected to repeated stress and apparent uncertainty of outcome can one confidently assume a leadership role. This may help explain why Amherst alumni extol the famous "old curriculum"—whatever they learned from it substantively, survivors learned that they could meet challenges, juggle an impossibly large and conflicting set of demands, and—despite inner turmoil—keep up a good front.[12]

Political Order: Social Stratification in Capitalist and Communist Societies, New York: Praeger, (1971).

[11] This line of analysis, applied to prep schools, is explored in Peter W. Cookson, Jr. and Caroline Hodges Persell, *Preparing for Power: America's Elite Boarding Schools,* New York: Basic Books, (1985).

[12] The strained relationship between the intense demands and learning set up at places like Amherst was delicately and movingly discussed in a recent letter to the alumni magazine, *Amherst* (Winter, 1987):38–40. Dr. Rice Leach, '62, a U.S. Public Health Service physician who has dedicated his life to work with American Indians, wrote to share with fellow alumni the response that greeted his remarks at his 25th reunion, at which he received an honorary degree. When asked by his classmates to say a few words, he spoke about how awkward and out of place he had felt during his college years because he did not do well at Amherst in the conventional sense of getting good grades. He expected to be thought again the fool and was surprised to learn that many others shared his feelings. He writes of his recollections of the conversations he had after his brief speech:

". . . As the evening progressed I learned that I had really said something meaningful to many of my classmates and their wives. At least a dozen and maybe more commented to me on how relieved they were that someone had acknowledged the frustration that comes from twenty-five years of feeling that they had not done as well as they should have while in college."

And yet, Leach, and presumably his classmates, at least those who return for

For all but the most brilliant or compulsive, doing all the reading and exercises assigned by a student's four instructors is virtually impossible. Faculty members, of course, do not lay on the work in order to help produce elites with clear consciences. Faculty do not think of themselves in those terms. We make demanding assignments to demonstrate to students how seriously we regard our work and to get students to take ideas —and themselves—seriously. But despite what we faculty think we are doing, the workload also prepares students to assume authority over others with confidence born of having demonstrated the qualities of mind and self-discipline which elites are expected to possess.

On the whole, students have a harder time seeing social reproduction at work among themselves than among poor people. Not only are students inclined to defend the workload, saying they would feel cheated if their days and nights weren't filled with studying; they also value the mastery of substance that is manifested, for them, in their grades. Some also justify this "hazing" by arguing that heavy demands made by their courses are good preparation for the intense demands they will face in the world of work. There is clear pride in being able to bear the weight, and reluctance to see the stress as merely a rite of passage that elites in egalitarian liberal society must endure.

Students are also visibly uncomfortable with an important implication of this analysis: in order to blunt the fact that outcomes are largely foregone conclusions, we have to create many occasions when future leaders are evaluated and measured. In this way, merit can be confirmed and subsequent placement in social hierarchies of work and community life can take on the appearance of having been determined objectively. It's not who your parents are, or who you know, but what you've learned. As in the Sennett and Cobb model, the grading is done by people who are culturally assigned the insight into inner qualities of mind and character that are otherwise opaque. Teachers are presumed to know not only arcane bodies of knowledge but also to be able to detect motivation, sincerity, and seriousness of purpose. Every test or assignment, then, exposes students to the risk of displaying some terrible flaw in their character.

Return, for a moment, to the workload. In the face of hundreds of

reunions, nonetheless thank Amherst for helping inspire them to do their best in whatever it is they devote themselves to. Regardless of grades, in other words, Amherst is preparing its graduates for leadership.

pages of reading, lab assignments, and papers to be written, the rational thing to do is to begin early and work regularly on each course. Students should allot time every day to the reading, start the research for term papers promptly, and write outlines and rough drafts of assignments well enough ahead of their due date to permit consultation, reflection and revision. As I describe these rational strategies to my students, looks of disbelief appear and ripples of laughter spread across the room. Virtually no one works that way. Most students write their papers the night before they are due. "Pulling all-nighters," as it's called, is a mark of fortitude, not a badge of irresolution or poor planning. Why?

The risk of getting a poor grade, of having an unwelcome truth revealed, is unbearably high, especially with so much appearing to ride on grades. By doing work at the last minute, students create a no-lose psychological condition. If the grade is low, they can point to the extenuating circumstances that prevented them from putting their best foot forward. If the grade is high, it means that their innate intelligence, their raw genius, has shown through. Doing work at the last minute is virtually the only way that students can redefine the situation in which they find themselves so that the most threatening implications of their predicament are neutralized.

At first, most students have a hard time accepting this analysis. It seems to diminish their accomplishments. For young men and women eager to be told yet again that they are destined to be important, to be at the center of things, it is deflating to realize the extent to which their actions have been significantly shaped by social structure.

More than deflation is involved, fortunately. I say "fortunately" because if all that this sort of discussion accomplished was take the wind out of bright young people's sails, discussion would be Hobbesian: nasty, brutish, and short. Though the general outcomes of the process of status placement are heavily influenced by structural determinants, the process itself is filled with uncertainties that make the outcomes seem problematic. Students experience uncertainty, not foregone conclusion. Their experience is with competition for scarce rewards—top grades, high test scores, glowing recommendations—not with easy, unproblematic movement from one achievement to another. It is a process in which success appears to depend upon having survived a continuing series of invidious distinctions based on criteria over which one has little control. As a result, even though the outcome can be structurally described as all but a sure thing, students experience status placement as a process that is marked by uncertainty, risk, and precariousness.[13]

As we work through the process, in both its abstract, structural and immediate, experiential dimensions, students come to realize that the experience of rigorous competition and the precarious claim to success is not false, however contrived and ritualized it might be. The fact that a course of action is heavily predetermined or is put to a use that one is unaware of does not rob that action of the meaning and purpose one attaches to it. To say, for example, that the maternal instinct is neither an instinct nor exclusively maternal but is, instead, a culturally encoded set of responses, does not empty mothering of its meaning for either the mother or the infant. That most Amherst graduates will end up pretty much where they began—in the upper middle class or above—is not to say they would have done so had they not studied hard. It is to say that studying hard means several things. Abstractly, it may be "merely" a rite of passage—it doesn't matter what one studies so long as one gets by and, in the process, comes to believe that one has what it takes to become someone others will look up to and be willing to follow.[14] But for the individuals involved, studying hard represents a choice, a decision to behave in ways that elders respect and reward.

By the same token, the poor behave in ways that make it likely that they will stay poor. But their behavior does not *cause* poverty, any more than studying hard and getting into a good school cause wealth. Poverty,

---

[13] This sense of uncertainty is also sustained by the admissions process. The fact that most students who get into selective colleges like Amherst come from affluent families does not mean that most sons and daughters of the affluent gain admission to such places. Affluence helps but is no guarantee. The same applies for admission to graduate and professional schools—an Amherst degree and family affluence help, but they cannot assure entry. Unlike an aristocracy, our upper classes cannot rest on their laurels: each generation must prove itself.

[14] So far as I know, there are very few instances in which the loose connection between formal preparation and subsequent placement in a hierarchy is explicitly acknowledged. The military is one of these. The cadet finishing last in class is ritually honored by his/her fellow cadets. This constitutes both a mocking of the faculty's standards and acknowledgement that the important line is not between ranks of cadets but between cadets and all others. Indeed, research on military careers has shown that academic standing has virtually no bearing on one's military career. Having played football for the academy is a better predictor of advancement to high rank than grades.

like wealth, is a structural feature of the society. Both arise by virtue of broad economic and political practices. We have extremes of poverty and wealth because we distribute economic rewards in a particular way and have done so with little variation for a century or more. Personal attributes —like being a high school drop-out, or an unwed mother—obviously increase an individual's chances of winding up poor; but neither quitting school nor pregnancy cause poverty.

At first, most students find it difficult to separate structural features of a society from the actions of individuals. In our culture we are taught to take responsibility for our actions. Sociological analysis does not dissolve individual responsibility, but it makes the connection between an action and the presumed consequences attached to that action far more complex than we commonly assume. For example, it could be argued that structural patterns and individual action create a setting in which one person's success condemns someone else to failure. Is the successful person, then, responsible not only for his or her success, but also for the other's failure? Or, if crime is generated by social conditions that we are able to alter, had we the will to do so, are criminals solely responsible for their acts? Or do we, the non-criminals, bear some of the responsibility?

Sociology has no answers to such questions. Indeed, the point of asking them is less to spur students to articulate answers than to make clear how fluid most answers are. With only slight shifts in assumptions about the relationship between the individual and the collectivity, very different answers—and thus quite different politics and policies—emerge. Not only do individuals choose to behave in certain ways, they also—perhaps less knowingly—choose to accept the meaning others attach to that behavior. And upon such choices, social order depends.

III.   Conclusion

AMHERST STUDENTS UNDERGO a complex process that readies them to assume positions of importance and responsibility in society. They are being educated—exposed to challenging ideas and inspired by the intellectual, artistic, and political accomplishments of the men and women whose works they are asked to study. They are also being groomed, assured that they deserve to go places in the world. The former has to be arduous to make the latter credible. But there are no guarantees. Order does not reproduce itself automatically. Education can whet appetites for change, just as it can help us understand the myths by which we live. In every act of reproduction there is risk.

The sense of risk is indeed high. Many of the students I encounter are convinced that access to jobs and a comfortable standard of living is becoming more difficult. The sharply rising costs of a liberal arts education increase the stakes even further. Many students know they will leave college with sizeable loans needing to be repaid. This must be at least partially responsible for the shift toward courses and majors that are linked, however loosely, to lucrative careers in law or business. It is harder for young men and women to feel free to pursue knowledge for the pure joy of discovery.

But their responses to the situation are interesting. One might expect students to become more grade-conscious, and find them shying away from courses reputed to be hard, or from subjects in which they do not feel well versed. Yet, in analyses of Amherst students' course selections, one finds plenty of risk-taking. Most students take at least two semesters of a foreign language, a majority take a math course or two, and most take at least one course in a laboratory science. And this occurs without any formal distribution requirement. Moreover, steadily increasing numbers of students elect to major in two disciplines, subjecting themselves to even more requirements and scheduling constraints. Clearly, the pressure to distinguish oneself, the better to be a compelling candidate for this or that plum, has given rise to strategies that demonstrate a willingness to take risks and combine unusual interests and talents.

But more than calculation is involved. For all the stress and anxiety placed on them, students remain lively, willing to try out new ideas and entertain, with healthy skepticism, heterodox opinions. Observers like Allan Bloom[15] are wrong when they claim that contemporary liberal arts education is closing students' minds. There are, obviously, biases of all sorts embedded in our educational system, and inevitably there are fads that arouse passions to a fever pitch before exhausting themselves. We may not be doing as well as we once did at conveying a body of facts— historical, geographical, and cultural—to the young. But there is no com-

---

[15] *The Closing of the American Mind: How Higher Education Has Failed Democracy and Impoverished the Souls of Today's Students,* New York: Simon and Schuster, (1987).

pelling evidence that we have killed curiosity or skepticism. To be sure, students feel the press of competition and the weight of debt, and—as I have noted—this may constrain some students' sense of freedom. But the students that I see are alive to the challenges of learning more deeply about themselves and the world they inhabit. They are open to seeing the connections between their own experiences and the larger structures that shape those experiences.

There is another way in which students perceive risk. However problematic they apprehend that their own futures may be, many sense a rather sharp disjunction between the pieties of our culture and how people actually behave. Growing numbers of our students—students, as we've seen, from "good homes"—contend with parents whose marriages are disintegrating. Whether in the deeply personal realm of intimate relationships, or in the public arena, uncertainty prevails and commitments can turn into betrayals. Hard work and achievement can turn hollow. Our culture is far from cohesive, and standards of both public and private conduct—from brokerage houses to crack parlors—are collapsing. But responsibility for this confusion and decline can scarcely be laid at the doorstep of our nation's colleges and universities.

The tradition that Bloom and others of his persuasion are defending is squarely a class tradition. Their critique of contemporary liberal arts curricula, of the faculties who teach and the students who study, reflects a desire to preserve a particular class culture and to bolster the self-assurance of a particular cultural elite. New disciplines and reconfigurations of older ones are a threat, not to the ancient project of knowing one's self and understanding the world, but to the more transient task of patching up a threadbare culture whose central purpose has steadily shrunk to that of getting and spending. It is that preoccupation that threatens the liberal arts, not the expansion of fields of study and the diversification of texts deemed worthy of serious attention.

The classroom remains an exciting place. The range of permissible questions is expanding, and the chances for fresh insight increase. Students are as willing as ever to explore the ways that societies reproduce themselves, even when that stirs anxieties about inequality, individual responsibility, and equity. If we use education only to bolster privilege, we will all be the poorer. The choice, as in all things social, is ours.

Teaching Philosophy

William E. Kennick
Professor of Philosophy

Diverse voci fanno dolci note.

—Dante

SIR ISAIAH BERLIN relates the following anecdote about himself and J. L. Austin when they were jointly teaching a course in philosophy in the mid-1930s:

> "If there are three vermilion patches on this piece of paper how many vermilions are there?" [Austin asked]. "One," said I. "I say there are three," said Austin, and we spent the rest of the term on this issue.

"Are there three vermilions, or is there only one?" is a beautiful example of a philosophical problem—indeed, an instance of the ancient problem of the One and the Many; and I begin with this seemingly footling and trivial case precisely because it does not at all look like a philosophical problem to most people.

One obstacle to the successful teaching of philosophy is a budget of entrenched misconceptions of the subject. Philosophy is occasionally taught in secondary schools, but it is still the rare student who comes to college with an inkling of what she is getting into if she takes a course in philosophy. She knows something of what it is to study literature or history, mathematics or chemistry; but for her conception of philosophy she is largely dependent on popular connotations of its name. There is, for instance, a vulgar use of the word "philosophy" in such phrases as "her philosophy of banking" or "his philosophy of life" where it signifies some, usually banal, maxim or policy of action. Here, for example, is a condom manufacturer on one of his advertising campaigns:

> The philosophy is that the issue of safe sex has to be relaxed before people are comfortable enough to buy condoms.

This is not what I teach.

This popular use of the word, however, did not come from nowhere. It has a nobler lineage, being an offshoot of a widespread misconception of philosophy that has come down to us from the late Stoics; the same people who brought us the idea, long entrenched in the language too, that to be philosophical is to be imperturbable in the face of any conceivable adversity. Philosophy, said Seneca, "is nothing but the knowledge of right living." A philosopher is a master of this art, a sage, a possessor and purveyor of wisdom. This way of thinking is abetted by that inane argument from etymology—which proves nothing in any case—repeated often enough by teachers of philosophy themselves: " 'Philosophy' means the love of wisdom, therefore . . ." Well, it means nothing of the sort. The Greek word *sophia* is, alas, usually translated into English as "wisdom" and the compound noun *philosophia* as "love of wisdom." But *sophia* had a much broader use than our "wisdom." Homer uses it to refer to the skill of a carpenter, Aristotle to refer to that of a master carver. Wherever intelligence could be used effectively—in the arts and crafts, in business, in practical affairs, in the sciences—there one could sensibly speak of *sophia*. So, *philosophia* is closer in meaning to "love of using one's mind to good effect" than it is to love of "wisdom."

Bad etymology notwithstanding, we seem to be stuck with the misconception of the philosopher as sage, and a first step in arriving at a more realistic notion of what it is I teach is to correct that conception.

Only a fool can have anything against wisdom, but there is no reason to expect it from philosophers as opposed to others. I have found much wisdom in the writings of philosophers (although never in Descartes or Carnap, for example), but when I am in a mood for wisdom I usually find myself turning to the poets and prophets: "Blunt Truths more mischief than nice Falsehoods do"; "The world is too much with us"; "Though I speak with the tongues of men and of angels, and have not charity, I am become as sounding brass, or a tinkling cymbal"; "Nothing, like something, happens everywhere"; "A living dog is better than a dead lion." Philosophers have no monopoly on wisdom, and wisdom, or even the love of it, is neither necessary nor sufficient to being a philosopher.

At this point one may feel in need of a definition of philosophy. As I advise my students, however, when one feels such a need it is generally best to lie down until the feeling passes. Definitions have their uses, but they are useless for telling someone what philosophy is. The only definitions worth paying attention to are those put forward by philosophers. Such definitions, however, are almost invariably tendentious and look as if they were designed to exclude from philosophy everything other than the work of their authors. "Philosophy is a battle against the bewitchment of our intelligence by means of language" (Wittgenstein). It is "the expressly accomplished correspondence which speaks in so far as it considers the appeal of the Being of being" (Heidegger). What is one meant to do with such sentences! Certainly, not hand them out to innocent inquirers who just want to know what philosophy is. As is the case with poetry too, the best way to find out what philosophy is is to read some. Although philosophers will never agree on what philosophy is, librarians seem to have an unerring sense of what it is. I have never heard anyone complain about their getting the philosophy books and journals in the wrong place. They know what goes with what, and they will head you in the right direction.

In reading books of philosophy the student finds different voices saying different things. Philosophy, like heaven, is a house of many mansions. Amid the striking diversity, however, the student should be struck by a characteristic, if not universal, feature of philosophy—one more noticeable in some authors (Thomas Aquinas) than in others (Nietzsche)—a feature in which I, as a teacher of philosophy, take a special interest and which, to my way of thinking, is the one feature that makes philosophy worth studying. To appreciate this feature of central importance, let us return to the difference between the sage and the philosopher.

In his *First Epistle to the Corinthians* the Apostle Paul, certainly one of the greatest of Christian sages however much contempt he may have had for the wisdom of this world, upbraids the members of the church of Corinth for taking one another to court, telling them that it would be better for them to suffer injustice or wrong (*adikeisthai*), *e.g.* to be robbed or assaulted, than to do injustice or wrong (*adikein*) to one another. Wise advice; or at least let us assume so for the sake of argument. Coming upon this passage the reader of Plato may remember having heard a similar message elsewhere. In his dialogue *Gorgias,* Plato depicts the philosopher Socrates and the rhetorician Polus debating the question whether it is worse to do wrong (*adikein*) than to suffer it (*adikeisthai*). Socrates holds that "to do wrong is the greatest of evils." Polus finds this opinion singularly perverse: it is obviously worse to suffer wrong than to do it; worse, for example, to be robbed or assaulted than to rob or assault someone else —assuming that one can get away with doing so. Socrates sets out to show that he is right and that Polus actually agrees with him.

He first gets Polus to concede that, although it may be worse to suffer wrong than to do it, it is more shameful, base, or disgraceful (*aischron*) to do wrong than to suffer it. Clearly, Polus must hold that something's being more base or shameful does not imply that it is worse, otherwise he would have contradicted himself at once. And, in fact, Polus holds that there is no logical connection between, on the one hand, the good (*agathon*) and the fair or beautiful (*kalon*) or, on the other hand, between the bad or evil (*kakon*) and the disgraceful, ugly, or base (*aischron*)—a conviction Socrates also tries to show him he cannot seriously hold.

Polus concedes that to judge something to be fair or beautiful, or the opposite, base or shameful, is to apply a standard or criterion. The criterion of the fair or beautiful is this: something is beautiful or fair just in case it is useful (and therefore good), or pleasurable, or both. Since the opposite of the beautiful or fair is the base, shameful, or ugly, the criterion of it is the opposite of that of the fair: something is base, shameful, or ugly just in case it is evil, or painful, or both. It follows from Polus's two concessions, however, that doing wrong, because it is more shameful than suffering wrong, is worse, or more painful, or both worse and more painful than suffering wrong. But he admits that it is not more painful to do wrong, *e.g.* to rob or assault someone else, than it is to suffer it, *e.g.* to be robbed or assaulted by someone else. Therefore, it cannot be worse *and* more painful to do wrong than to suffer it. It must, then, be simply *worse* to do wrong than to suffer it—precisely the opposite of what Polus initially maintained and identical with what Socrates maintained!

Here we have an interesting phenomenon. Both the Apostle Paul and Socrates seem to be saying much the same thing, that it is better to suffer a wrong than to do one. There is nothing peculiarly philosophical about this view. What is it, then, that makes Socrates's claim philosophically interesting, where Paul's claim, however important (and it may well have been of greater immediate importance than Socrates's), is just a piece of wise advice? It is that Socrates's view appears as the outcome or conclusion of an argument or line of reasoning. Examples are easily multiplied, but let one more suffice. "He who lives under the guidance of reason strives, as far as he can, to repay another's hatred, anger, and contempt with love and generosity." Again, a wise saying. But it is not just that. It is Proposition 46 of Part Four of Spinoza's *Ethics* and is accompanied by a six-step "demonstration." Without the demonstration it would be no less wise, but it would be devoid of philosophical interest.

This gives us a key to the nature of at least one large class of philosophical questions. They are questions answers to which can be supported by reasoning or argument alone. Take the question with which we began: if there are three vermilion patches on a piece of paper, how many vermilions are there? No facts of physics or physiology will answer this question. Nor are any so much as relevant, as far as I can see. What, then, does a philosophical argument for an answer to the question look like? Berlin tells us that he and Austin spent the balance of an academic term arguing the matter (and the suggestion is that the question arose early in the term), but he does not tell us what arguments were advanced. We know of arguments, however, that have been advanced. Here is a crude sketch of three of them.

Aristotle would argue that both Berlin and Austin are right, albeit in different ways. Just as there are—and must be, if a species, unlike the species dinosaur, is to be an existing one—particular members of species in the category of things, for example, particular members of the species dog (*e.g.* Argos and Bounce), so there are, and must be if the species is to be an existing one, particular members of species in categories other than that of things. Vermilion is a species of color, therefore a species in the category of qualities. *Ex hypothesi* it is an existing species of color, unlike, say, some discontinued shade of lipstick every trace of which has vanished.

Therefore, although there is but *one species* of color, *viz.* vermilion (thereby making Berlin right), there are *three members* of that species, *viz.* the color inherent in this patch, the color inherent in that patch, and the color inherent in the remaining patch, any one of which could disappear, *e.g.* fade, leaving the other two extant (thereby making Austin right).

But the reality of universals, here species and genera, has been unacceptable to other philosophers who would reject Aristotle's answer on nominalistic grounds. Hobbes, for example, holds that there is "nothing in the world Universal but Names; for the things named, are every one of them Individual and singular," and Berkeley and Hume agree. This being the case, since there are three vermilion patches, there are three vermilions, all called by one name, "vermilion," in virtue of their similitude or resemblance to one another. (So, Austin was right.)

A young contemporary philosopher, R. Fahrnkopf, will have none of this. He takes the idea that "colors are individuated in virtue of the things that they color" to be "arbitrary and counter-intuitive." Think of a uniformly dyed piece of cloth that has been cut in two.

> Whereas the original piece of cloth was of one color, the two cut pieces are—on nominalist principles—no longer of one color, but are rather of two resembling colors. Were these pieces of cloth divided in turn, there would result four resembling colors, and so on. Finally, were all these pieces sewn back together, we would again have one uniformly colored cloth.

Since the nominalist's position has this ridiculous consequence, it is unacceptable. Colors, *e.g.* vermilions, ought not to be multiplied beyond necessity. There is one vermilion only. (So, Berlin was right.)

At this point it is not unnatural for the student to ask, "Well who *is* right? How many vermilions *are* there?" (To which my maddening answer is, "You know as well as Aristotle, or Hobbes, or Fahrnkopf, or I do. So, how many *are* there?") The student, however, has unwittingly put his finger on a fascinating feature of philosophical problems, one that has often puzzled philosophers and non-philosophers alike and that Sidney Hook has called "the scandal of philosophical disagreement": despite the lifelong efforts of persons of intellectual genius, no problem of philosophy seems to have been *solved*. Answered, yes—when it comes to answers, philosophy suffers from an embarrassment of riches; but solved, no.

In his *Discourse on the Method* of 1637 Descartes complained that although philosophy "has been cultivated by the most excellent minds that have appeared in this world in many centuries past, nevertheless every one of its propositions is still subject to dispute." Like others before him, he set out to remedy this situation, with a result that is well known. He is often referred to as "the father of modern philosophy," not because he achieved his aim of finally solving its problems with the certainty and finality with which he solved some problems in mathematics, nor even because he provided us with a method for their solution, but because like others before him, notably Plato and Aristotle, he sired new problems, especially those of modern epistemology, thereby increasing the population he sought to reduce.

Friedrich Waismann has noted that

> in philosophy there are no proofs; there are no theorems; and there are no questions which can be decided, Yes or No. In saying that there are no proofs I do not mean to say that there are no arguments. Arguments certainly there are, and first-rate philosophers are recognized by the originality of their arguments; only these do not work in the sort of way they do in mathematics and in the sciences.

This fact, which I think is incontestable, has proved to be a stumbling block to the further pursuit of philosophy on the part of many bright students—although it has also proved to be an incentive to others. The idea that in answering a philosophical question there is a sense in which one does not add to the store of human knowledge has suggested to many that philosophical inquiry is futile. Sir Isaiah Berlin, who in the 1930s was embarked on a very promising career in philosophy, reports having had a conversation in the mid-1940s with the logician H. M. Sheffer that "made a profound impression" upon him.

> In the months that followed, I asked myself whether I wished to devote the rest of my life to a study, however fascinating and important in itself, which, transforming as its achievements undoubtedly were, would not, any more than criticism or poetry, add to the store of positive human knowledge. I gradually came to the conclusion that I would prefer a field in which one could hope to know more at the end of one's

life than when one had begun; and so I left philosophy for the field of
the history of ideas, which had for many years been of absorbing interest
to me.

The suggestion that a poet or critic cannot hope to know more at the end
of his life than when he began to write strikes me as rather quaint, but
one sees what Sir Isaiah is driving at. "To write down lists of propositions
'proved' by Plato or Kant," or, he might have added, by any other philosopher, is, says Waismann again, "a pastime strongly to be recommended";
confident, as I too would be, that our papers will remain blank. It would
be easy, of course, to make a list of philosophical propositions with which
one *agrees,* but that is another matter entirely. At different times and in
different circles it has also been *fashionable* to espouse certain philosophical
views and to think of them as having somehow (but how?) been defini-
tively established. It is a plain fact, however, that no philosophical problem has been solved in the way that at least some problems in
mathematics, in logic, or in the sciences have been solved, namely, to the
satisfaction of all competent inquirers. The history of philosophy, indeed,
gives us ample reason to wonder whether we so much as understand what
it would be to solve a philosophical problem.[1]

The same point can be made by a brief consideration of doubts. Doubts
about matters of contingent fact, be they of the humble quotidian variety,
like the doubt about whether one left the engine of the car running, or of
the more recondite scientific variety, like the doubt about whether Alz-
heimer's Disease is hereditary, can ordinarily be settled by established or
devisable procedures of observation or experiment; which is not to say
that all such doubts are in practice resolvable. In some cases—Is he really
in love? Is it really a stroke?—some observable facts point to one conclusion while others point to a contrary one, but even in these cases we know
what it would be like to resolve the doubt, and we can continue to look
for fresh evidence that will settle it.

---

[1] One might reply to this, as some have, that unless there is a solution, or
unless we know at least what it would be to solve a problem, we have no problem
to solve, merely a pseudo-problem. But, first, although many have tried, no one
has yet shown that the problems of philosophy are pseudo-problems. All such
attempts have merely added to the store of philosophical problems. Second,
whether there can be solutionless problems—in the sense of "solution" that I have
been using—is itself on all fours with other problems of philosophy.

An analogous situation obtains in the area of such "formal" sciences as mathematics. In his *Brief Lives* John Aubrey relates the following amusing story about Thomas Hobbes:

> He was forty years old before he looked on Geometry; which happened accidentally. Being in a Gentleman's library, Euclid's *Elements* lay open, and 'twas the 47 *El. libri I* [In any right-angled triangle, the square which is described on the side subtending the right angle is equal to the squares described on the sides which contain the right angle]. *By G—,* sayd he (he would now and then sweare an emphaticall Oath by way of emphasis) *this is impossible!* So he reads the Demonstration of it, which referred him back to such a Proposition; which proposition he read. That referred him back to another. *Et sic deinceps* that at last he was demonstratively convinced of that trueth.

Should any other reasonable person have Hobbes's doubt, or any doubt sufficiently like it, her doubt could, at least in principle, always be resolved in a similar way, *viz.* by producing a demonstration.

Philosophical doubts are not like that. What demonstration will resolve the doubt whether some Evil Power is constantly deceiving me—or one of its modern equivalents, whether I am really nothing but a brain in a vat being fed stimuli of some experimenter's whimsical choosing; whether mental events are identical with brain processes; whether the rightness of an act is a function of the amount of pleasure it produces; whether existence is ever a property; and so on? Had it been Spinoza's *Ethics* that lay open to Pt. IV, Prop. 46, and had Hobbes read the "demonstration" of it, does anyone seriously suppose that Hobbes would have been unreasonable had he continued to doubt that a reasonable person necessarily strives, as far as possible, to repay another's hatred, anger, and contempt with love and generosity?

Although philosophers constantly claim the discovery of mistakes, fallacies, howlers, errors, and so on, in the arguments of other philosophers (after all, that is part of the game), there is something odd about many such purported discoveries. No one wishes to say that philosophers never make genuine mistakes in reasoning. Hobbes was notoriously bad with modal arguments. To prove that every occurrence, "how *contingent* soever it seem, or how *voluntary* soever it be, is produced *necessarily*," he offers the following argument:

> Let the case be put, for example, of the weather. *It is necessary that tomorrow it shall rain or not rain.* If therefore it be not *necessary* it shall rain, it is *necessary* it shall not rain, otherwise there is no necessity that the proposition, *it shall rain or not rain,* be true.

He knows that this will not wash with some of his readers, but he thinks he has an answer for them:

> I know there be some that say, it may necessarily be true that one of the two shall come to pass, but not, singly that it shall rain, or that it shall not rain, which is as much to say, *one* of them is *necessary,* yet neither of them *necessary* . . .

Alas, it is not as much as to say anything of the sort. It is rather to say that it is necessary that one of them shall be true, but neither of them is necessary. Hobbes confuses (1) "Necessarily: either it will rain or it will not rain" with (2) "Either it is necessary that it will rain or it is necessary that it will not rain." He is entitled by the Law of Excluded Middle to (1) but not to (2); yet only with (2) will the argument work.

This sort of egregious logical error, however, is not the sort of error one philosopher usually finds in another's reasoning. Philosophers rarely accuse one another of committing the familiar formal and material fallacies of the textbooks, but fallacies for which special names are needed: Whitehead's "fallacy of misplaced concreteness," Collingwood's "fallacy of precarious margins," G. E. Moore's "naturalistic fallacy" and John Searle's "naturalistic fallacy fallacy," Ryle's "category mistakes," Austin's "descriptivist fallacy," and so on. These fallacies appear to be peculiar to philosophy and to be such that every purported instance of them is disputable. Does one who says that "I know that . . ." is a descriptive phrase really commit a fallacy, namely, the descriptivist fallacy? Austin says he does; others, including some who have read Austin, say he doesn't; and still others may be of two minds on the matter. And does one who, like Descartes, says "There are minds and there are bodies" make a mistake, namely a category mistake of the same order as the person who says "I saw the three battalions and the regiment march past" (as though the regiment were something in addition to the battalions of which it is composed)? Is Cartesian dualism nothing but a bad joke?

Closely related to this feature of philosophical differences is another, which Hilary Putnam has put this way: "Things once refuted don't stay refuted forever." Put another way, philosophy is constantly threatened by the return of the repressed. Philosophical views thought to have been discredited get rehabilitated. In *An Examination of Sir William Hamilton's Philosophy* John Stuart Mill wrote the obituary of metaphysical realism, the view, in his words, that "General Names are the names of General Things," or that in addition to individual things there are universals. This doctrine, he says, "is now universally abandoned"; "it could not . . . permanently resist philosophical criticism, and it perished"; "it is no longer extant, nor likely to be revived." Like similar announcements in the history of philosophy—demonstrations of the impossibility of metaphysics come to mind—Mill's obituary was premature. The doctrine was not dead, or, if dead, was resurrected by, among others, Mill's godson (if an infidel can have a godson), Bertrand Russell.

A final noteworthy feature of philosophical disagreements is that in many, if not all, cases, everything is already known that seems to be relevant and necessary to the settlement of them. In this, as Kant suggests in his preface to the Transcendental Deduction of the Categories in his *Critique of Pure Reason,* they appear to be more like lawyers' arguments over points of law, over questions *quid juris,* where both sides agree on the facts of the case. As Wittgenstein remarked about philosophical puzzlement over the nature of time, "it is not new facts about time which we want to know. All the facts that concern us lie open before us." Rival philosophers have the same facts—empirical, mathematical, and verbal—at their disposal. Yet they reach, by argument, what appear to be logically incompatible conclusions: "There are three vermilions." "No, there is only one."

In a famous passage of *Pragmatism* William James tells of returning from a walk in the mountains to find a party of his friends "engaged in a ferocious metaphysical dispute."

> The *corpus* of the dispute was a squirrel—a live squirrel supposed to be clinging to one side of a tree trunk, while over against the tree's opposite side a human being was imagined to stand. This human witness tries to get sight of the squirrel by moving rapidly round the tree, but no matter how fast he goes, the squirrel moves as fast in the opposite direction, and always keeps the tree between himself and the man, so that never a glimpse of him is caught. The resultant metaphysical problem now is

this: *Does the man go round the squirrel or not?* He goes round the tree, sure enough, and the squirrel is on the tree; but does he go round the squirrel?

James's "solution" to this problem is well known:

> "Which party is right," I said, "depends on what you *practically mean* by 'going round' the squirrel. If you mean passing from the north of him to the east, then to the south, then to the west, and then to the north of him again, obviously the man does go round him. But if on the contrary you mean being first in front of him, then on the right of him, then behind him, then on his left, and finally in front again, it is quite obvious that the man fails to go round him . . . Make the distinction, and there is no occasion for any further dispute. . . ."

But did James, by making this move, solve the problem? John Wisdom, who propounds a similar puzzle involving a dog and a cow, thinks not. To those like James who say that there's a sense in which he goes round and a sense in which he doesn't, Wisdom replies, "But this is untrue. There are not in English two senses of 'go round' in one of which the answer is 'Yes' while in the other it is 'No.' " Even James's disputants were not all satisfied with his "solution," and James's comment at this point is interesting:

> Although one or two of the hotter disputants called my speech a shuf-fling evasion, saying they wanted no quibbling or scholastic hair-split-ting, but meant just plain honest English "round," the majority seemed to think that the distinction had assuaged the dispute.

James seemed not to notice that his proposed "solution" had simply cre-ated a new problem of exactly the same type as the original, *viz.* Did James *solve* the problem or didn't he?

Here persons who have the same information—about the squirrel, the tree, the man, and the English language—disagree about whether the man has gone round the squirrel or whether James has solved the problem. Although this dispute, unlike the one about the vermilion patches, has not been taken seriously by philosophers—it does not connect up with much else—it invites more than passing comparison with disputes philos-ophers have long taken seriously.

Now, the features of philosophical argument I have been discussing can be viewed in different lights. Some see them as adding up to a kind of indictment of philosophy, or an embarrassment or, to use Sidney Hook's word, a "scandal." I see them as nothing of the sort. The idea that perpetual philosophical disagreement is an embarrassment or scandal comes from thinking that philosophy is, or ought to be, a science (in the modern sense of "science"); either a formal science analogous to mathematics (Spinoza) or an empirical science analogous to psychology (Hume). "Philosophers," said Wittgenstein, "constantly have the method of science [or, he might have added, of mathematics] before their eyes . . . and this leads to complete darkness." Were philosophy a science it would be a mystery deeper than that of the Holy Trinity that after over two millennia it has produced no results analogous to those of chemistry, geology, or arithmetic. "Science of philosophy" (as opposed to "philosophy of science") is an oxymoron. Within at least certain limits, one has a right to expect conclusive answers to questions in mathematics and the sciences ("What is the square root of 9?", "What is the atomic weight of iron?"), if sometimes only in principle. One has no right to expect this in philosophy, even in principle. The kind of disagreement I have been discussing is intrinsic to philosophy. Were it to cease to exist, philosophy would cease to exist; the word "philosophy" would mean something different from what I have been talking about. "The spirit of contradiction (*Widerspruchsgeist*)," as Hegel saw, is the lifeblood of philosophy. I can understand how someone might find philosophical disagreement, with its attendant uncertainties, intolerable, but that is no reason for wishing philosophy were something it is not and cannot be.[2]

_____

[2] I know of no one who thinks explicitly of philosophy as one of the natural sciences. Quine comes closest. He thinks of philosophy as "continuous with science, even as a part of science," but it is hard to know what this means. Wittgenstein says, "Philosophy is not one of the natural sciences. (The word 'philosophy' must mean something whose place is above or below the natural sciences, not beside them)," and the words in parentheses seem to imply that philosophy is neither continuous with nor a part of science. If they do, we have here a disagreement which science cannot, even in principle, settle. The issue is a very complicated one, however, and cannot be examined here. Suffice it to note one historical irony in the relationship between philosophy and the sciences. Legend has it that philosophy is the fissiparous parent of most, if not all, of the sciences. Not very long ago physics and chemistry, biology and psychology, as we know them, did

Another possible response to the situation in philosophy as I have depicted it, one that may seem to be invited by James's answer to the puzzle about the man and the squirrel (although James himself knew better) and one that I receive frequently from students, is "It's all just a matter of semantics"; meaning, I take it, that it is merely a matter of what one chooses to say, it being understood that it makes no difference what one chooses to say. One's response to this mindless view will depend on how kind one wishes to be. My own customary reply, which I consider quite gentle, takes the form of a couple of questions that seem to do the trick of prompting second thoughts: "Does it make no difference, is it a matter of 'mere semantics,' whether we call a human fetus a human being, a person? Does it make no difference, is it a matter of 'mere semantics,' whether we call homosexuality a sin, a disease, or simply a matter of sexual preference?" There is obviously a verbal difference between "Homosexuality is a sin" and "Homosexuality is a disease," but to think that there is a *mere* verbal difference is like thinking that there is a mere verbal differ-

---

not exist. It was then not uncommon for philosophers to speculate about answers to such questions as "What are bodies composed of?"—Democritus: "Atoms and void"; Aristotle: "Fire, air, water, and earth"—or "How are the stars and planets related to us?"—Aristotle: "They are attached to revolving aetherial spheres homocentric with the earth." Such questions were seen as belonging properly to philosophy. (The word "philosophy" meant something different in those days.) One might think that when such questions were, in Austin's colorful phrase, "kicked upstairs," philosophy would gradually have diminished. On the contrary. As mathematics and the sciences have evolved they have generated further philosophical problems. There is now, for example, a philosophy of quantum mechanics. And the philosophy of mind, which is where a lot of the action is these days, complicated enough in the classical sources—Aristotle, Descartes, Hume, Hegel, and others—has been further complicated and enriched by developments in psychology, psychoanalysis, computer science, and neurophysiology. Another very active area these days, the philosophy of language (not to be confused with linguistic philosophy, whose basic idea, that "All philosophy is 'critique of language,' " we owe to Wittgenstein) arose largely from the work of a mathematician, Gottlob Frege. These are but a few examples of many testifying to the fact that with the development of the sciences and mathematics philosophy has expanded, not contracted, making it a more difficult subject to teach now than it was, say, forty years ago. Allan Bloom assures his readers that "philosophy hardly exists today," but nothing could be further from the truth. Only a man blinded by the megalomaniacal idea that philosophy is coextensive with his own interpretation of Plato's *Republic* could say such a silly thing.

ence between "involuntary manslaughter" and "first-degree murder." Sins are to be repented; diseases, cured; mere matters of preference, left to the discretion of persons concerned. It makes a difference what we call something, because what we call it is intimately connected with how we feel about it and are prepared to behave towards it. This is one place where philosophy touches life.[3]

A third response is the skeptical one, also rather popular among students: There's no way to know what the solution to a philosophical problem is, no way to tell whether any given answer to it is true or false. My response to this is more mischievous than that to the "mere semantics" fellow: "If you are looking for truth, consult the telephone directory. For all its errors, it contains more truth than the whole of world philosophy." The point is to remind the skeptic that he is working with a philosophically contestable picture of knowledge and of truth (as well as of philosophy as a quest for something that answers to that picture); which, like the first complainant's picture of science, lies at the root of his complaint. Junk that picture, and the skepticism has nothing to stand on.

Still, the skeptic's challenge is a useful one. It prompts us to ask ourselves what is attainable in philosophy and whether that might be something that is not merely capriciously called "knowledge."

Philosophical questions come in many forms, but the basic forms, those to which the others (like "How many vermilions are there?") are usually subordinate, can be represented as follows: What is it to . . . ? ("What is it to act rightly?," "What is it to count colors?"), What is . . . ? ("What is Justice?," "What is a color?"), Is/are there . . . ? ("Is there a God?," "Are there individual members of a species of color?"); where the first blank is to be filled by a verb-phrase, the other two blanks by noun-phrases. Not just any verb- or noun-phrase will do, however. "What is it to castle in chess," "What is defalcation?" and "Are there tigers in Japan?" are not philosophical questions. The first can be answered by consulting a rule book for chess or a competent player of the game; the second, by consulting a dictionary or a person acquainted with the meaning of "defalcation"; the third, by someone knowledgeable about the fauna of Japan. To generate philosophical questions, substitutions of appropriate verb- or noun-

---

[3] There is a serious and profound philosophical theory, as much subject to dispute as any other such theory, according to which philosophical problems are at bottom linguistic, but that is not what is at issue here.

phrases should result in what the Schoolmen aptly called disputed questions (*quaestiones disputatae*); very roughly, and negatively, questions that cannot be answered by appeal to rule books, manuals, atlases, tables, dictionaries, and the like; or by calculating ("What is the sum of 5^3 and 6^7?"), or by demonstration ("Is there a greatest prime number?"), or by counting ("How many students are in the class?"), or by consulting an instrument ("What is the time?"), or by observation ("Is there any jam left in the jar?"), or by experiment ("What is the result of the electrolysis of a solution of common salt?"), or by appeal to a statute ("Are there in the Commonwealth of Massachusetts grounds for divorce other than adultery?"). Disputed questions are not amenable to the decision procedures, such as they are, that we employ in answering most of the questions we ask in daily life or in the sciences, formal or empirical. As we noted earlier, they are not scientific questions, except in some Pickwickian sense of "scientific."

Some philosophers, Quine among them, hold that philosophical questions are merely *more general* than scientific ones. Quine writes:

> A physicist will tell us about causal connections between events of certain sorts; a biologist will tell us about causal connections between events of other sorts; but the philosopher asks about causal connections in general—what is it for one event to cause another? Or again a physicist or zoologist will tell us that there are electrons, that there are wombats; a mathematician will tell us that there are no end of prime numbers; but the philosopher wants to know . . . what sorts of things there are altogether.

"What is it for one event to cause another?" and "What sorts of things are there altogether?" are philosophical questions, all right, but they are not simply more general than "What is the cause of lightning?" or "What is the cause of AIDS?" This is shown, I think, by the fact that the philosopher who, like Bradley or McTaggart, denies the reality of time does not thereby deny the historical fact that the War of 1812 took place prior to the Civil War; and solipsists like Christine Ladd Franklin are not behaving irrationally in writing letters to Bertrand Russell; and Bishop Berkeley, who denied the reality of matter, was not refuted by Dr. Johnson's kicking a stone and bellowing "Thus I refute Berkeley!" Whether time is real or there are persons other than myself in the world or material objects exist independently of their being perceived are questions logically discontinuous with the questions whether one war took place prior to another, whether one's sister is still alive, or whether there are metamorphic rocks on the moon.

If the essentially disputable character of the questions of philosophy is not a direct function merely of their generality, it is also not a function merely of their vagueness or indefiniteness either. Most of the concepts we employ lack precise conditions of application, lack sharp boundaries. (And you have to be a Frege to say, "Therefore they aren't concepts at all.") We get along well enough with them despite that. The existence of possible borderline cases—"Is psychoanalysis scientific?", "Are children's drawings art?"—does not as a rule prompt much philosophical reflection. Far more interesting is the fact that what may seem to be clear, central, even paradigmatic cases of a concept can become philosophically questionable. For example, what Descartes took to be paradigms of knowledge, *viz.* "I think," "I exist," have been held by Wittgenstein not to be cases of knowledge at all! And what strikes most of us as surely being real things, *viz.* physical objects such as chairs and tables, have been held by Plato and many other philosophers to be nothing of the sort. This the student of philosophy must learn to expect.

In answering a disputed question the philosopher aims at a "theory" of that which the question is about: a theory of knowledge or of justice, of history or of art, of beauty or of truth, of language or of law, of reference or of identity, of meaning or of intelligibility, of time or of causality. Such a theory is philosophically supportable solely by arguments the premises, or at least the key premises, of which are alone supportable in the same way. That is why the aim of the student of philosophy is, and ought to be, the understanding, analysis, and criticism of the arguments of other philosophers and the devising of arguments of her own. The aim of the arguments is, as Plato taught us long ago, a dialectically defensible theory; by which I mean one that satisfies at least four conditions: (1) it is coherent or intelligible; (2) it is internally consistent, a condition that will guarantee that its logical consequences will also be consistent with one another; (3) it is consistent with one's other beliefs; and (4) it is such that it can meet proposed objections to it, especially such that putative counterexamples can be shown not to be genuine ones. Dialectical defensibility is very difficult to achieve and has rarely been achieved, but it is a worthy object of endeavor; more worthy perhaps than truth, most of which comes cheap. If one wishes to think of dialectical defensibility as truth of a sort and to think of one who occupies a dialectically defensible position as having knowledge, I have no objections.

In his *Tractatus Logico-Philosophicus* (1921) Wittgenstein believed he had worked out a dialectically defensible theory of the nature of a proposition, and with it defensible answers to a host of other philosophical questions. In his Preface he says, "the *truth* of the thoughts here set forth seems to me unassailable and definitive. I therefore believe myself to have found, on all essential points, the final solution to the problems." Having achieved his goal, or so he thought, he gave up philosophy for ten years. When he returned to it he subjected the *Tractatus* to the most ruthless criticism it has ever received, and, in doing so, worked out a whole new philosophy. Although Wittgenstein is not entirely alone in the reasoned rejection of his earlier views—Plato also comes to mind—this is one of the more moving chapters in the history of philosophy.

That philosophical arguments are not conclusive in the way arguments in mathematics and elsewhere sometimes are, and that different dialectically defensible answers to the same philosophical question, *e.g.* different theories of justice or of knowledge, are possible, is—as I noted earlier—intolerable to some. It does not bother me. It is a further philosophical question whether different answers to the same philosophical question are necessarily logically incompatible or whether it even makes sense to ask which theory is, in some unqualified sense, true. My own answer to these questions is negative. I find that I can not only tolerate but rejoice in a world that, for example, contains both Hume and Heidegger on human nature; or, as Heidegger might prefer, on what it is for a human to be.

Philosophically interesting concepts are, of course, not peculiar to the thought and language of philosophers. We all employ such notions—of rightness, fairness, meaningfulness, sameness, truth, evidence, liberty, causality, and the like—as a matter of course in thinking about what is the case and about what to do. Most of us have other things to do than spend our time worrying about such things as what memory is when we claim to remember, or about what art is when we go to a museum or fume at the use of public money for the purchase of something we consider rubbish. Still, there is surely room in this world for the Socrates who occasionally stops us and invites us to think about what we are doing and saying. Although philosophy is often thought of as productive of nothing but foolishness and confusion, it can help to make us more responsible for our words and deeds, can help to keep us honest, whether it always, or even usually, does so.

In recent years there has been increasing interest in what might be thought of as applied philosophy, the application of philosophical competence to the clarification of problems of public policy, *e.g.* abortion and the death penalty, to biomedical ethics, to feminist theory, and to other issues having a direct bearing on how we conduct our lives. This one can only applaud. My own attitude towards philosophy, however, is that its principal value, like that of music, lies not in any practical applications it may have, but is intrinsic. Simply, it is inherently worth pursuing, and I try to teach it in such a way that my students will see that not only does it beat watching wrestling on TV, it is worthy of Milton's words:

> How charming is divine Philosophy!
> Not harsh and crabbed as dull fools suppose
> But musical as in *Apollo's* lute,
> And a perpetual feast of nectar'd sweets,
> Where no crude surfeit reigns.

Reading the Equations and Confronting the Phenomena—The Delights and Dilemmas of Physics Teaching

Robert H. Romer
Professor of Physics

I.   Sylvia Plath's View of Physics

"The day I went into physics class it was death." Not every student would put it as starkly as did Sylvia Plath, yet there is no doubt that physics bears a special burden within the liberal arts curriculum. Surely physics *is* one of the liberal arts, in the best sense of the term, but there are many students, even many physics professors, who would find that claim an odd one. We suffer from a powerful collection of misleading, largely erroneous and even self-contradictory impressions and misconceptions.

Physics is boring. So are physics books, not to mention physics professors, few of whom have any interests or knowledge outside their subject or perhaps even outside their own narrow research specialty. Physicists are cool, dispassionate, unemotional, even about their own subject. Physics is impossibly difficult; no one can begin to comprehend it without advanced courses in mathematics. Physics consists primarily of a vast collection of mysterious and unconnected formulas (all of which must be periodically memorized), into which one must plug equally mysterious numbers in the hopes of passing the course (to satisfy a pre-med requirement?) and getting on to more interesting things. If there is a logical structure to the subject, it is so abstruse as to be inaccessible to ordinary mortals. And physics is not new, at least not what you will get in college; that part was finished a century ago, and even 19th-century physics has nothing to do with everyday phenomena. Certainly ongoing physics research, all of which is enormously expensive and is carried out only at huge national laboratories, deals only with subnuclear or cosmological phenomena and has no influence, not even an indirect one, on what transpires in undergraduate classes and laboratories. Physicists (especially experimentalists) are merely technicians, who follow a set procedure ("the scientific method"?), in their repetitive and ultimately boring search for "truth." And once a new truth has been found, the issue is settled; unlike other fields where new results are tentative and can be argued about, science is cut and dried, scientific truths are final, our truth is *absolute* truth.

Physics does carry a handicap because of the ways in which so many outsiders (and entering students) view us and our subject. We have a special burden, but also a wonderful opportunity because most (but not all) of the views described above are simply false. Ours is a delightful and beautiful subject, and if we can convey even a small fraction of that delight and beauty to our students, we will probably have far exceeded their expectations. To be sure, we have only ourselves to blame for many of the popular misconceptions about physics, and there is at least a bit of truth to some of the accusations. Indeed, sad to say, there are not a few physicists and physics teachers who would subscribe to most of the views described above. Many, probably most, physics books *are* dull and badly written and manage to conceal everything that is beautiful, interesting and intellectually stimulating. Much of what passes for teaching *does* present physics as a set of unconnected and uninteresting formulas, ignoring the logical structure and the beauty to be found there. I received a good dose of that myself as a student; it really is a wonder that any of us survived. Surely, many students do not stay with us. How many thoughtful students do we lose because of the way we teach?

In *The Bell Jar,* Sylvia Plath went on to describe how she came to terms with her Smith College physics class. She sat in the back row, writing poetry while managing to give the appearance of rapt attention to the lecturer. "Mr. Manzi" assumed she was faithfully transcribing every formula he put on the board. Both parties were happy. All of us, of course, entertain the hope of engaging our students somewhat more intensely. We have a wonderful subject. Those who are fortunate enough to teach physics, the subject that is the most fun to teach and study and learn, have a rare opportunity. Physics can be a vehicle for providing some of the best of what a liberal arts education should be. I will try to describe some of the things I try to keep in mind when I am teaching, some of the ways I try to teach, the ways I wish that I did teach, the ways that perhaps I do teach on the better days.

II.   Reading the Equations

IF THERE IS ANY one thing that illustrates the way of doing physics that I try to encourage, it is a thoughtful approach to the interpretation, the "reading," of equations. I am often impressed by the way in which an artist can read a painting for me, showing me all manner of things I could never have seen on my own, or by the way an English professor can interpret a poem or a short story. Rather than try to describe in the abstract what I mean by *reading an equation,* it seems far better to give a specific illustration. Here is a humble example of an equation, a "formula," one that will be found in an early chapter of virtually every introductory physics text:

$$R = \frac{2\,v_0^2 \sin \Theta \cos \Theta}{g}.$$

This equation is one I have chosen because it is complicated enough to be interesting, to require a bit of effort in its interpretation, yet simple enough to be read without advanced training in either mathematics or physics. All too often, it is only the bare equation that we write down on the board, and that is what the students write down and memorize for the quiz. But, as we will see, students and teachers who are so easily satisfied are missing most of the joys to be found in our subject.

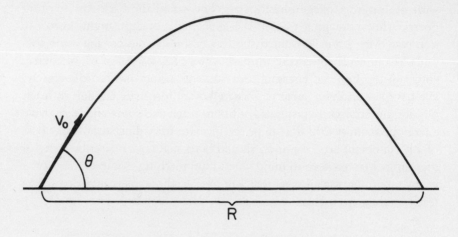

Figure 1. Projectile motion. An object is projected with
an initial speed v_o, at an angle Θ with respect to the
horizontal. Its horizontal *range* is denoted by R.

One obvious remark should dispel for good the thought that physics is
"nothing but a collection of formulas." By itself, that equation (or any
other) is absolutely useless. Some sort of textual accompaniment is
needed, what I call the "hidden text" because we are usually too busy to
write it down or even give a verbal summary. At the very least, we must
explain what those symbols mean, in what context the equation is supposed to be applicable. The context here is that of "projectile motion" (see
Figure 1): a child tossing a ball, or a battleship firing a shell at a distant
target. Here v_0 is the speed (or velocity) with which the ball leaves the
child's hand, θ is the angle between the ground and the initial direction
of motion, and g is the so-called "acceleration due to gravity," a quantity
perhaps all too familiar to anyone who has studied introductory physics.
(In Henry Adams's famous autobiography, *The Education of Henry Adams,*
there is just one equation—and it appears twice—an equation that was
perhaps the only detail that Adams remembered from studying physics at
Harvard:

$$s = \frac{gt^2}{2}.$$

The symbol g has been used for well over a century to denote the acceleration due to gravity, and Henry Adams used this equation to symbolize what could be achieved by applying *mathematics* to natural phenomena.)

In the equation I propose to read, R, the "left-hand side," is the *range* of the projectile, the horizontal distance it travels before returning to earth. It was assumed in the derivation of this equation that the projectile was fired exactly from ground level. Why? Because it makes the problem an easier one to work out, the resulting equation much simpler than it would otherwise be. That neither battleships nor children fire their projectiles from ground level but rather from some distance above is conveniently ignored; that, for better or worse, is typical of physicists and the problems they pose for themselves and their students.

In this equation, "sin" and "cos" are the trigonometric functions, sine and cosine, familiar to everyone from school experiences with triangles. I could easily have chosen an illustrative example with no trigonometry, but to do so would have been misleading. I deliberately chose this equation, trigonometry and all, to emphasize the point that one cannot do serious physics without some mathematics. As in many other cases, Galileo (a master of scientific prose) made the point most eloquently:

> Philosophy is written in that great book which ever lies before our eyes —I mean the universe—but we cannot understand it if we do not first learn the language in which it is written. The book is written in the *mathematical* language, without whose help it is impossible to comprehend a single word, without which one wanders in vain through a dark labyrinth.

In stating what the symbols mean, we have only just *begun* to provide the hidden text that goes with this equation. What are some of the other components of the accompanying text? First we should ask about the *logical status* of the equation. We deal with many equations in physics, all of which have in common the fact that they contain an "equals" sign, but various equations play very different roles. Some equations are even wrong. Some are "true" but only tautologically so, because they are just definitions. Of course, we should not sneer at definitions; we could not get along without carefully framed, unambiguous and useful definitions. In retrospect, much of the effort in physics over the centuries has been expended in deciding *what* quantities are important enough to *merit* definitions. Logically, one can define anything; in practice, which quantities (such as velocity) or combinations of quantities (such as kinetic energy, defined as one half the mass of an object times the square of its velocity) are *useful* to define, concepts worth naming, is something that is determined by the nature of the universe, not by us.

Indeed it is sometimes difficult to decide whether a particular equation is an expression of a law of nature or a definition or some of both. I have seen colleagues nearly come to blows while arguing about the logical status of Newton's famous "second law of motion," $F = ma$, which relates force, mass, and acceleration. Is it really an expression of a physical law, or is it a *definition* of force? Or is it something more complicated, an equation that one cannot readily put in either of those two categories? Furthermore, some equations with "physical content," *i.e.,* those that are not simply definitions, express fundamental laws of nature, whereas others state more specialized and narrowly applicable results. There is no democracy among equations: some are extremely important, and others are not; some are beautiful and others are ugly. We must ourselves be aware of these distinctions and teach our students to discriminate among the various equations they will meet.

My illustrative range equation is definitely not a *definition* of the "range" of a projectile. But though it does have physical content (by which we really mean that it *could* be wrong, it is not *necessarily* correct; in Karl Popper's terms, it is *falsifiable*), it is not in any sense a *fundamental* law of physics. Instead it is a rather special result, applicable only to a rather restricted set of phenomena, war and baseball, for example. Having said that, we then want to know whether this equation is simply a mathematical expression of an *empirically* discovered regularity or whether it was logically *derived* from a more fundamental physical law. It was in fact derived from other, more basic, results, and what those other results are is an important part of the hidden text, as is the derivation itself.

Virtually everything we do in physics requires idealizations and approximations. Progress would be impossible without simplification. Had Galileo and Newton insisted on an "exact" description of falling objects and orbiting planets, modern science could never have gotten started. Clearly this set of idealizations and approximations is an important part of the text that accompanies an equation. Without knowledge of these idealizations, we would have no idea of the range of applicability of a theoretical result such as the range equation, *how* accurate we might expect it to be, when and how we might expect it to fail.

So much of the art and pleasure of physics lies in deciding what idealizations to make, what approximations are desirable to make a theoretical treatment possible without destroying the essence of the problem. How do we make these decisions, and—more importantly—how can we let students in on the process? All too rarely do we articulate this process, and the result is that this crucial and fascinating part of doing physics is totally hidden from our students. Our advanced students, those who go on to be research scientists and physics teachers, may get it later, but unfortunately even some of *them* never become explicitly aware of this important part of our subject. It is easy to see why we rarely discuss these matters with our students. It takes time, it hurts "coverage," we are impatient to get on to the next topic. The students really want to know (or think they want to know) how to answer the straightforward problems of the type they think (usually correctly) will be on the exam. We are self-conscious, for some reason, about articulating the thinking that we must go through in idealizing a problem sufficiently to make it soluble without idealizing it so much that we remove its interesting features. To put it bluntly, we are uneasy about discussing with students the truly interesting and important aspects of what we do. It is easier just to go through the mathematical steps of the derivation, as if it were pure logic that connected one equation with another; yet there really is a connecting argument, a *physical* justification, a plausible approximation, that is required at almost every step.

What *are* some of the idealizations that were made in deriving the range equation? One is that we ignored the spatial extent of the projectile itself (baseball or shell), treating it as a "point mass." Otherwise, we could not talk simply about *the* range—throw a chair across a room, and some parts of the chair will travel farther than other parts. Furthermore, the chair will rotate, and the rotation too we have ignored. Air resistance is something else that has been idealized away. Why? To keep the problem one that *can* be solved by elementary methods and with a result that can be expressed by a relatively simple equation. Was it a "good approximation" to neglect air resistance? That depends. If we want to predict to within 100 feet or so how far a baseball will go, then it probably *is* a good approximation to neglect air resistance; if we want to predict its range to within 5 feet, it is not such a good idea. (Physicists often neglect air resistance; outfielders do not.) Notice that what constitutes a "good approximation" depends not only on the physical situation but also on the *question* being asked. Is it a good approximation to idealize the Earth as a geometrical point, in considering the orbits of Earth and Moon around the sun? That seems like a reasonable question, but in fact it is not. Yes, it is a good approximation if we are calculating the time between one full moon and the next; but obviously not, if we want to calculate the duration of a lunar eclipse, when the Moon passes through the Earth's shadow, for the extent of the shadow is directly related to the size of the object that casts it. In other words, and this is a general observation about approximations, whether a particular approximation is a "good" one or not depends not only on the physical situation but on the *question* we are asking about it and, of course, on the needed precision of the answer.

More idealizations. We have taken g, the "acceleration due to gravity," to be simply a constant, the same value at every point on the projectile's flight. Of course, it is not really a constant; Newton taught us that the Earth's gravitational effect gets weaker in a specific way as the distance from the Earth increases. It is also implicit in the range equation that the Earth is *flat!* We might well guess that the flat-Earth approximation is an excellent one for baseballs but not so good for ICBMs, and we note for possible future reference that the problem of projectile motion on a *round, rotating* Earth, with varying gravitational acceleration taken into account, is a good deal more challenging. (The rotation of the Earth does make a difference. When the British fleet sailed to the Falkland Islands a few years ago, the sights on their guns had to be adjusted because the direction of the Earth's rotation, relative to the "up" direction, is different in the southern hemisphere.) The truly careful and experienced equation reader would know, without being told, that our range formula did not allow for the rotation of the Earth and its roundness, because surely, if it did, the formula would include symbols denoting the diameter and rotation rate of the Earth. Our students are not, to begin with, experienced at reading equations; it is our responsibility to open their minds to the pleasures to be found here.

Much is left for more advanced courses. Physics is almost invariably taught using a "spiral" approach. We do not "finish" electromagnetism, for instance, in the freshman course; we do study electromagnetism there, but the serious physics student will formally study it at least twice more, once in an advanced undergraduate course, again in one of the most important courses that all graduate students take. Along the way, topics in electromagnetism come up in virtually every other course, and if you are lucky enough to be a physics professor, especially one with the good fortune of occasionally teaching that advanced undergraduate course, you will go on studying electromagnetism all your life.

We could go on with more discussion of the approximations and idealizations (implicit or explicit) that were made in arriving at the range equation, but perhaps it is time to begin some serious *reading* of our chosen equation. The first thing a careful reader will do is make sure that the *units* are correct, or—as we say—that the equation is "dimensionally consistent." By this we mean that because the left-hand side of the equation represents a *distance* or *length,* R, so must the right-hand side in order to avoid absurdity, even though the nature of the right-hand side is concealed in a combination of speeds, angles, etc. To take a simpler example, consider the familiar formula for the equation of a rectangle: area = width × height. Width and height both have "dimensions" of *length* (and are measured in meters or miles or yards, according to one's preference). We say that an area has dimensions of length × length, or length^2. The equation for the area of a *circle* of radius r is this: area = πr^2, a formula that is dimensionally correct because, like the formula for the area of a rectangle, the right-hand side has dimensions of length^2. (The number π is just a number, it has no dimensions; that is, it does not matter whether distances are being measured in inches or meters, the value of π is still approximately 3.14159 . . .) Consider a hypothetical formula for the area of a circle: area = πr^3; this equation can immediately be dismissed as erroneous—it is *dimensionally inconsistent.*

Let us make a dimensional check of our range formula. The combination of quantities on the right-hand side must somehow have dimensions of *length*. The 2 and the trigonometric functions (sin θ and cos θ) are simply numbers, of the same dimensional status as π. Now v_0 is a *speed,* something measured in miles/hour or meters/second; it has *dimensions* of length/time. The quantity g is an *acceleration,* measured in, say, meters per second per second (meters/second^2); that is, its dimensions are length/time^2. Thus the dimensions of the combination

$$\frac{2\ v_0{}^2\ \sin\ \theta\ \cos\ \theta}{g}$$

are simply

$$\frac{\text{length}^2/\text{time}^2}{\text{length}/\text{time}^2}.$$

After carrying out the appropriate cancellations, we see that indeed the right-hand side of our equation has dimensions of *length,* as it must if the equation is not to represent nonsense.

Now let us get on to some more interesting reading. But let me mention in passing the type of "reading" that is all too common in our physics textbooks. A typical homework problem is something like this: "A rock is projected at an angle of 29°, with an initial speed of 14 meters/second; what is its range?" The only reasonable answer to that, one that no student I have ever met has been brave enough to give, is: "Who cares? Unless it is a real rock, which someone is aiming at *me,* I am just not interested in the mechanical task of plugging numbers into that formula." The question that *is* interesting is this: "A rock is projected at an angle θ, with an initial speed v_0; what is its range?" *That* is a question that our range formula allows us to answer, and it is interesting largely because of the reading we are about to do. And, of course, our general range formula allows us to calculate the answer to any and all numerical homework problems of this sort, (v_0 = 14 meters/second or 22 meters/second, θ = 29° or 38° or anything else), whenever or if ever we care to do so.

One of the first questions we might ask, on reading such a formula, is something like this: "What if the initial speed were increased or decreased? How would the range change?" The answer is clear from looking at the formula: if v_0 were made larger, the value of R would get larger as well. That is not surprising, but our lack of surprise partially confirms the correctness of the formula. (Once in a while, our simple expectation about "What if . . . ?" turns out to be wrong. In such a case, life gets more interesting, and we have a real chance to learn something truly new. I will give an example later in this section.) Another simple question we might ask is this: "What if the value of g were larger or smaller?" The inexperienced equation reader might never think of asking this question, or might even object if the teacher asks it. "After all, g is what it is, 9.8 meters/second^2 as a matter of fact. It *isn't* larger or smaller." One can squelch such an objection by pointing out that if we were playing baseball (or making war) on the surface of the *moon,* the value of g *would* be different from the usual value, but such a comment misses the point. Even if g had the same value *everywhere,* it would still be interesting and educational to ask "What if . . . ?" Here the answer to "What if . . . ?" is this. Look at the formula: "g" is in the *denominator,* so if you were to *increase* its numerical value, the resulting value of R would *decrease.* That is reasonable, of course; other things being equal, if the strength of gravity could be made larger, the range of a projectile *should* get smaller. Physics does make a little sense, but this minor insight could not have been obtained had we only substituted specific numerical values to get the answer to a homework problem, or if we had not been adventurous enough to ask what would happen if somehow the value of g were altered.

One of the most useful and educational things we like to do with any equation is to look at "limiting cases." In physics, this often means asking what would happen if some physical quantity were equal to zero, or were infinitely large. Physicists often find it fruitful to look at limiting cases, in talking with each other about physics, or with nonphysicists, about totally different, even nonscientific, subjects. Here one might ask, for instance: "What if we fire a projectile with zero speed?" Clearly, our formula says it won't go anywhere ($R = 0$), surely an unsurprising result. What if there were no gravity ($g = 0$)? The g is in the denominator, and our formula would give an *infinite* range. With some qualifications, that does indeed make sense. This result reminds us of some of the things we have left out of our discussion: we assumed there was no air resistance, and that the Earth was flat. (An unlimited size was implicit.)

Now let us see how things vary when the *angle* of firing is altered. The appropriate limiting cases are these: $\theta = 0°$ and $\theta = 90°$. If $\theta = 0°$, that simply means that the ball (or shell) is projected horizontally. But the trigonometric sine of an angle of $0°$ is zero, so in that case the range predicted by our formula is zero as well. How can that be? If you fire a gun horizontally, its range is *not* zero; instead it may travel for quite a distance, until it has fallen far enough to hit the ground. Yes, but remember, one of the assumptions made in deriving the range formula was that the projectile is fired from ground level; if so, it has no distance to fall, and so it immediately hits the ground. In spite of a momentary doubt, the range formula does make sense in that limiting case. The other limiting case is $\theta = 90°$. Now although $\sin 90° = 1$, $\cos 90° = 0$. Once again, though for a different reason, our range formula gives $R = 0$. This, too, makes sense. If you throw a baseball (or fire a bullet) vertically upward, it will come back and hit you. It may take a long time to do so, but its *range* (its horizontal range, that is what R means) will be zero.

Thus as far as the limiting cases are concerned, the angular factors do make sense. Let us proceed a bit further. If $R = 0$ both for $\theta = 0°$ and for $\theta = 90°$, and since it is obvious (both from experience and from looking at the formula) that R is not zero for intermediate angles, it is natural to ask what angle, other things being equal, will give the *maximum* value for the range. Halfway between, $\theta = 45°$, is a plausible guess. But at this point, that is merely a conjecture, though a correct one as it turns out. Let us see how to put that on more solid ground. One reasonable approach, one made feasible by the pocket calculator, is to plug in some numbers; just calculate the value of (sin θ cos θ) for various angles. You will quickly find that the result is larger for 45° than for 44° or 46°. Narrow it down: a little bit larger for 45° than for 44.9° or 45.1°. The guess is looking good, though no mathematician would accept these numbers as proof. Another approach, almost a reflexive one for a calculus student, is to wheel out some of the heavy artillery from a first course in calculus, where we learn powerful methods for finding maxima and minima of mathematical expressions.

Perhaps a more interesting way of exploring this question, though, is to *rewrite* our formula. Rewriting a formula, rearranging it mathematically, and then examining the new version, is a perfectly legitimate part of "reading an equation." Here the useful manipulation is provided by one of the "trigonometric identities" that most of us memorized in school (they *are* good for something after all):

$$2 \sin \theta \cos \theta = \sin(2\theta).$$

Using this, we can reexpress our range formula as

$$R = \frac{v_0{}^2}{g} \sin(2\theta).$$

Now it is simpler, in a way—only one trigonometric term [sin (2θ)] instead of two. Everyone remembers, we hope, that the sine function gives its maximum value when the quantity whose sine we are calculating is equal to 90°. Thus R is a maximum when $2\theta = 90°$, or, therefore, when $\theta = 45°$. Our conjecture is confirmed. And we can go further. Perhaps we remember that the sine of an angle not only is a maximum at 90°, but also that it has the same value at angles that are above and below 90° by the same amount. The sine of 80° is the same as that of 100°, for instance. But if $2\theta = 80°$ or 100°, then θ itself is 40° or 50°. For two angles, above and below 45° by equal amounts, the range formula gives exactly the same results. Few of us find that prediction "intuitively obvious." We have arrived at a famous result first proved by Galileo, who exulted in this discovery:

> The force of rigorous demonstrations such as occur only by use of mathematics fills me with wonder and delight. From accounts given by gunners, I was already aware of the fact that in the use of cannon and mortars, the maximum range, that is, the one in which the shot goes farthest, is obtained when the elevation is 45°; but to understand *why* this happens far outweighs the mere information obtained by the testimony of others or even by repeated experiment. The knowledge of a single effect apprehended through its cause opens the mind to understand and ascertain other facts without need of recourse to experiment, precisely as in the present case, where, having won by demonstration the certainty that the maximum range occurs when the elevation is 45°, the author [Galileo] demonstrates what has perhaps never been observed in practice, namely, that for elevations that exceed or fall short of 45° by equal amounts, the ranges are equal.

Or, as Virgil put it,

> "Felix qui potuit rerum cognoscere causas."—"Happy is the person who can understand the causes of phenomena!"

Onward—more reading of this equation. The thoughtful equation reader may notice that something seems to be missing from our range equation. Why doesn't the mass or weight of the projectile appear there? I am reminded of a famous passage from Arthur Conan Doyle's "Silver Blaze."

> "Is there any point to which you would wish to draw my attention?", said Inspector Gregory. "To the curious incident of the dog in the night-time," said Sherlock Holmes. "But," said Inspector Gregory, "the dog did nothing in the night-time." "That was the curious incident," remarked Holmes.

The point, of course, was that the dog did not bark; hence the intruder was undoubtedly someone who was no stranger to the dog. The *absence* of barking was itself interesting and informative. Here it is the absence of the properties of the projectile itself from the range formula that is curious and potentially very important. At first sight, this absence is an absurdity —after all, one *can* throw a baseball farther than one can throw a refrigerator. But then we realize that what our formula tells us is that if we throw a refrigerator and a baseball, both at the same angle and with the *same initial speed,* they will travel the same distance. Maybe if we *could* throw the refrigerator with the same speed as the baseball, it *would* travel as far. It is not absurd, at least not totally absurd, after all. But it is still extremely interesting, if properly considered. It seems odd that, even with identical speeds and angles, those two objects would travel exactly the same distance. The more one thinks about that, the more mysterious it seems. The point is not a trivial one. Einstein pondered this mystery, and eventually he made it the cornerstone of his General Theory of Relativity, the most successful theory of gravity we have ever found.

We are not yet done with our reading of this equation. I observed earlier that the formula tells us (correctly) that if v_0 is increased, the resulting range (other things being equal) will be larger. But there is a somewhat more subtle reading we can make. The equation contains the quantity v_0^2, speed *times* speed. The speed appears not just once but *twice.* Can we somehow understand this double significance of the initial speed? I think we can. First of all, if it is fired with a larger speed, then (other things being equal, as usual) it will travel a greater horizontal *distance* in any specific length of time. Second, the greater the speed with which it is fired, the greater the *time* that will elapse before it returns to earth. These are really two separate effects (though it is easy to be led astray and do some double counting by mistake), and so it is not hard to see (at least in retrospect!) that there *should* be two factors of speed in the result. That argument is only a plausible one. It is a helpful argument, it leads to a kind of understanding that builds confidence and enhances one's physical intuition, but it should be regarded as a supplement to, not a substitute for, the careful work that had to be done in order to find that formula in the first place.

I end the discussion of this equation by observing, once more, that I have not made any pretense of including the *derivation* of the range formula from more basic results. In fact, I have deliberately omitted those steps, just because in the usual way of teaching physics, it is those steps—

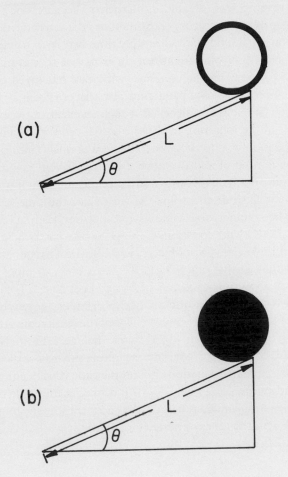

Figure 2. End views of two cylinders, one hollow (a)
and one solid (b), being rolled down inclined planes.

steps that the students are usually expected to memorize and be able to reproduce—that are usually emphasized to the exclusion of what is really interesting—the rest of the hidden text that goes with the formula and the reading and interpretation of the formula once we have it.

Usually when one reads an equation, what one finds may be at first sight surprising but turns out, upon reflection, to seem quite reasonable after all. The reading was valuable, nonetheless, because one's physical intuition ends up better and stronger. Sometimes the interpretation, reading, examination of "limiting cases," simply does not seem to make sense at all. What then? More often than not, it turns out that a mistake has been made, and so reading the equation with care has saved one from professional disaster (if one is a practicing physicist) or from an unnecessarily poor grade (if one is a student). But such an event is more exciting, more profitable in the long run, in those unusual cases in which it turns out that the equation is indeed correct, that it was one's "intuition" that was wrong and in need of improvement. I cannot give an example using the range formula, but here is another situation, again from introductory physics, that may illustrate the point. At least since the time of Galileo, physicists have been rolling objects down tilted planes, both in reality and in our imaginations (with equations). Suppose one has two identically tilted planes, and two cylindrical objects, with identical masses and diameters, differing only in that one is hollow (like a piece of pipe) and the other solid, such as an unopened can of corned beef hash. (To make the masses equal, we could perhaps use a wooden cylinder as one object and a short piece of lead pipe as the other.) The two experiments are shown in Fig. 2a and Fig. 2b. Which object wins the race? From Newton's fundamental laws of motion, the same basic physics that underlies projectile motion, one can derive equations giving the time it takes either object to reach the end of the tilted plane. With θ denoting the angle of tilt, L the length of the plane, and g, as before, the "acceleration due to gravity," the two formulas for the times of descent (t) are these:

$$t_{hollow} = \sqrt{\frac{4L}{g\sin\theta}};$$

$$t_{solid} = \sqrt{\frac{3L}{g\sin\theta}}.$$

It is strange that the weight or mass of the rolling object does not appear in these equations, but perhaps after the failure of the weight of the projectile to appear in the range formula discussed earlier, that might not seem so bizarre any more. It is even more strange that the *size* (radius or diameter) of the cylinder does not appear in either formula. Is it really true, for instance, that a large can and a small can would reach the bottom in a dead heat, both obeying the second of the two equations given above? The answer, by the way, is "Yes."

There is much more that we could do by way of reading these equations, to try to make sense of the square-root sign, for instance, but let us just concentrate on the question of which object, hollow pipe or solid cylinder, wins the race. The formulas are identical except that one contains the square root of 4 where the other has the square root of 3. No higher mathematics is needed to understand that $\sqrt{3}$ is less than $\sqrt{4}$. The time for the solid object (the cylinder) is less than that for the hollow one (the piece of pipe). The solid cylinder wins the race. (Remember, by the way, that I assumed for simplicity that the weights of the two objects are identical.)

I do not now find, I have never found, that result, that the solid cylinder wins the race, to be intuitively reasonable, let alone obvious. Somehow, it seems to me, the hollow object, with its weight concentrated at the rim to get it turning, to get it *rolling* faster, should be the winner. Not so. My intuition is wrong. The derivation that led to those two formulas was indeed correct, and (most important!) those theoretical predictions *do* agree with experimental observations. Deep in my heart, I still think the hollow pipe should win, but it does not. I have learned to live with this, and what I have really learned from this very modest example is that although our universe does not always behave as I naively think it should, with persistence and cleverness and some mathematics we can nevertheless describe and even "understand" its mysteries. True understanding must come not only from the heart but also, of course, from the mind.

This example of the solid and hollow cylinders is a wonderfully useful example for teaching purposes. Ask students, fresh to the subject, what they think about the outcome of such a race. Some intuitions are like mine, others differ; on the average, a typical class will be evenly split in its predictions, but almost no one is really confident of the experimental outcome.

By the way, the answer in the back of the book to the range question posed earlier ("What is the range of a rock projected at an angle of 29° with an initial speed of 14 meters/second?") is R = 17 meters. But I hope that by now the reader is persuaded that the correct answer to *that* question is: "Who cares?"

III. Confronting the Phenomena

PHYSICISTS ARE CONSTANTLY TRYING to improve their understanding, at the most fundamental level, of the universe in which we live. Although we sometimes appear to have forgotten it, our subject matter does not consist of the chalk marks on our blackboards but of natural phenomena and real objects: balls, tricycles, electrons, water, stars. . . . That is what makes physics different from mathematics, harder than mathematics in some ways but easier in others. Physics is harder than mathematics because the real world of phenomena and data is always out there, waiting to check up on us, shooting down our speculative ideas. No matter how mathematically beautiful and elegant a physical theory may be, if it does not correspond to experimental facts, it is wrong. But in some ways physics is *easier* than mathematics, simply because it must be based on and checked by physical phenomena. We can afford to be somewhat nonrigorous, more speculative in our thinking, for if we are seriously off the track, it will not be long before nature lets us know.

A teacher who does not contrive to have his or her students somehow confront the phenomena is failing in an important way. In fact, I think this is where most of us who teach physics in colleges and universities exhibit our most egregious inadequacies. Ever since I began teaching (and long before), physics teachers have been debating the purposes of laboratory work, writing papers on the role of "labs," attending conferences on the subject, agonizing in the privacy of their offices. In spite of all that has been said and written, the variations that have been tried, we are really no closer now than we were thirty years ago to making the most out of labs in our courses, or even to having a shared rationale for their existence.

Why *do* we have labs accompanying most of our physics courses? Some teachers cling to the hope that during the weekly lab period, their students will discover (!) the significant laws of physics. Surely no one can seriously believe that students who enter the lab ignorant of, say, the law of conservation of momentum, will *discover* it during the next few hours. We may lay out a procedure that if scrupulously followed might be described (by a truly generous observer) as a condensed version of the way in which such a law was, or might have been, discovered. But one only has to recall how many decades it took scientists to fumble their way toward a clear formulation of the law of conservation of momentum to realize the absurdity of thinking that our students will in any real sense reenact that process in an afternoon.

Though it may be absurd to think that innocent students will "discover" a physical law during the lab period, we can at least hope that they will be *testing* a known law. Though this more modest goal is at least closer to what is possible, it too is unrealistic. To see this, one need only consider what we and our students actually do when an experiment "comes out wrong." Do we conclude that the law of conservation of momentum is wrong? Of course not, even though a naive application of Karl Popper's philosophy of science might lead us to reject the law on the basis of one failure. Instead, if time permits, the students go back to the apparatus, back to their notebooks, to try to find out exactly what did "go wrong" with the equipment, what data they may have incorrectly recorded, where their arithmetic went astray. If time does not permit (after all, even the most dedicated teachers and students enjoy eating dinner), we simply conclude that *somewhere* a mistake of some kind was made. Sometimes the *teacher* will return, late at night, to try to understand the problem. It is a very rare student who has the time to do so, and besides, the lab is usually locked. There are real possibilities here, though, for changing the format of our courses so as to make it more feasible for persistent students to return to the laboratory and for us to encourage and reward those who do.

No one is going to test, let alone *discover*, a law of nature during an afternoon lab period. Any serious introduction to the experience of scientific research and discovery requires *time:* time to fumble, to err, to break things (and repair them), to go home, sleep, rethink and repeat, to become gradually more skilled at asking and answering questions of nature. Rarely is anything remotely like that possible in the setting of a "course." It does happen, and happens frequently, during a year-long senior thesis experience, and when it works well, it is a wonderful experience for all concerned.

My own—possibly too modest—view of what labs can and should do reduces to the following: they remind us of the elementary but easily forgotten fact that physics deals with the real world of natural phenomena. Labs must force our students to confront *some* of those phenomena (exactly which ones is not terribly important), with all their stubborn idiosyncrasies, their refusal to conform precisely to our neat and oversimplified equations, and with real physical objects. Experimental data are imperfect, subject to error and uncertainty; graphs that "should be" straight lines are never exactly so. Real springs and strings, not the "weightless" ones that populate our homework problems, *do* have weight, apparatus does break or get stuck or go up in smoke. Air resistance, which may be made negligible by professorial decree in a homework problem, may or may not be negligible in the lab.

In our tests and homework problems, physical objects are idealized and abstracted so as to be unrecognizable. Electrical circuits, even the simplest, provide a wonderful example of the distance between real objects and their representations. Fig. 3a is a typical diagram of a simple circuit, a battery heating several interconnected resistors, with a couple of meters to measure current and voltage. Compare Fig. 3a, with its neat square corners and abstract symbols, with Fig. 3b, a photograph of the real thing. Labs require students to make the connection between physical reality and its representation. Every year I seem to have forgotten how hard it is for novices to make this connection, and every year I enjoy watching a new group struggle with the task of assembling an assortment of flexible, drooping wires of various lengths and colors in order to create the physical realization of something like Fig. 3a. It is always a battle, but they always learn something, something very important. And therefore, of course, we must refuse to use the "efficient" approach of having a professor or teaching assistant connect the students' wires for them.

Real experiments produce *real* (imperfect) data. Real equipment sometimes sticks or breaks. Momentum is not exactly conserved in any real experiment, no matter what the "law" says it should do. Humility in the face of these facts is one thing we want our students to take away from a lab, and the distance between a physical object and its abstract representation is another. Some teachers use *computer simulations* of physical phenomena as a substitute for labs. It's easier, the equipment never breaks, there is always enough of everything, and the results are always excellent. Clearly a simulated "experiment" is the creation of the devil, and the temptation to use one must be stoutly resisted.

We should be cautious, but cautiously adventurous, about using computers in the teaching labs. Properly used, computers "interfaced" to physical apparatus can be marvelous teaching tools. They can allow our students to gather large amounts of precise data and relieve much of the drudgery of routine data analysis. Yet if we are not careful, we can fall prey to the "blinking light syndrome." The computer can be rigged to do

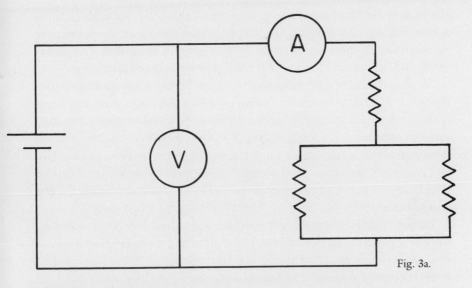

Fig. 3a.

Fig. 3b.

Figure 3. A simple electrical circuit: (a) its abstract
representation, and (b) the real thing.

the experiment "for" the student, who has little to do but push buttons and be entranced by the seductive display screen and has little opportunity or incentive to think about what is going on. I have seen computer-interfaced labs like this, and clearly they are of no educational value.

Similar concerns can be voiced about *lecture demonstrations,* too, though I say this as one who intensely enjoys planning, designing, and showing demonstrations. Demonstrations serve a real purpose, but they cannot substitute for student laboratory experience. For reasons of expediency (time, money), I have taught a number of courses without a lab, and I do many demonstrations—especially in those courses—but I do not delude myself into thinking that demonstrations can compensate for the absence of a lab.

I enjoy designing new demonstrations, and indeed I feel that *my* enjoyment is a perfectly legitimate reason for including a demonstration, even if not every demonstration shows convincingly what it was supposed to show. Better, of course, if it does convey the desired message, but I do not believe that we should flatly prohibit complicated demonstrations that most of the students will not understand. I am probably the first physics professor ever to argue in print that there may be indirect benefits from such demonstrations. Not too many mysterious demonstrations, of course, but after all, most physicists do enjoy things and phenomena, as well as equations, and physics professors are humans, too; we should take advantage of every opportunity to keep the professors keyed up about courses and subjects they may have taught many times. I find it hard to imagine teaching a whole course with nothing but books and chalk; even when I teach calculus, as I have a number of times, I often have a piece of demonstration apparatus in my hand as I leave for class.

Not every demonstration "works," and once in a while one of those that "fails" turns out to be one of the best. I always delight in observing, and showing to a class, Faraday's great discovery, that a moving magnet can make electrical currents flow in a nearby wire, simply by virtue of the changing magnetic field, without any contact whatever. Set up an electrical circuit, including a meter and a large coil of wire. Thrust one end of an ordinary magnet into the empty space in the center of the coil, and observe with awe the resulting deflection of the meter. One day I did this for a class, inserting the "north" end of the magnet into the coil and seeing the meter move to the right. Some minutes later, after some discussion, I posed the question: "What if we simply repeat that experiment, but turn the magnet around first, and insert the "*south*" end into the coil?" Everyone knew what would happen. So did I. Of course, the meter would now move to the *left*. Great was our astonishment (especially mine!) when the meter moved to the *right,* just as it had in the initial demonstration. What to do? The experienced demonstrator has a number of responses ready when an experiment fails. Sometimes you have some well chosen words ready, so that you can point out "what they would have seen if. . . ."; some teachers look hopefully at the clock, waiting for the bell to ring. Luckily, I had my wits about me that day, because the period was not about to end. I had no idea what had gone wrong, but we had some other equipment available, magnets and compasses and iron filings and the like; we talked about the strange nature of what we had seen, and eventually "we" (but in this case, *I* certainly was the director) did a number of simple experiments and learned that the magnet we had been using was a most unusual one; it did indeed have "north poles" at *both* ends, and a very strong "south pole" in the middle. Whether by design or by accident, it had been magnetized in a strange way and acted exactly like two magnets glued together. That was a wonderful class. Even though I had to lead the way, I had time enough so that we could all understand the simple diagnostic tests I was carrying out. And my perplexity was genuine; they saw my dismay at the beginning, and we shared the pleasure of figuring it all out. I wish I could repeat that class, and of course I have saved that peculiar magnet, but although I continue to use it, I am not very good at feigning incomprehension.

There is another reason for having lab work associated with physics courses. I refer to the human interactions that can take place, between one student and another, and between student and professor. In a small course, lab or no lab, it is not long before we know one another, and I begin to become aware of each student's strengths and weaknesses and peculiar perspectives and interests. But in a large course (30 or more students, say) this is very difficult. However, if the course has a lab, as our introductory courses do, it almost always happens during the first or second lab meeting that the mass of faces and names turns into a collection of individuals. I may not have lengthy conversations in lab with each student, but I usually manage, without special effort, to talk to each one, and so—after the first week or two—we are not quite the strangers we were during the first few days of the semester. Once in a while I have taught a fairly large class for nonscience majors, without a lab, and I find it painful to realize, as Christmas draws near, that there are still a few people on my list who might as well be anonymous. Our colleagues in the nonscience departments have many reasons to be jealous of us, and one of them is the built-in opportunity for human contact with our students that the teaching laboratory provides.

IV.   Chaos and Nonlinearity—A Welcome
Dilemma for the Physics Teacher

IN AN EARLIER SECTION I described the equation for the range of a projectile, a 300-year-old topic, to illustrate the general approach that I try to use. I try to take a similarly thoughtful approach toward more recent and more advanced topics, for instance toward Maxwell's electromagnetic theory, my own number-one passion in physics, a theory that dates from the late 19th century; but the sometimes embarrassing fact is that little of the explicit content of undergraduate physics courses, even those for junior and senior majors, is *new*. Even the special theory of relativity is by now a venerable and well-tested theory.

Does this mean that there is no place for contemporary physics in the undergraduate classroom and laboratory? I believe that some of the most pervasive and influential developments of the last few decades do in fact permeate the teaching of most us who teach undergraduate physics, even though this is by no means evident from a superficial examination of catalogs and course syllabi. I do not mean that we explicitly include the latest theories and experimental discoveries in our courses, but rather that recent developments have permanently and drastically altered the ways in which physicists view the world, and that these changes in attitude have had profound effects on the ways we approach even such time-honored topics as Newtonian mechanics.

The quest for unity has been an important theme in the discipline of natural philosophy (my preferred term for physics) for centuries. Nothing excites us more than the creation of a single theory that can encompass, at a deeper level, two or more parts of our subject previously thought to be disparate. Newton, to oversimplify his achievement, unified the sciences of terrestrial and celestial mechanics by showing that falling apples and orbiting planets obey the same natural laws. Maxwell showed that light (optics) is just a branch of electromagnetism. And within the past twenty years, great strides have been made toward the physicists' Holy Grail, a single unified theory of *all* the fundamental forces of nature. Though the advances of the past two decades cannot readily be incorporated in a responsible way into undergraduate courses, our curriculum does reflect these steps toward unity. Far less often than when I was an undergraduate is physics presented as a series of apparently unrelated subjects: mechanics, heat, sound, light, electricity. . . . And far more frequently do professors explicitly call attention to the unity of the subject.

"Conservation laws," too, (conservation, the constancy in time, of energy, momentum, angular momentum, etc.), play a much more important role in our teaching than they did when I was a student. (The past tense is inappropriate; I am *still* a student, though now instead of my paying tuition, they pay me.) At any rate, back around 1950, conservation of energy, say, seemed to be regarded by my teachers as a technical trick for solving some problems without laborious calculations, rather than as a grand and deep principle. During the past forty years, the community of professional physicists has been paying more and more attention to conservation laws of all sorts, and our reverent attitude toward them is reflected in what we say about the tried-and-true conservation laws such as conservation of energy.

There are many other advances that have been made in the past few decades, deep shifts in our attitude about what things are truly fundamental, that affect—at least indirectly—what we do and say in the undergraduate classroom. But rather than continue with a list of such topics, I want to discuss what I see as perhaps the most exciting development of recent decades, the realization of the importance of *nonlinearity* and the related emergence of *chaos* as an important area of research, and especially the dilemma that nonlinearity and chaos pose for thinking about how we should respond to these developments in our undergraduate curriculum.

In my office, I have a simple piece of physics demonstration apparatus. (See Fig. 4.) (Or perhaps it is a toy; my students and colleagues are fond of pointing out that in *my* office, the line is a fine one.) Its most important component is a wooden stick, about one foot long, suspended so that it can swing freely in all directions. Attached to the bottom of the stick is a small magnet, and fixed to the table top below are 8 or 10 similar magnets, laid out either in a symmetrical pattern or at random, according to my whim. Some of the magnets are oriented so as to *attract* the swinging magnet; others, "upside down," exert a *repulsive* force.

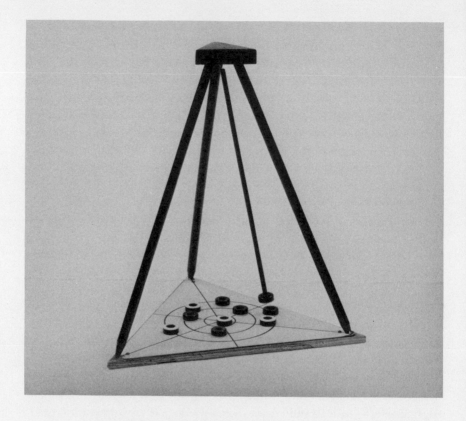

Figure 4. The magnetic pendulum "toy."

If one pulls the stick with its magnet aside and releases it, at first the moving magnet swings wildly, swooping about among the fixed magnets, perhaps circling close to one of the attracting ones for a while, then darting off, finding a path among the repelling magnets to an erratic haven near another attracting magnet. No matter what happens, sooner or later friction inevitably takes its toll, and the swinging magnet settles in near one of the attracting magnets; but before its motion ceases altogether, it vibrates back and forth above the attractor, just as it would if it were simply a weight on the end of the pivoted stick, a simple pendulum of the type that Galileo and Newton were so fond of.

Until a very few years ago, my excuse for having this apparatus in my office was this. In spite of the wild, unpredictable, chaotic initial motions of the swinging magnet, it will always settle down near *some* point of "stable equilibrium." Which particular position it will find one cannot tell in advance; its motion is just too *sensitive* to the precise conditions under which it was released. But when it does find the region in which it will eventually come to rest, its dying vibrations, no matter which final position it chooses, no matter how the magnets are arranged, are indistinguishable from the small oscillations of a gently swinging pendulum. "Every oscillatory motion is physically (and mathematically) identical to that of a simple pendulum, provided that the motion is of quite small amplitude." That was what I saw in the behavior of that toy; that is what I wanted my students to see.

Now I see other aspects of its behavior, features that were staring me in the face all the time but to which I was almost literally blind. That is what the exciting topic of "chaos and nonlinear dynamics" is all about, and I want to say something about this area and in particular about the quandaries that it creates for teachers of physics.

For many generations, the culture of physics has been permeated by the idea of *linearity*. We have almost worshipped linear equations; in those rare circumstances in which nonlinear equations appeared in the mathematical statement of physical laws, after trying to overcome our initial revulsion we would usually turn the entire area over to someone else—to the aeronautical engineers or the meteorologists, for instance, because the fundamental equations of hydrodynamics are intrinsically and inescapably nonlinear. Even though flowing liquids, air streams, and hurricanes are undeniably part of the real world we live in, we have managed, by our disdainful attitude, to declare them by fiat not respectable subjects for physicists to study.

Let me try to explain what I mean by "linearity." The equation $y = 5x$ is a "linear equation," its graph is a *straight line,* whereas $y = x^2$ and $y = 7x - 3x^3$ are *non*linear equations. A relationship between y and x described by the equation $y = 5x$ has the simple property that if, for instance, you double the value of x, the corresponding value of y is also doubled. Or, consider the value $x = 7$ and the corresponding value of y, $y = 35$, and consider likewise the pair $x = 3$ and $y = 15$. What if you now consider as "input" to that equation an x whose value is the *sum* of the two just considered: $x = 7 + 3 = 10$? The corresponding value of y, the "output" of the equation $y = 5x$, is of course just $y = 50$, simply the sum of the two previous outputs, $35 + 15$. No such properties hold for even the simplest *nonlinear* equation. (Just try it for the example given earlier, $y = x^2$.)

Similar examples can be found in the outside world. The sales tax on a $15 item is the sum of the sales tax amounts on a $5 item and a $10 item. But the income tax on an income of $100,000 is *not* the sum of the taxes on incomes of $30,000 and $70,000, at least not if the graduated income tax is working the way it was intended to work. The sales tax is *linear;* the graduated, progressive income tax is *nonlinear.*

Physicists are fond of linear equations because of their simplicity. The mathematics is something we can deal with. In particular, a physical situation described by linear equations is often one we can handle with the scientists' favorite tool, reductionism. We can break a complex problem into several simpler problems, solve *them,* and then add up the answers to get the answer to the original problem. The answer to the "sum of the problems" is just the sum of the individual answers, as seen above, both in the case of the linear equation ($y = 5x$) and the case of the sales tax.

We have a large collection of powerful mathematical tools for dealing with linear equations and linear systems. We have a long list of brilliant successes in this area. Linear physics often leads to *exact* solutions, solutions "of closed form," by which we mean solutions that can be expressed by formulas, like the range equation discussed at length in Section II. Those are solutions that we can examine at our leisure, ones on which we can bring to bear all the things we have learned about "reading equations." Specific numerical solutions are often not needed, indeed are often a hindrance. No computers, only calculus, algebra and the like, are necessary to get the solution.

Why are we so enamored of linearity? One might suspect that it is just because problems described by linear equations so often *do* have fairly simple solutions, solutions that we can lovingly examine and read, that we ignore those aspects of nature that cannot be described by linear equations, that we may even use linear equations when they are inappropriate. Indeed, there is just enough truth in such suspicions to make us a bit uncomfortable. There is more to it than that, however. First of all, many of the underlying equations describing phenomena at their most basic level are indeed linear equations, at least so far as we know today what those equations are. Newton's second law of motion, relating force to acceleration, $F = ma$, is linear; that is, if one doubles the force, one gets double the acceleration. So are Maxwell's equations, the equations that concisely describe electromagnetism; double the amount of electric charge and you double the resulting electric field in the surrounding space. So is Schrödinger's equation, the fundamental equation of quantum mechanics. That does not mean that all the phenomena *described* by those equations are simple and can be expressed in closed form, but still the basic equations in the underlying theories are *linear* equations. Second, though many natural phenomena are nonlinear (pull hard on a rope and it stretches a bit; pull twice as hard, and it may *break,* rather than just stretching twice as much), there are many, many phenomena that are *nearly* linear: pull gently on a rope and you may increase its length by one centimeter, say; pull twice as hard, but still gently, and you will increase its length by almost exactly two centimeters.

Curiously, though, one of our theories most widely admired for its elegance, as well as for its successes in describing natural phenomena, is intrinsically nonlinear: general relativity, Einstein's theory of gravity, his crowning achievement and one that still stands as our most successful description of gravity. Why we have largely failed to learn from this the lesson one might think we should have learned, that nonlinearity *can* be beautiful, is something I find somewhat mysterious. I suspect that the reason is that for most physicists, general relativity is simply not part of our daily experience. This is certainly true in my own case. We have little competence in this area, we do not use it in our own work, we do not teach it. It is "there," and we admire it (for good reasons!), but we are not constantly thrown up against its nonlinearities. Indeed, when those physicists who *are* truly competent in general relativity attempt to explain it to those of us who are not, they often try to do so by "linearizing" it(!), by treating it in an approximate but linear way, so that their explanations can exploit our linear experience and intuitions. And thus, I think, they perpetuate our ignorance of what general relativity is all about, while at the same time reinforcing our commitment to linearity.

The *resonant* behavior of a mechanical or electrical system provides a simple example of the sort of linear behavior that physicists have come to know and love. Consider a steel hacksaw blade, clamped at one end. (See Fig. 5.) Pull the free end of the blade aside with a finger and release it; it will vibrate back and forth for a few seconds, with a natural frequency of oscillation that is determined by the dimensions of the blade and the properties of the steel from which it is made. But now apply not just a momentary deflecting force with a finger but rather a sustained periodic

Figure 5. A hacksaw-blade oscillator, with a nearby
electromagnet to provide an oscillatory driving force.

"driving force," using an electromagnet that can periodically pull the end
of the blade, with a force whose size and frequency are under our control.
Whatever the frequency of the driving force, the blade will respond by
settling into a sustained oscillation at that frequency, with an amplitude
of vibration that depends on how close the frequency of the driving force
is to the natural frequency of oscillation of the blade.

Start with the driving frequency well below that natural frequency.
Observe the amplitude of vibration of the blade once it has settled into a
steady state, then increase the driving frequency and observe again. What
happens as you gradually increase the frequency of the driving force is
shown in Fig. 6. For a long time, nothing remarkable happens; the *frequency* of oscillation of the blade changes in response to the changing

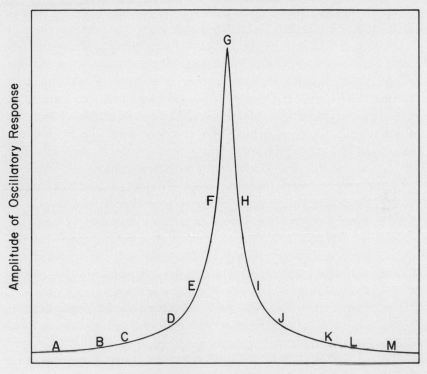

Figure 6. The hacksaw-blade oscillator: resonance!
Amplitude of oscillation of the hacksaw-blade for a
driving force of relatively small size. Maximum response
occurs when the frequency of the driving force matches
the natural vibration frequency of the saw blade.

frequency of the driving force, but there is little change in amplitude
(ABC in Fig. 6). Then as the frequency of the driving force approaches
the natural oscillation frequency of the blade, the amplitude of the response begins to increase significantly. Continue to increase the frequency
of the driving force, and the amplitude increases still further, perhaps
enormously, as indicated by DEFG in Fig. 6. Increase the frequency a bit
further, and the response diminishes in amplitude (GHI . . .). We have
passed through "resonance," we have "traced out the resonance curve

ABCD . . . JKLM." We can retrace the curve at our leisure, going back to lower frequencies (MLKJ . . . DCBA), tracing out the resonance curve in the opposite direction. Resonance is a fascinating thing to observe and to measure and—even better—to understand. The hacksaw blade is but one example; there are numerous other *mechanical* examples of resonance, and the same behavior is exhibited in many, many nonmechanical situations —electrical circuits, atomic vibrations, and indeed in almost all subfields of physics. This is a phenomenon that we can describe with *linear* equations, equations that we can solve exactly, whose "closed form" solutions we can read and dissect and interpret to our hearts' content.

Unlike many things in life, the resonant response of a linear system becomes more interesting, not less, upon repetition. It is a wonderful thing for veteran physicists to see, in large part just *because* we have that accumulated exposure to so many examples, have literally *lived* with the equations that describe it. It may not be so stimulating to beginning students who have not been immersed in the culture of linearity. Part of our job, of course, is to convey some of that excitement.

The physics community collectively has accumulated a vast amount of familiarity with linear phenomena—our strongest and apparently most reliable "physical intuitions" lie here. But physical intuition is not something one is born with; intuition is really just a synonym for accumulated experience. Is it "intuitively obvious that the basic equations of the physical world should be linear differential equations"? Not to most people. Not to the beginning physicist. But, at least in past decades, yes, that proposition does seem obvious by the time he or she has acquired a Ph.D. and has been doing and teaching physics for a decade or two.

Now it is time to describe what happens when the hacksaw blade's response becomes seriously *non*linear. The blade is a linear system when the deflecting force is quite small, but if the deflecting force is substantially increased, the blade's behavior is no longer linear. If one pushes gently on the blade, it bends through a small angle. Push twice as hard, and it will bend through approximately twice the angle. Double the force again, and now, if the force is substantial, the deflection will *not* double. It may be more than, or less than, a doubling, for blades are not all the same, but the deflection will not be precisely proportional to the deflecting force.

What happens if we repeat the experiment described earlier, but with a larger oscillatory driving force, large enough so that nonlinearity plays a significant role? The results are markedly different and quite unexpected. Start once more with the frequency of the driving force well below the natural resonant frequency of the blade. At first, there is nothing really new; the vibration of the blade has a larger amplitude, but that was only to be expected with a larger driving force. As the frequency of the driving force is again increased, it is "intuitively obvious" that we will again trace out a resonance curve, though one of generally larger size, a greater amplitude at any given frequency. But that intuition is *linear* intuition, and it is totally incorrect.

Instead, as we gradually increase the frequency, and watch the amplitude of the response get larger and larger (ABCDEF in Fig. 7), anticipating further growth in the response as we approach the peak, the vibration of the blade abruptly comes to an almost complete stop, as indicated by the line FGH in Fig. 7. It is almost as if the whole apparatus had been dipped in molasses. "Something is broken" was my first reaction, the first time I observed this phenomenon. As we then continue to increase the driving frequency, the response, now small, gradually decreases further (HIJK). Now let us retrace our steps, gradually lowering the frequency of the driving force. We confidently expect to retrace our path, not a smooth resonance curve, but at least we expect to see in reverse the behavior we saw on the way up. But this is not to be. Instead of following the path KJIHGFEDCBA, when the driving frequency reaches point H, the amplitude of oscillation does *not* jump up to F; instead it persists at a fairly low level, as indicated by the curve HLM. Finally, at M, it does jump up to the earlier amplitude and then, at last, again follows the earlier path in the reverse direction: DCBA. On occasion, it has been said that it is an "absolutely necessary condition" for scientific investigation that if we apply a given force and get a particular response, then if we later apply the *same* force, we *must* get the same response; observations must be reproducible. Not so. Consider the two points E and L in Fig. 7. The size and frequency of the driving force were identical, but the resulting amplitudes of response totally different. The only things that differed were the past histories, which way we approached this driving frequency (from above or below), and surely it is intuitively obvious (!) that—especially because friction is present—this hacksaw blade will not continue to "remember" from which direction the experimental conditions were approached. It may be intuitively obvious, but that is a *linear* intuition, and it is wrong. Our linear experience ill equips us to understand the behavior of even rather simple nonlinear systems.

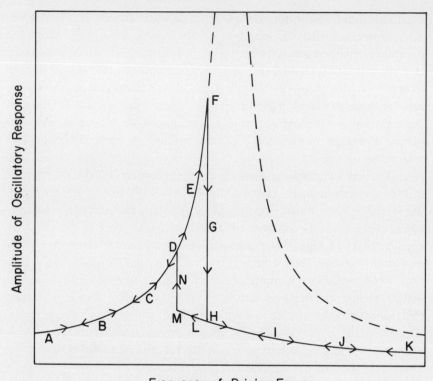

Figure 7. The hacksaw-blade oscillator in the presence
of nonlinearity. The way in which the amplitude
changes as the driving frequency is changed depends
markedly on whether the experimenter is increasing or
decreasing the frequency, as indicated by the arrows.
(The dashed curve shows part of the resonance curve
that would be obtained if there were no nonlinearity.)

For still larger driving forces, we have *chaos*. By this I do not mean that
the behavior of the hacksaw blade is random, though it certainly may look
that way. Rather, "deterministic chaos" is the more complete name; the
underlying equations that describe the blade are still the rather simple
ones that describe the behavior with *small* driving forces, but the resulting
behavior is anything but simple. In the nonlinear regime described in the

preceding paragraphs, though the hacksaw blade behaved in counterintui-
tive fashion, at least when we applied a periodic driving force, the blade
eventually settled down in *some* steady oscillatory motion. Not so in the
strongly nonlinear, chaotic regime. Apply a periodic driving force, with a
frequency in the vicinity of the natural oscillation frequency of the blade,
and the blade will *never* settle into a steady oscillation. It may vibrate for
a bit, then almost come to a stop, then begin vibrating more wildly than
before. Just how it moves is *in practice* unpredictable (though not in
principle—that is why we call it *deterministic* chaos). The blade exhibits
what is called "sensitivity to initial conditions." Suppose on one trial that
the blade happens to be precisely at rest when we turn on the driving
force, and that on another trial, it has instead a barely perceptible initial
motion. The initial conditions in the two trials are virtually identical, yet
after a few vibrations of the blade, the resulting motions and positions
will be very, very different. (Compulsive honesty—an annoying habit—
requires a confession at this point. Though I have built hacksaw blade
oscillators and observed the striking behavior described in Fig. 7, my
electromagnet was not strong enough to drive them into the chaotic
regime. What I have described in this paragraph is the behavior that *is*
observed when physical systems mathematically identical to my hacksaw
blade oscillators are driven with sufficiently strong forces.)

Nonlinear physical systems such as hacksaw blades are not the only
ones to exhibit deterministic chaos. I have a number of "chaos toys," many
of them purchased in airport gift shops, in which a metallic contraption is
allowed to swing back and forth and is given a periodic magnetic kick
every time it passes through the low point of its motion. The behavior of
such a toy may also be chaotic: periods of wild oscillation, followed by
intervals of little motion at all, then steady motion at moderate amplitudes, and so on, with no apparent pattern at all. And it is not only
mechanical systems that behave this way. Fluid flow at low velocities is
smooth and regular; at high velocities, turbulence sets in. The "onset of
turbulence" has long been a mystery, and the new science of chaos and
nonlinear systems may be on the verge of giving us some insights into this
problem.

My abbreviated discussion might give the unwary reader the impression that chaos is exciting only because of the replacement of linear equations with nonlinear ones (and nonlinearity *is* an essential ingredient for
producing chaos), but there is much more to it than that. It is "sensitivity

to initial conditions" that most clearly characterizes "chaotic" behavior, and one of the striking developments of recent years is that even quite *simple* physical systems (such as the hacksaw blade and the toys described above) and simple sets of mathematical equations can—given a modest amount of nonlinearity—exhibit such sensitivity.

Complex physical systems can of course also exhibit complicated behavior and sensitivity to initial conditions. The atmosphere is a prime example, and the modern science of chaos may be said to have originated in the discovery in the 1960s that computer models for predicting the weather were incredibly sensitive to the precise numbers chosen for initial conditions. This sensitivity is sometimes described as the "Butterfly Effect." What will the weather be a year from today? The answer may depend on whether a particular butterfly on the other side of the world flaps its wings (or if you twitch your little finger) during the next several seconds. Though such a claim is untestable, and hence unscientific, it does capture the essential idea of the unpredictability of many physical systems, even those whose underlying equations are perfectly deterministic. (What I have been describing is sometimes called "classical [i.e., non-quantum mechanical] chaos." It has nothing to do with quantum mechanics and the Heisenberg uncertainty principle. Indeed, whether or not there is anything like classical chaos at the quantum level is right now an open question.)

If two such different systems as the hacksaw blade and the Earth's atmosphere *behave* in some ways that are similar, perhaps an understanding of *simple* chaotic systems will eventually lead to a better understanding of *complex* systems. Perhaps we will gain more insight into meteorology, the turbulent behavior of flowing water, perhaps even into economics, "the dismal science." For a survey of the entire field, I recommend what is perhaps the best "popular" science book I have ever read, one of those truly rare books that is simultaneously accurate, insightful, and well written, James Gleick's 1987 best-seller, *Chaos*.

My brief description of chaos barely begins to explain what it is all about and why so many of us find it so interesting. My main point is that this is a new and fast-moving field of physics that did not exist fifteen years ago, and it is largely based on simple physical systems and simple mathematics; much of it is readily accessible to undergraduates. Had we cared to look, we could have been studying many of these phenomena thirty years ago, though I must admit that most of our serious studies of chaos would be impossible without digital computers.

Chaos and nonlinearity are exciting partly because of their intrinsic interest, but also because they are new, and—for physicists of my generation—because we have had several decades of indoctrination into the linear culture of physics. For one like me who has been a professional physicist for over thirty years, it is a bit like my belated discovery of cross-country skiing when I was 40: "*Why* didn't someone tell me about this earlier?" Now that my eyes are at least partially open, I see familiar equations and familiar apparatus in new ways. I have not forgotten my heritage, though. Linear insights and linear intuition are real and valuable. The search for exact solutions, the reading of equations, this is a large part of what has made, and still makes, physics intellectually exciting. Linearity and nonlinearity are both fascinating. Even though I myself am not doing professional research in chaos and nonlinear dynamics, I am having a grand time learning about these new developments.

But here is an interesting and real dilemma for the conscientious physics teacher. I want my students, and all future physicists, to be thoroughly initiated into linearity. This cannot be done quickly. To do it right requires years of living with the phenomena and with the equations, and it requires developing a certain amount of disdain for ugly, nonlinear phenomena. I also hope that my students will have the fun of repeating the experience I am now having, of learning the shocking facts of nonlinearity *after* years of linearity. For them to learn about nonlinearity now would prevent this. But I *also* want them to have *now,* early in their education, while their intuitions are still in the formative stage, an exposure to the new world of nonlinearity; I want them to acquire early in life the nonlinear intuition that will prepare them for contemporary physics.

To observe that the things I want for my students are mutually incompatible is a clear understatement. What is the best way of introducing them to nonlinearity without diluting too much their appreciation of linearity? Different physics teachers will have different solutions to this dilemma, and I doubt that there is a single best solution, one that is best for all teachers and all students. What my own solution is I do not yet know, but the problem cannot be avoided by doing nothing, by continuing to teach about electrical circuits and about mechanics in the same ways we have taught those subjects before. When I discuss linear physics now, my knowledge of nonlinearity makes me articulate more carefully what we are doing when we make approximations in order to make a problem a linear one, and to point out that if we overlook the nonlinearity, we *may* be throwing away something very interesting and qualitatively different.

We certainly cannot and should not hide nonlinearity from our undergraduates; some aspects of nonlinear dynamics are sufficiently simple so
that we can, and we are, introducing them into the first college course.
We have real opportunities here for enriching undergraduate physics education. I hope that it will be done with care, to preserve an appreciation
for linearity while still introducing our students to the wonderful world
of nonlinear phenomena.

What is it that I *now* see in that magnetic-pendulum toy described much
earlier in this section? The answer is obvious to anyone who has read the
preceding paragraphs. Now it is not the final small oscillations (the *linear*
behavior) that I see. Instead, my eye and mind focus on the initial wild
swinging from one attractive magnet to another, the darting through the
repulsive regions, the impossibility of predicting when I release the stick
where it will end up, the "sensitivity to initial conditions" that we now
know to be so characteristic of chaos and strongly nonlinear behavior. To
which of these two aspects of its behavior do I call attention when I show
this toy to my students? Both, of course, but I am sure that my attempts
to wax poetic about the linear behavior at the end, as it settles in to its
final resting place, are diluted by my simultaneously emphasizing the nonlinearity and the sensitivity to initial conditions, to which my own mind
has so recently been opened.

V.   Some Final Thoughts

I TRY TO ENCOURAGE a thoughtful approach to physics, I want to teach
the enjoyment of reading equations, I hope that my students will pay
attention to the logical structure of our subject. Am I always successful?
Of course not. Am I sometimes successful? I hope so. But surely many
physics students, my students and others, leave us as they came to us,
perhaps reinforced in their belief in some of the misconceptions about our
subject that I described at the beginning of this essay.

Students *are* interested in more than getting an answer that agrees with
the one "in the back of the book," but we have to cooperate. We have to
cooperate by making room in the syllabus and by our choice of what we
put on the exams, not just by what we profess to be interested in. Not
long ago, when teaching the first-semester calculus course in the mathematics department, I spent a period trying to discuss the difference be-

tween a theorem and its converse. "If the sun is shining, they are playing tennis" is not the same proposition as "If they are playing tennis, the sun is shining." The distinction is an elementary point of logic; both sentences might be true, both might be false, or one false and the other true, but they are *not* logically equivalent. Obvious though the distinction is in ordinary discourse, it somehow seems baffling when it comes up in the context of physics or mathematics, surrounded by equations. I could not go on with the syllabus, knowing that many of the students did not get the point. Physics and mathematics, after all, are about clear and logical thinking as much as they are about natural phenomena and derivatives and integrals. I postponed the assigned subject matter and spent the entire period on this one logical point, yet I would judge that class a failure. Almost none of the students got the idea or understood why I was bothered. And when it was over, I found myself an entire period behind, and in a cooperatively taught staff course, that can be a disaster. We must make room for discussions of those things we really care about, and—not least—we must see to it that our grading somehow rewards students for paying attention to these issues.

I think now that the glazed eyes I saw during that discussion of logic resulted from the students' instinctive knowledge that it would "not be on the exam." Of course, one reason for not putting it on the exam was that it would have been a tough question to grade. Once, in the second-semester introductory physics course, I put the following question on an exam very early in the semester:

> Write an essay of about two pages on Gauss's law. Here is the equation. (No need to have memorized it.) The choice of topics is up to you, and space is limited, but among other things you might consider are these. Is it a *definition* of something, or an empirical law, or was it derived from something else? If derived from something else, from what? What is its range of validity? What is it useful for?

That *was* successful. It was not an easy question to grade, but it helped persuade those students that I was interested in more than how good they were at memorizing formulas or substituting numbers for symbols. That would not have been a particularly useful question for the *final* exam; its purpose was to indicate some of my priorities *early* in the course.

It takes time to deal with a basic logical point such as the difference between a theorem and its converse. It takes time to pause and articulate the hidden text that goes with an equation. We are always impatient to get on with the new material. There are often other courses for which ours is a prerequisite, and we feel a responsibility to "cover" the assigned subject matter, lest our students be at a disadvantage in the next course. (I have always felt a bit uncomfortable about that verb, "to cover." Somehow it suggests burial, whereas I believe our role is to *un*cover, not to conceal.) So often we show our impatience when responding to students' questions. Whether in class or in my office, when students ask, for instance, about an assigned problem on which they are stumped, it is very tempting just to "do the problem for them," rather than deal honestly with *their* difficulties. It is so much more efficient to do it my way, the *best* way. Why fuss around with their misconceptions? If it's in my office, and I have other things waiting to be done, it will answer their question and get them out of the office more quickly. And, in most cases, that's probably what they want too (or what just then they *think* they want). It is so much easier to watch me than to think about it themselves, with my help; it is so much easier for *me* to do it *for* them than to watch their painful struggles.

Like anyone else, I often succumb to those temptations, but occasionally I resist. One of my best hours as a teacher came when a student came to my office to ask for help one afternoon. "I'm stuck on Problem 17," she announced. Instead of doing it, my way, I said "Why don't you show me how you got started, and then we'll see where you went astray?" For the next hour I said nothing more. She worked at the blackboard, making heavy use of the eraser, with many long pauses. I tried to look interested the whole time. (That was not hard; I *was* interested.) I am sure that although I did not actually say anything, I did participate by frowning, or by looking optimistic when her progress warranted it. At the end of a long struggle, she emerged, triumphant, with the desired result. No need to ask me for confirmation; at that point, she *knew* it was right. As she turned to leave, she said: "Thank you very much, Mr. Romer, for doing that problem for me." At that point, of course, I did speak: "Think for a minute. *Who* did the problem?" I remember with pleasure the look on her face as she realized the answer. Would that all my physics conversations worked the way that one did!

In spite of my passion for reading equations and my frequent uncertainty about what laboratory work is good for, I do make an effort to remember that physics deals with the real world, and that there are remarkable and beautiful phenomena to be observed around us, often with no auxiliary equipment whatever, sometimes with very little. An Amherst colleague described in a recent book review how he carries in his wallet a small polarizing filter (such as you could make for yourself by taking one of the tinted pieces from a pair of "Polaroid" sunglasses) so that he can check the state of polarization of light from some unexpected optical phenomenon in the sky. In *my* wallet, I always have *three* such filters, in case I meet someone who has never seen what I call the "Three-Polaroid experiment." Put two such filters on top of one another, but at right angles so that they block the light. Observe the darkness as the pair is held up to the sky. Then insert a *third* such filter (apparently just a piece of grayish plastic) between the other two, as the "meat" in the sandwich, at a 45° angle to each of the other two. Now as you look through the triplet of filters, where there was darkness before, light comes pouring through. Anyone who has not seen this effect should go try it, at once. Who is not moved by witnessing this phenomenon? Who does not feel compelled to understand it at some level?

As Einstein said, the most incomprehensible thing about the universe is that it is comprehensible. I believe that physics teachers are among the most fortunate inhabitants of this universe. How lucky we are to live in a world where so many interesting things happen, where we *can* understand some of them, and where we have the opportunity to try to understand others while simultaneously introducing a new generation to this search for understanding, this search for the true beauty of the universe in which we live.

The Education of a Painter

Robert Sweeney
Professor of Fine Arts

TEACHING HAS ALWAYS BEEN for me a natural and necessary component of being a painter. Both of my parents were artists, and both were teachers.

My approach to teaching is based on the premise that drawing is a language in which one needs to become conversant before being able to create or profoundly understand works of art. The issue is not the extent of one's eye-hand coordination. In grade school there are always some students singled out who can "draw." They are able to make marks that have a strong resemblance to nature. I have seen no evidence that these children are thinking in a visually innovative manner, but rather they seem to have a natural skill for visual mimicry. However, the result of this singling out is that all the rest of the children view drawing as something they are incapable of doing.

The art student must begin by studying works of art. The masters who created these pieces are the student's artistic ancestors. From a very early period in the student's development, they can provide an artistic grounding. I remember being taken as a young child to the Metropolitan Museum in New York and being shown the painting *A Woman Cutting her Nails,* at that time thought to be a Rembrandt. My parents would talk about certain paintings at home and these works would become legends. This painting was one such legend. Although I was consequently prepared to some extent to focus on this painting, I was moved by its intensity and the force of its light. I was intrigued by the way a person could make something that contained all that sense of illusion and story. I also was very impressed that I could look closely at the surface and see the drag of the brush evident in the paint. I was especially pleased to make intimate contact with the artist's hand that had passed that way 300 years ago. Here I was seeing the hand and the total illusion of the work at one time. This presence of the artist in the work remains for me a potent element, and one that rarely occurs in other art forms. Consider the excitement there would be if all of Shakespeare's works were to be discovered in original manuscript form.

Although one is able to see evidence of the artist's hand in a final work of art, such evidence does not fully reveal how the picture emerged. For students, this mystery is coupled with the attempt to find qualities in the work that will help them find their own voices as artists.

In my family, drawing was a normal activity. Hence for most of my childhood I did not make a conscious decision to have a stronger interest in art than other intellectual activities. In fact, upon entering high school I was determined to be something other than an artist, although I took art as an elective. My father was my high school art teacher for my first two years and after his death my mother was my teacher for my last two years. I worked from nature for those four years, studying formal elements of perspective, using lights and darks to create an illusion of form, and using watercolor and oil paint to establish color. My focus seemed to be on surface elements such as the illusion of texture, and on small details of natural forms. When a few of my paintings appeared to go beyond a recording of such details, I was not yet aware of why. Today I look back to those few paintings as critical signposts for what became future directions in my work. By my senior year I had become completely engrossed in painting and decided to devote my energies entirely to the study of art.

I applied and was accepted to a four-year art school. It was a highly competitive environment. The program stressed learning essential fundamentals. It was here that I finally made a major cognitive breakthrough concerning drawing. I had heard all of the words before, both in high school and during my first couple of years of art school, but I was not intellectually mature enough or desperate enough to comprehend. I had been very busy up to that point with drawing or painting an image as a finished illusion of form. In some cases this approach had been very useful, in learning about concentrated observation and a lack of compromise.

The major element missing from my thinking at this point, however, was an ability to let go of the surface of the finished work, or to ignore the direct one-to-one relationship of illusion of form to creation of form. A process of profound abstraction was lacking. When drawing a figure, I would make marks that referred only to the shape, proportion, and space that were visible on the surface. Although these studies ultimately would produce a decent record of those various elements, it was becoming increasingly clear to me that they were visually lifeless. Realizing this, I forced myself to give up the need to have every mark become part of a "finished" image. In fact, I gave up the idea of finish altogether. I put my faith and ego into the quality of the investigation. I concentrated on understanding the interconnection of certain elements, by making marks that would merely designate their relationships rather than representing the objects themselves. When drawing a figure, I made points that would deliberately reflect the location of key anatomical elements, or marks that would correspond to observations of large overarching shapes. These points, I discovered, were just the footprints of the investigative process. Making the judgments that produced them was the exciting and difficult part. Similarly, learning how to create the illusion of an object no longer had any relevance. What mattered was the discovery of some elemental truths of space, shape and structure that were not on the surface. Not surprisingly, this kind of drawing would not necessarily be meaningful to the casual viewer. However, as far as it went, it would establish without compromise an essential set of abstractions that were derived rigorously from nature but had a new life of their own within the image. This meant that I was free to explore and discover, no longer shackled by the need to make an object that "looked good." I realized with an exhilarating shock that there was another world. It had existed beneath my nose without my knowledge. I was now able to see works of art that I thought I knew very well with much more insight. I began to discover visual suborders that created powerful organization in these works. All of my thinking was radically altered. The most mysterious part of this process of course is the fact that in one sense I had "known" about this approach to drawing, and yet was unable to make any use of it, or to be able actually to see in this manner. This mystery of learning continues to intrigue, drive and at times frustrate my work as a teacher.

That basic understanding of the potential of thoughtful drawing cleared the way for me to begin my journey as an artist. I now recognized the inherent power a shape can have even before any representational form is discovered. One day I looked at a small Corot in the Boston Museum of Fine Arts from two galleries away, too far away to make sense of its beautiful illusion of buildings, water and light that I had studied many times. I saw for the first time its underlying set of three major interlocking shapes. This newly perceived artistic unity created a presence of such powerful mood that I was stunned. This pictorial effect was not accidental. It was too grandly formed. Upon moving closer to the picture, I became transfixed by how non-representational shapes became intertwined with the illusion of a landscape. I realized that two parts of a simultaneous and yet separate structure existed in one exquisite relationship, with one part deriving meaning from the other. I began to see years of studying "composition" in design classes in a new light. Formerly, I had approached the construction of a painting the way one would use a coat rack and hangers: once I had established support and had arranged the hangers according to design principles, I then painted with great care the images that interested me. Because the images were placed on these pre-arranged "hangers," I could be assured of a competent and attractive organization. But, dissatisfied with the result, I tried to put myself in Corot's place. The whole point I had missed was that drawing *is* design. Corot looked at those stuccoed structures reflected in the Tiber River and was obviously moved by the particular combination of shapes that then became the armature of the painting. Of course, there were innumerable elements at work in this environment—light steadily shifting, water moving, tremendous amounts of architectural and organic information, all demanding attention. He had to strip away everything that was not essential in order to uncover what had attracted him to this place. He also had to see clear relationships between these basic shapes and the edges of a picture plane. Indeed, those edges defined many of the shapes he had seen in the first place. He worked until the large organizing shapes took on a resonance. Smaller shapes and other details of information that established the illusions of building, reflections, light and atmosphere grew out of this larger order. They were not superimposed on it. I began to see that composition or design was not a separate element, but was the very basis of drawing.

As I looked at many of my favorite Degas pastels of ballet dancers, I saw more clearly this emphasis on the rhythm of shapes. I understood now that drawing was not a matter of rendering a leg, or a torso, but designing a work that consisted of a combination of irreducible shapes discovered by observing nature. In the process of abstracting what I saw, I learned that I could actually create the illusion of the very forms I had unsuccessfully been trying to copy from nature. I had been working under the assumption that if you worked hard enough you would be able to copy those impressions of form, space, light or texture that you saw in nature. Now I know that that was absurd. Nature is too complex, and it doesn't hold still. I had forgotten that I was dealing with a two-dimensional image that requires a translation from the three-dimensional world. In short, I had been so busy doing an artistic equivalent of push-ups in my training that I had lost sight of what had driven me to become a painter.

An artist has to move from opposite directions. First you must view nature as though you had just landed from outer space, with no preconceived notions about the way things ought to look. You must look at nature willing to see familiar forms as one new shape. In this way you will see what is wonderfully unique in a situation that otherwise might appear to be banal. I also discovered the importance of seeing nature as if it were a flat screen, with no spatial quality. That way of seeing requires a deliberate discipline. Our normal three-dimensional perception blocks our ability to see the tapestry of interlocking shapes that exists in nature. In "flat seeing," the composition analogizes these shapes. In continuing to study other artists, I realized that every work I responded to had a set of shape relationships that established an emblematic quality. Even when I looked at the most delicate Vermeer, squinting my eyes revealed a provocative arrangement of three or four key shapes subdividing the picture plane.

As I saw nature flatly, I also needed to understand profoundly the substructure of form. I knew I must also go in an opposing direction, from the inside out, in order to know much more about the form than would ever be apparent on the surface. Although I had been working from the figure extensively at art school, to learn anatomy, I now was beginning to see another value in this study. The figures I mentioned earlier were lifeless not only because I was not seeing the flat shapes clearly, but also because I was not abstracting a series of rhythms that existed in the core of the forms. I was studying human anatomy, but that alone is just an understanding of detailed parts of the substructure. I had to work until I began to have a spatial understanding of the major underlying forms and a kinetic understanding of how they moved through space. Thoughtful drawing reveals how the figure is capable of movement and yet, of course, is fixed on the paper. That result is not accomplished by freezing the figure in one moment, but by drawing it in a way that shows how the figure came to be in a particular position, and how it could move out of its position, and yet possess, undeniably, a sense of energy that lives forever in the present form. A Michelangelo figure study may have an elaborately suggested description of musculature, but the supple sense of underlying tension to the whole pose, the expressive quality of this very tension, remains movingly palpable. As I compared figure studies by Michelangelo, Leonardo, Degas, Dürer and Raphael, I saw that each artist had created his own re-invention of nature. A Michelangelo arm could not convincingly exist within a Leonardo figure, or a Leonardo arm within a Michelangelo figure. This phenomenon is not just a question of styles. The Michelangelo arm would look anatomically incorrect, actually badly drawn within the Leonardo, because all elements that combine to deliver a convincing illusion do so only within the world they themselves have created. Hence it is futile to try to make a "correct" or accurate figure, for there is no such single image.

A photograph is considered by many to be an "accurate" recording of reality. After all, the camera can be seen as a scientific instrument. Yet, how many photographs actually drive home the likeness of the sitter? To achieve this goal, an artist uses a camera as a tool, much as a painter uses a brush. An artist must always combine essential elements of form, gesture and underlying structure, dramatizing certain qualities of the model to produce a distillation which in some peculiar way looks more familiar than the actual person. Likewise, drawing that struggles with the elemental issues seems to produce images with the most character, worthy of sustained viewing. I no longer drew to achieve the fewest possible errors, but with an eye to making artistic sense. This discovery was, of course, my reinventing the wheel. Artists have always come to this conclusion at some point. What I had learned is that you must earn this knowledge through a process of individual trial and error, no matter how clearly its concepts have been presented by an instructor.

UNTIL THIS POINT, I had been drawing with pencil, charcoal, and conte crayon. They provided the directness and immediacy that were essential

Jean-Baptiste-Simeon Chardin, *Fruit, Jug, and a Glass*

to my abstract search. Converting the results of this basic research into paint, however, combined with the intractable problems of color, required another leap. Here Chardin's painting *Fruit, Jug and Glass* in the National Gallery served my needs. I set up a similar still life in the studio, and tried to make something happen. Having looked at the Chardin closely, I studied my still life intensively and worked hard on my painting. The result was a lot of fussy little forms, but none of the space, drama or luminosity of the Chardin. In the heightened awareness created by my dismay, I realized that I had not established any overarching value structure to the painting. When I went back to the Chardin and squinted my eyes I saw how clearly he had made a powerful light and dark pattern of the picture plane and had reserved his greatest value changes for those planes that created the illusion of forms.

It became clear that here again I had to use the brush to refer to elements that were not on the surface of the finished form. Changes in light and dark—changes in what the artist calls "value"—had to be observed in nature in a clear hierarchy. The first thing I had to give up was trying to compete directly with nature in terms of value. What I had available to me in paint for a light and a dark didn't come close to the range of lightness and darkness present in nature. I had to become sensitive to the relative nature of value, and the optical illusion nature creates. For example, a square of a middle value placed on a dark background would appear to be much lighter than the same middle value placed on a light background. The fact is that the mind makes a comparative judgment in reading each value. In the first case the square read as a light and in the second as a dark. The artist needs to ask a third question by looking back and forth and eliminating the background, in order to see the difference between just the two squares. In this example the difference is zero. This small and obvious problem actually represents a principle that works through all of painting. An artist becomes a juggler—manipulating countless separate elements. Until he throws all of these elements in the air and begins to find a balance for them he doesn't have a painting. Major elements of light, middle and dark values all need to be present and precisely controlled. Even the value of the ground on the canvas is an issue. A white ground makes every value look darker than it will ultimately appear in the finished painting. Only when the white that needs to be eliminated is replaced by the desired value, will further pictorial decisions be possible. What becomes clear is that the artist does not measure in absolute terms, but in relative terms. Ratio becomes the dominant issue. One form is three times bigger than another, one value is one quarter from the top of the lightest light compared to the darkest dark. These judgments of ratio can then be translated in a variety of ways, depending upon the aesthetic resonance the artist seeks to establish. Many of these judgments are made on an intuitive level, with the artist experimenting widely to discover a personal direction.

I learned that only through understanding value could I begin to make use of color in a meaningful way. I had been using color in my paintings, but with nothing more than a mechanically muted system. When a large Cézanne show came to Boston, I spent two weeks doing watercolor studies from the paintings. What a revelation! I realized that there was a distinct value structure underlying his color decisions, but I also discovered that in his small chips of paint he made startling color judgments, with no prejudice. For example, a person's head might be dark blue on one half and a light yellow orange on the other. Up to this point, if I were going to paint the dark side of someone's head, I would try to mix a color that I thought of as a dark flesh color. The problem is I didn't realize that there is no absolute "flesh color." Cézanne demonstrated that in a given painting you can make the dark side of someone's head blue and because it relates to other colors in the painting in a particular manner it works. Blue in that painting is flesh color. I began looking at color without prejudice and began discovering very exciting color relationships. Cézanne had shown me the way to discover color ideas that were not tied to some pre-conceived notion of "correct" color. I began to put together a way of exploring that would bring order to my questions and help sustain my ability to proceed as an artist.

I CANNOT ENTIRELY SEPARATE a discussion of my teaching from my development as an artist. My teaching evolves directly from many of the ideas that had a dramatic impact on my painting. My continuing growth as an artist is intertwined with my role as a teacher. Consequently, neither enterprise can hold still. Painting occurs in a private world. Teaching is an opportunity to step out of the studio and to give a precise public shape to those issues which thrive in that world.

The process of art school consisted of many voices speaking to me both literally and figuratively over my shoulder. These were the voices of artists who were carrying on the tradition of imparting knowledge that really can only be done orally and through demonstration. Although I respected what these voices had to say, I discovered that I often would not really digest something that one of them said until a couple of years later, when the concept would suddenly take on real force. Leaving art school and striking out on my own didn't mean I automatically had a clear artistic direction.

Eventually I realized that the best work I had done had always involved subjects that I deeply understood and that offered me some significant insight. I began painting still lifes and interiors in my studio, trying to strike a spark. The experience was painful, tedious and frustrating. However, I had come to understand the artistic process well enough to know that this effort was unavoidable in order to have a chance to bring some ideas to life. I continued to paint very complex interiors, including arrangements of discarded machine parts. Some of this painting involved working from imagination as well as working directly from life. I had begun to develop a cast of characters that would appear in various combinations.

I was becoming increasingly aware of a "feel" evoked by certain forms, structured spatially in an atmosphere that would create a complete world within the picture plane. I was on to something. The voices over my shoulder were replaced to a large extent by the paintings talking to me. My aim was to eliminate all unnecessary elements in the painting. Anything that could be removed without affecting the mood of the painting had to go. I saw that, even though I might have been initially attracted to a certain still life containing many bottles, my real interest was in a certain color pattern that could be most dramatically established in a painting with no bottles at all. As I pursued these thoughts it became apparent to me that my paintings were too cluttered. My real concern was to create a sense of atmosphere by precisely ordering color shapes. I took one large interior I had just finished and, realizing I was more interested in the light on the wall than I was in many of the objects in front of it, I painted over much of the picture eliminating a large cluster of objects, leaving only a small table and two doors as the nominal subject of the painting. In this instance the painting had been freed because I saw what had been lurking under its surface. I also learned that a special way of seeing color was becoming central to my thinking. This color that is not decorative, but charged with some meaning, is what I see out of the corner of my eye. If I turn to stare at it, it is gone. I began to respond much more to this ephemeral sense of the image, knowing that this intuitive exploration of color is something that can happen only when you have developed enough confidence in your abilities to handle those other issues of drawing that do hold still when you look at them. I realized through my working process that my initial marking on the canvas essentially established a non-representational image. I needed to work towards a strong gestural impact and a firm hold of overall color until an essential quality began to emerge. It was only then that I could begin to intensify my ideas by having representational images of form and space emerge.

Through this interest in light and color working within the geometric structure of the interior I found myself drawn to the work of Piero della Francesca. I received a Miner D. Crary Fellowship from Amherst College to support a trip to Italy to study Piero's frescoes. The combination of seeing his work and doing a series of pastel landscapes further focused my thinking about color and painting. The experience informed many of the ideas I am pursuing today. My current work comprises a series of paintings, using the same subject a number of times, to try through comparison to discover common perceptions. I have become intrigued by the energy that lies in the seams between a form in nature and the light and atmosphere that surround it.

A painter teaches to a large extent out of a sense of responsibility to act as a guide to students who are just starting their education. I feel especially strongly about this because both of my parents were artists and teachers and because I had such dedicated instructors at Boston University School of the Arts. My instructors were artists who believed in providing a rigorous training and applied themselves to that mission with diligence. I was fortunate to have had some teaching experience while I was a graduate student, which gave me a chance, while still in art school, to see if some of my thoughts about educating artists had merit. I had not considered what I would do to make a living when I graduated because I believed that learning to become a good painter was so difficult that, if I were able to succeed, how hard could it be to earn a living by comparison? I basically still hold to that philosophy. Upon graduation from art school I was faced with the choice of continuing to teach at Boston or accepting a position at a liberal arts college. A difficult and complex process led to the decision to come to Amherst College for several reasons, not the least being a change in environment. Of course, one of the obvious differences in teaching at Amherst was the liberal arts curriculum. My education and the teaching I had done were all in a professional art school. In art school I worked with a four-year structured curriculum, in which all of my students had the same education and continued on in a predictable sequence. At Amherst I realized that my painting or drawing course could be a student's first and only art course. Ideas or approaches that I took for granted in my teaching at art school needed to be re-evaluated. It is that very process that I find so useful to me as a painter. I have to backtrack and analyze decisions I have made in order to understand how I came to be at my present state. It is a process one employs as both a painter and teacher.

A teacher of painting confronts students who have been bombarded with an ever-increasing amount of visual information, and who have learned to see only in the most rudimentary manner. Consequently one has to slow the sheer amount of visual information to enable them to understand and order it. The challenge is to teach the basic language of vision, but at the same time try to point the way to posing, or at least recognizing, the larger aesthetic and moral question that is at work. Over the last seventeen years I have focused on the development of fundamental issues that I believe are essential for the education of the student. The umbrella that covers these issues is the concept of drawing.

My idea of drawing includes learning to observe or, more specifically, to frame questions that are directed at discovering abstract relationships of form, space, shape and color. It also includes learning to establish the means of visual manipulation through a vigorous experimentation with various artistic media, a process that ultimately challenges those original observations with a powerful reconstruction and re-invention of those relationships. Students need to draw in a manner similar to certain aspects of scientific inquiry. They must learn to establish a constant or control against which a number of variables are measured. The student must understand that the artist's measure is one of relativity and ratio, and that these abstract relationships are at least as clear a truth as an absolute measure made with a ruler or weight scale. As their drawing develops, students will discover a basic dichotomy. They must approach nature as if they had never seen it before so that the matters of pattern, form, and color are not derived from preconceived notions. This procedure gives the student the opportunity to glimpse the possibility of new orders, not biased by prior convictions. At the same time the student needs a profound understanding of nature, of natural orders that exist beneath the surface, so as to be able to create a personal structure that resonates with those perceptions that establish a painting as a work of art. Unlike the scientist, the artist discovers and creates a world not accountable to natural law. Art is the opposite of scientific experimentation in that it is not reproducible. Drawing must give shape to the process by which it is conceived and created. Ironically, a critical point for a student is the realization that good drawing is not made by trying to make a "drawing" that looks good. The student is then freed to concentrate on pursuing truths instead of making clever facsimiles of the truth. The teacher is there to help the students improve first on the quality of the questions, and then on the precision and insight of the answers that the students fashion.

The teacher of art must walk the line between a curriculum that emphasizes skill development for a significant period of time before actively trying to "make art," so that the work has strong underpinnings, and a curriculum that eschews any basic instruction (essentially leaving the students to discover these elements on their own) and focuses entirely, instead, on developing an aesthetic sophistication. Applied exclusively, the former approach would retard artistic growth by not encouraging students to extend their imagination. The latter approach often leads to students making objects that look like art, but which have no substantial visual or aesthetic base. What happens is that a student who has not studied underlying principles and worked hard to attain some level of skill is really trapped into working off the surface of other art in order to create something that has an interesting appearance. It is difficult to redress this problem in a student's education because the glamor of working on a ten-foot-long canvas with buckets of paint is heady stuff compared to working for two months with an ebony pencil on a studio exercise. There is no substitute for scaling down the superficial ambition of the process to concentrate on beginning to learn to "see," or in other words to draw.

It has to be taken on faith that at an early stage in an artist's career, the work will bear little resemblance to work at the mature stage. If a student is interested in a particular artist's work, the student needs to discover what artists influenced that artist and study their work. In this way the student will gain insight into the processes and choices that were made in the development of that artist's work. In being drawn to another artist, the student may find a kindred spirit. The point is not simply to make your own work look like the other artist's, but rather to understand the underlying directions. What the student can discover looking closely at the development of another artist is important in trying to develop an attitude that will sustain artistic development. It takes a long time for visual artists to reach a point where their work speaks clearly. Students must have many varied learning experiences, therefore, that will give them a substantial base of knowledge and nurture them during this long process of self-realization.

An example of the type of experience I believe is essential for a serious student of the fine arts is the study of human anatomy. As an isolated study, Gross Anatomy will be of minimal use to the art student. But if the focus is on first gaining a strong understanding of the human skeletal and muscular forms that are common to all figures, a student can then predict certain spatial relationships and understand what is not superficially visible. The student now has the constant against which to compare the infinite variety of human physiognomy and an opportunity to measure the tension between a general knowledge of nature and its unique manifestations. It is a reconciliation among the terms of this equation that the artist pursues. Whereas the scientist can measure the wavelengths of light and establish absolutes for color, the artist understands that his world of color exists between that scientific measure and the way that color appears when found in combination in nature.

Because of their extensive exposure to photographic images of nature, students have come to equate photographic with "real." The student does not understand that the photographic image has abstracted a relatively narrow range of information. One element that is sharply limited is the record of space. The camera "sees" with one eye; we have two. We tend to see by moving our head slightly to see around forms. The camera doesn't. The photograph tends to lose many tonal variations in very light or very dark areas. Our pupils are constantly adjusting as we look at a wide value range, to allow us to absorb a great deal of information. Many of us, however, have been trained to see by the photograph, resulting in a remarkably limited ability to see form and space. I have often shown students a painting such as a Chardin still life that is rich with form, space and even a surface texture along with a work by a photo realist painter such as Richard Estes. Estes usually impresses them as the artist delivering the most illusionistic image, even though the sense of weight and volume of the forms in the painting is relatively thin. One would expect, from the exposure to photography they have had, that students could read flat-shape organization. But I find that this ability is restricted to small pieces. Practically all of my students can recognize a friend by the shape of the back of his or her head—a fairly sophisticated flat-shape analysis. But finding larger flat shapes made up of smaller ones is more of a problem. Occasionally, to address this situation, I ask my students to select a complicated photograph and then create a flat shape analysis of the work. I also ask them to turn the photo upside down. This reversal makes it harder for them to recognize objects and helps them to discover the new shapes created by combination of smaller objects. They should discover three or four large shapes that control the surface of the photo. In most cases none of the shapes corresponds to a single object. For this reason, the student gradually begins to see that these three or four abstracted shapes are every bit as "real" as any object in the photograph.

The next problem for the student is to look at nature and read the flat shapes that they see. It is important to note that the shapes each individual perceives will be quite different, and that it is right here that real artistic choices begin to be made. Potentially, there is no limit to artistic depth in any apparently simple problem. Reading nature as a flat pattern is extremely difficult for most students. To force a totally flattened view from one's natural depth perception takes a great deal of discipline. This approach is important not only for discovering rich, two-dimensional patterns, but also for controlling the optical illusions of form and space that nature creates. For example, a student looking at a box will see a front plane with no distortion, but will normally see the top plane of the box with a foreshortened view in which it appears to be shorter than it actually is. The problem I have observed with beginning students is that as soon as they recognize a foreshortened situation, they can no longer accurately gauge the actual dimension. Such students will considerably "un-foreshorten" or exaggerate the plane. Paradoxically, one has to learn to read nature as a flat pattern in order to capture the essential flat shape relationships that create the illusion of space. Consequently, it is important for a student to develop this "unnatural" relationship with nature early on. Drawing is the process of trying to possess nature, to crawl inside, to find the way things work in order to be all the more surprised by how different the next experience is. Reading flat shapes allows the student to encounter nature directly and then unlock the spatial information that is contained within the flat-shaped organization. The perspective system invented during the Renaissance, which assumes flat-shape integrity, is actually mimicked by the modern photographic camera. This so-called linear perspective was based on a single, fixed-eye view. Using an eye-level line and vanishing points the artist could order some of nature's optical illusions. For example, two parallel lines moving away from us appear to converge, thus breaking the geometric definition of parallel lines. Also, objects appear to get smaller as they move away from us. How many children have "held" a distant airplane between two fingers and wondered how something that small could carry all those people? Obviously we have learned to translate these illusions, otherwise countless people would run off all these roads that seem to be getting much narrower in the distance. This learning requires "flat shape" recognition and drawing entails its manipulation.

The critical element in any artistic pursuit is an obsessiveness that leads to the standard of settling for nothing but the best effort at every stage. That is why an apparently simple problem may encompass a great experience. One could ask a student to draw a sphere using value—that is, lights and darks. Only a student who is really imagining a sphere in its complete sense of being a totally round volume will be able, with great effort, to construct an image that embodies this reality. The mystery here is that this study of the sphere will tell us as much about that half of the sphere we don't see as the one we do. Take the situation a step further and have a student draw an egg using value. The student now finds that everything that was predictable in the sphere becomes unpredictable in the egg, despite the fact that both are generally "round." Although the objects are mundane, the concentration required to reach an effective realization of these forms is extraordinary. The alert student will see a glimmer of what transformations lie ahead through the process of shaping a personal vision and reconciling the inherent tensions between two- and three-dimensional forms.

ONE OF THE MOST interesting aspects of painting and drawing is that the completed work can literally be seen in one moment. Other art forms such as literature, music, theater, dance, film, and even sculpture reveal their aesthetic structure in an unfolding series of events through time. In listening to a symphony one relates the current notes to the ones remembered from five seconds ago and a half hour before. The artist literally controls the amount of time the listener will spend with each stage of the composition. A sculpture requires viewers to walk around the piece connecting a memory of a form on one side with the presence of the part of the form seen in front of them with the anticipation of that part of the form to be seen next. Even low-relief sculpture, despite its pictorial appearance, creates a sense of a whole form and experience that can never literally be seen at one time. Painting, on the other hand, has to create its own time. The artist does this by establishing many levels on which the image can be understood. The nature of these levels ranges widely from artist to artist or even within a single artist's body of work. They account for the resonance in a strong piece that seems to create a dominant mood and yet a presence that never holds still. One of the most powerful ways that a painting carves out a time sequence is in the play between its two-dimensional impact and three-dimensional illusion. Much of the energy and character of the painting is found in the tension between the flat shapes on the taut picture plane and the illusion of space they create. In Cézanne's *Mt. St. Victoire* in Philadelphia, the triangles and rectangles that subdivide the picture plane into increasingly smaller units, right down to the blocky brush strokes, also appear to move back and forth spatially because of their hue, value and intensity. Trying to separate one impression from the other is impossible. The illusion of the magnificent sense of the mountains, air and clouds, and the plain below, thrills us in its rightness but also intrigues us because of its equally compelling sense of pictorial structure. The feeling emerges of nature having been constructed as an odd masonry monument. Cézanne requires your time because he is instructing you anew in how to see nature and, ultimately, to see his art.

We most often see paintings exhibited in an environment poorly suited to appreciating and understanding the work. When we enter most museums, we are confronted with room after room filled with paintings. It is perfectly natural for unwary individuals to think that they are supposed to march along and look at every painting. This idea is as crazy as going to the public library and expecting to read all of the books. But because of the nature of painting, what often happens is that people walk around with earphones, essentially collecting autographs of each of the well known works by checking the identification plate, glancing up, and moving on. This procedure makes it impossible to enter the world of any given painting. One is left, instead, with a fleeting impression of each work, not much different from the relationship between a brief obituary and the actual fabric of a person's life. I suggest to my students that they explore a museum first, just to establish what and where those works are that most interest them. Then they should come back with a folding seat and a small drawing pad and make a pencil study of a painting. By doing this the student is forced to slow down and consider how the artist constructed the piece. As this happens, the student is brought into an intimacy with the work and the artist's sensibilities. Paintings should not just be stared at any more than books. They should be read. They also need to be viewed, as with color, literally out of the corner of the eye in order to discern the less literal aspects of the ensemble, such as the twist of related rhythms woven through the surface, or any number of unique qualities that constitute the life of that painting. One consistent aspect of a work

Paul Cézanne; *Mont Sainte-Victoire*

of art is that, at its root, there always seems to be something surprising about the image. In other words, the reinvention of nature, even in a non-representational work, evokes a sharp sense of personal recognition in the viewer, and yet, at the same time, a clear feeling that this world has been turned slightly askew. Through this cockeyed view, greater clarity is some-how reached.

Another reason that it is important for students to study a whole range of artists, is to compare the nature the artist was working from and the resulting variety of abstractions. Look at a photo of Mt. St. Victoire taken from where Cézanne created the Philadelphia painting and you will rec-ognize the landscape. Yet what becomes disturbing is the confusing clutter of information in the photo, and the sense of a lack of purpose to the landscape, compared to the clear order in the Cézanne. In the painting you can see the artist abstracting what he felt were key relationships, reordering the landscape through his own priorities concerning space, color, form, and texture. Because he presented his logic in such compelling dramatic fashion, he convinces you of the existence of his world. The uniqueness of Cézanne's landscape is not the result of his being from a different planet than Ruisdael's, Monet's, or O'Keefe's. Rather, each artist found in nature elements to be dramatized and manipulated to form a complete new vision. These visions serve to instruct individuals in new ways of seeing and approaching nature. One cannot literally or figuratively see the world in the same way again after experiencing a great work of art. The test of a truly great painting is the way it continues to haunt the imagination and becomes a part of one's whole perception.

Students often become confused about the difference between a painting that is primarily descriptive or narrative and one that combines narrative with an inherently vigorous image. Compare Norman Rockwell's *Freedom from Want* with Chardin's *Fruit, Jug and Glass*. Rockwell, as an illustrator, combines images that have literal meaning to tell a particular story. He has to edit and refine these images so that nothing distracts from the message he wishes to present. With great skill, he creates a view of Thanksgiving that crystallizes an idealized notion of the average American family drawn together at holiday time. He does this through a presentation of narrative elements that Rockwell knows will strike certain chords. Essentially, the illustration is a handsome ensemble of familiar symbols at the center of which is the turkey—the most recognizable element of the American Thanksgiving dinner. However, like all the other objects portrayed in the work, the turkey has no inherent power due to its shape, color and form. As a matter of fact, it really has at best a bland quality that makes it look wooden. Unfortunately, the longer you look, the less you will see. The Chardin painting, whose narrative seems to be nothing more than a genre anecdote about objects found on a kitchen table, is charged with drama. The pile of peaches, while they speak of the rich color and velvet texture of the fruit, is transformed into a fortress with a strange flickering light, creating a landscape-like atmosphere. The play between our preconceptions of peaches and Chardin's contrasting reordering of these forms is characteristic of a strong painting whose impact on the willing viewer is endless. The intent of the two individuals, then, was very different. Rockwell would not have wanted his turkey to distract the viewer by going beyond its prop-like presence.

As students begin to see the differences in these two approaches they can begin to ask more of their drawing or painting than merely description. Their role is as Chardin's was, to discover fresh visual metaphors and create a new world. One of the great 15th-century Italian teachers was Cennino Cennini who wrote the *Craftman's Handbook*. A passage in that book distills much of what I am attempting to express about painting. "And this is an occupation known as painting, which calls for imagination and skill of hand, in order to discover things not seen, hiding themselves under the shadow of natural objects, and to fix them with the hand, presenting to plain sight what does not actually exist."

The obvious truth is that students of fine art need to be challenged from many directions. A basic program which involves the study of form, space, shape, value and color through observation and work from memory and imagination in both the two-dimensional and three-dimensional disciplines is critical before narrowing one's focus to a particular direction. The student also needs a complete grounding in the craft of art, not just to satisfy immediate needs but to prepare for future possibilities. The student will then develop an informed respect for the craft that underlies the fabric of a work of art. This preparation must include a study of basic principles and values in culture generally, including history, philosophy, literature, and science, not as a dietary supplement but as an integral part of a coherent education.

Those basic principles are the basis for all of the courses in drawing and painting that I teach. The amount of information that can be literally imparted is relatively small compared to the levels of understanding of that given information. That is why I have to work individually with students, responding to their questions and solutions to urge them to a more complex and ultimately personal level of comprehension. I have supervised successful studio senior honors theses in which the student has worked hard to create a focused subject that is little different, on the surface, from a three-week drawing problem I would give a basic drawing class.

A number of my students at Amherst have gone on to work as artists. But the great majority pursue other fields upon graduation. That, of course, is the nature of a liberal arts college. When I first came to Amherst I knew that I could base my teaching on only one set of educational principles. Consequently the intensity of study was at least at the same level as my teaching in art school. I was concerned whether liberal arts students had the drive and ability to engage the issues I set forth. I was thrilled to discover that their commitment and drive were tremendous. I also soon learned that their broad range of intellectual interests created a rich resource with which the visual discipline could interact. Among those students who have gone on to make their way as artists over the last seventeen years, there has been a very low attrition rate, much lower than I have observed in art schools. I think this is partially due to their level of emotional and intellectual maturity when they make the decision to pursue art as a career. Students entering art school have already made this key decision by the age of eighteen. In addition, the breadth of the liberal arts education prepares students well for the complex choices they will have as artists.

Several years ago, two of my colleagues and I planned an ILS course, which is an introductory freshman course designed to move beyond departmental boundaries and engage students in learning how to question and make independent intellectual connections. We were a geologist, a mathematician and an artist. What interested us was how our methods of investigation overlapped and also polarized. We developed a course we called "Order: Proportion and Perception."

I was encouraged in the ILS class to see that the students were able to deal with some fairly complex aesthetic issues presented through a combination of lectures and out-of-class drawing assignments. Up until this point, the only students I had seen in my classes were those who had already made the decision that they wanted and were capable of learning how to draw. Many of the ILS students were not prepared for the fact that they would be drawing, and probably would not have selected a drawing course if they had known. But they discovered that drawing is a language that can be learned like any other, and that a whole area of visual discourse that they had assumed was unavailable to them was now accessible. I was exhilarated to have reached a group of students and to have involved them in a mode of thought that I view as vital, and about which they otherwise would have remained absurdly ignorant. It struck me as ridiculous that in this age, with all of our reliance on visual imagery, many students at a liberal arts college would not take at least an introductory drawing course. The decisions we constantly make that demand some sense of aesthetic structure need to have a base in formal education. It is a tragedy that bright, vital young men and women should be visually illiterate. I believe that this handicap creates a deadness in the imagination, leaving a person incapable of being nourished by the visual richness around us.

I am first and foremost a painter. I believe that being an artist includes a responsibility to contribute to the education of students. The principles at work in my teaching necessarily develop from my formal education along with my understanding of other artists' work and ultimately from what I discover in my own studio. The studio is the place to challenge the artistic attitudes one has formalized. To date I have managed a productive relationship between my teaching and my painting. Because the painting is a very private enterprise, teaching becomes a complementary public forum for ideas pushed around at the easel. My contribution as a teacher can come only from my continuing work as an artist, pursuing the issues that have increasingly absorbed my attention and have led into my current work.

Unique combinations of color suggesting illusions of light, form, and space not only set loose an emotional response, they inspire intellectual clarity. I am at a point in my career where I have confidence in my ability to ask provocative questions of my painting and explore an unlimited number of ideas. It is exciting to realize that my future work is still a mystery and yet know that the next painting will provide another clue in the search for a personal artistic vision. Teaching affords me the privilege of sharing these discoveries with my students.